D0049575

This Business of Writing

This Business of Writing

GREGG LEVOY

Writer's
Digest
Books

CINCINNATI, OHIO

This hardcover edition of *This Business of Writing* features a "self-jacket" that eliminates the need for a separate dust jacket. It provides sturdy protection for your book while it saves paper, trees and energy.

96   95   94   93   92   5   4   3   2   1

Library of Congress Cataloging-in-Publication Data

Levoy, Gregg
  This business of writing / by Gregg Levoy. — 1st ed.
       p.   cm.
  Includes bibliographical references and index.
  ISBN 0-89879-505-2
  1. Authorship.   I. Title.
  PN145.L39   1992
  808'.02 — dc20   91-34733
                                                         CIP

Edited by Nan Dibble
Designed by Sandy Conopeotis

Gregg Levoy is a full-time freelance writer who has written for the *New York Times Magazine*, *Omni*, *Psychology Today*, *American Health*, *Washington Post*, *Reader's Digest* and others, as well as for promotional, corporate and television projects. A former columnist and reporter for the *Cincinnati Enquirer* and *USA Today*, and the recipient of a first-place feature-writing award from The Associated Press, he is also a college instructor, lecturer and writing consultant.

DEDICATION

To Robin
For your love and sustenance, and for bearing up with grace the challenge of being an author's companion.

And to John Brady
For having faith in me, and for opening doors.

ACKNOWLEDGMENTS

A tip of the hat and a grateful bow to the following people:

Dorothy Linder, "who chopped up her students to tinder," for shepherding my writing long before it was recognizable as such, and for introducing me to Scheherazade.

My family, for giving me support, counsel and lots of material to write about.

The folks at Writer's Digest Books — Bill Brohaugh, Nan Dibble, Terri Boemker, Kate Morrow, Jo Hoff, Christy Pretzinger, Sue Ann Stein — for walking me through my first book with patience, generosity and expertise.

Brad Bunnin, for being a gentleman fighter.

Stephen Altschuler, for the friendship and commiseration.

Larry Harrison and Leslie Handmacher, also for their friendship, and for always having ice cream in the freezer for me.

Gail Haar, reference librarian extraordinaire, for not ducking when she saw me coming.

Virginia Fossel, wherever you are.

And to the memory of my father, who taught me the love of stories.

Fall Down Seven Times, Stand Up Eight:
How to Handle Rejection

CHAPTER TWO

Goals: Setting Your Course for Success

Procrastination: Cholesterol in the Arteries of Success

Getting in Focus: The Power of Clarity

Write It Down: Making Simple Maps of the Territory

Divide and Conquer: Making Molehills Out of Mountains

Are You Having Fun Yet? Rewarding Yourself Along the Way

Whose Idea Is It Anyway? An Aviso

The 80 Percent Solution: Choosing Attainable Goals

Clearing the Decks: Making Room for New Goals

Count Your Chickens: How to Get All the Help You Can Get

Finding Your Passions: There's Goals in Them Thar Hills

Skillful Means: Finding Salable Skills

CHAPTER THREE

Market Research: Looking Before You Leap

CHAPTER FOUR

The Writer's Workshop: Setting Up an Office

CHAPTER FIVE

Promotion: The Art of Getting Attention

CHAPTER SIX

More Than Money: How to (Really) Support Yourself as a Writer

CHAPTER SEVEN

The Art of Negotiation: How to Get Paid What You're Worth

CHAPTER EIGHT

Research: The Happiness of Pursuit

INTRODUCTION

Giving Your Writing the Business

When I was twenty and informed my college advisor that I wanted to be a writer, she said, "Excellent. A noble profession. I'm signing you up for some business classes next semester."

Bewildered, I said, "What do you mean, business classes? I want to be a writer."

She patiently explained that in her experience writers, who so often fear sullying their creative spirits with the vulgarities of business, too often end up sullying them by *not* studying the craft of business along with the craft of writing.

Without a firm grounding, she said, in how a product sells—and writing is eminently a product—they end up unable to make a living, or any part of a living, doing what they love, and that has a far more vulgar and ruinous effect on their spirits than business ever will.

Creative satisfaction may come primarily from the writing itself, but the stability and growth of your enterprise as a whole comes from the business.

Writers write, she said, for many reasons: to change the world; to live twice; to redress old grievances; because they must. They write to send letters to the world, to slow time down (though it won't), and to hold the words up to their ears, like empty shells, and listen to the roar of their own lives.

But ultimately they write not just to express themselves but to *share* those expressions; not just to write but to be read. Assuming that you write more than just notes to yourself that you stick under fruit magnets on the refrigerator door, writing is an act of communication, and communication demands that you give it to someone, that you find mediums for your messages. And getting your work into even one person's hands requires, by definition, a business transaction, specifically promotion, which simply means "moving something in a positive direction." That is, out into the world.

Business is the vehicle by which your writing is given to the world, and without minding your business, you produce but you don't sell, and your Great American Writing sits on shelves collecting Great American Dust.

Writing is a demanding enough calling as it is, my advisor counseled, without adding to it the disillusionment of not being able to sell your writing. Trying to become a successful writer without engaging wholeheartedly in the business side of it, she said, is like trying to ice-skate without taking the rubber off the blades.

So, over the next few semesters I stepped out onto what was, for me, thin ice. I slogged my way through classes in economics, marketing, management, advertising and design, in addition to Survey of Western Lit, English Comp, Expository Writing, and American Fiction 1912-1945.

And I didn't have to wait long for the payoff. Within six months of graduating, I landed a staff position at a good-sized city newspaper—*The Cincinnati Enquirer*, formerly the flagship paper of the Gannett chain before *USA Today* was born—as their youngest-ever full-time columnist and feature writer.

What got me that job, in part, was that I sold myself to them as their first singles columnist, backed up by a few insights I picked up in those business classes—for example, the importance of paying attention to my market, my audience and my timing.

For starters, I went to the public library and gathered figures on the number of single people in the county (as well as their statistical buying power) and compared this with the reader demographics from the newspaper's own ad-rate sheets. This showed that they were sitting on an untapped reserve of readers.

As for timing, I also pointed out the trends at the time into which a singles column would fit neatly, such as the disco craze, the singles bar scene, the divorce trend, the rise of the single-parent household, and what was then being called the Me Decade.

I helped the editors discover a viable and profitable niche, and then promoted myself as the person to inhabit it. I was single, possessed a native New Yorker's resolve, had plenty of column ideas and a sense for trends, and could write.

In the years since then, I have written features, columns, essays, book reviews, even poetry for many of the magazines on the rack at the corner convenience store; applied my writing and business skills to promotional material, corporate in-house magazines, newsletters and press releases; worked as an editor, college instructor, writing consultant and lecturer; and even narrated a Planned Parenthood television film on male contraception.

Today, the mailbox ouside my house reads "Gregg Levoy—World Headquarters." This, however, is not the delusion of grandeur it would appear. I am a one-man business, true, but I am also a worldwide operation. My writing not only reaches the far corners of the globe, but occasionally takes me there, too. Business is good.

It turns out that my college advisor—bless her farsighted soul—was right. Business and writing not only do mix but must! So whether you're a ghostwriter, grantswriter or gonzo journalist, whether you write about politics, parenthood, or passionate, tragic love affairs, you as a writer must learn not only the King's English, but the dialects of the business world. You must study them the way Michelangelo studied science and biology and the corpses down at the local morgue to see just how the knee bone connected to the thigh bone.

The Writing Business Is Not an Oxymoron

On the back of a one dollar bill, above the eye on the pyramid, are the Latin words *Annuit Coeptis*, which translated mean "Our undertakings are favored."

Printed right on the most basic medium of exchange in our culture is this small article of faith, a vote of confidence in our endeavors, a kind of financial backing if you will. And I cannot imagine who needs the encouragement more than the self-employed, in particular the artistic self-employed such as writers, whose relationship to the financial and business world has customarily been a bit like that of one warring nation trying to maintain trade agreements with another.

The fact that not even writers—whose very merchandise is the meaning of words—know the meaning of those printed on a dollar bill betrays a telling lack of familiarity with even the basics of business.

Throughout history, writers have often labored under the misapprehension that creativity and business were somehow an unholy alliance, or at best an extremely limited partnership. One was not to tarnish the purity of art with business. To make matters worse, writers have frequently operated on the assumption that to be of note they must demonstrate some misanthropic vice, or at least a few melancholy and eccentric virtues. Many have thus taken it as an oath of office and sworn duty to hover artfully on the brink of insanity, mumble incoherently in public, maintain passionate, tragic love affairs, and disregard all mortal laws.

The public, for its part, has just as dutifully obliged all this unbusinesslike behavior by looking upon writers as generally temperamental, unreliable, dreamy, self-centered, and altogether difficult to live with.

Rounding out this conspiracy are editors, who have often seemed possessed of the idea that genius flourishes best in penury.

Consequently, the notion of a writer with business acumen is, to this day, something of an oxymoron, a self-canceling concept like "relaxation exercises" or "a good spanking." It is a reputation, of course, not without some justification, but one that is also, in some sense, merely symptomatic of the culture that helped create it.

For example, because I travel a lot on assignment, I am frequently asked, "Is this trip for business or pleasure?" It is a revealing remark, testifying to a widespread belief—nowhere more obvious than among creative people such as writers—that business and pleasure, professional life and personal life, indeed, commerce and creativity do not mix.

Furthermore, we have all heard that we are supposed to keep our "personal lives," especially our emotions, out of the office, and most of us have worked for companies where this was certainly one of the unwritten codes of conduct. The fear is that emotions are irrational, and thus make us ill-prepared to voice opinions on matters of the bottom line; that if we are fully ourselves, fully human, our capacities will be somehow diminished and we will be less than productive.

But this is an untenable position to take if your life is indistinguishable from your work, as it is for writers. This approach to business may or may not work in the nine-to-five world, but it certainly won't work if you are in business for yourself, especially in a profession that draws so heavily on the passions.

Work is extremely personal, unavoidably personal, and if we do not bring our full repertoire — head *and* heart — to bear upon the challenges of business, we are effectively locking half our salesforce out of the office.

When Sigmund Freud was asked once what constituted mental health, he said, "Arbeiten und lieben," to work and to love. They are, in my mind, one and the same, and to be successful in business, to write for prosperity as well as posterity, we must consult not just the facts and figures, but also our own desires, fears and intuitions; the emotions as well as the equations.

For instance, the question "What am I worth?" which is discussed in the chapter on the writer's relationship to money, is far more than a financial question, and answering it requires far more than a cursory look at what the market will bear or what the competition is charging.

Procrastination, too, which is certainly a business concern and discussed in the chapter on goal setting, is less a logistical issue than an emotional one, less a problem of not having the right tools or time than one of clarity and commitment.

The explorer Jacques Cousteau once said that when you enter the ocean you enter the food chain — and you do not necessarily enter at the top. The same applies to the world of freelancing. There is a lot of food-chain activity going on out there, and dreams get devoured at an alarming rate. The best defense is a clear understanding of the territory and the active participation of every resource at your command.

The desire to help mend the rift between creativity and business, the personal and the professional, has tremendously inspired me in writing this book; my purpose is to bring business to life. Not just in the sense of bringing the power of business to your writing career so that it bears fruit, but of exploring and describing business as something vivid, dynamic and personal.

In painting an intimate portrait of the writer as merchant, I hope to encourage in writers — whether just setting out, struggling to stay afloat, or starting up again after a stall — the conviction that the tasks involved in getting your writing out into the world are every bit as noble, essential and even creative as the writing itself. In fact, the business and the writing require, I think, the same kind of courage and discipline and are strengthened by each other.

This book, therefore, is as much about inspiration as information. It is as much for the heart as for the head, because business must have heart, and heart must work in the real world. If you are inspired and are propelled by a clarity of purpose, you will be far more willing to do what it takes to succeed.

The how-to alone will simply not carry you through, as anyone who has a problem with procrastination knows.

This book, though, is also filled with nuts and bolts: nitty-gritty, rubber-meets-the-road advice on making it as a working writer of fiction or nonfiction, from someone who does it every day for a living, and has for nearly half his life. It is a guerrilla guide to living by your wits in a field where half of those who become self-employed will be working for someone else again within a year, two-thirds within five years (although, if it's any consolation, editors and publishers don't fare much better; worse, actually: Of the two hundred or so publications that start up each year in the United States, fully 80 to 90 percent will fold within those same five years).

What separates those who sell their writing from those who don't is as much business smarts as talent, perhaps more (though the combination is unbeatable). We have all run across writing about which we have found ourselves muttering, "I could have written that." It's just that the other guy knew how to get it published. This book shows you how.

The Fate of Scheherazade

Scheherazade was the queen whose stories make up the *Arabian Nights*. She became the wife of the Sultan of Persia, by whose decree every girl he married would be killed on the morning after the wedding—a man with a serious intimacy problem.

On the day of their wedding, Scheherazade began telling him a story, but stopped just short of the climax. The Sultan agreed to let her live so that she could finish the story the next day. On the next day, she finished it and began another, and again the Sultan let her live in order to finish her story. After 1,001 nights and 1,001 stories, the Sultan, who by now had fallen in love with Scheherazade, finally agreed to repeal his onerous law.

To endure a career as a writer, you must be driven by a quality of faith not unlike Scheherazade's—the certainty that if you stop telling your stories, if you stop writing, you will die, or perhaps worse, your life will be bereft of meaning.

This book is written for those who share the fate of Scheherazade and who are committed to following it wherever it leads and whatever it demands of you.

Annuit Coeptis

CHAPTER ONE

Dragons at the Edge of the Map: The Life of the Freelance Writer

At the edges of old maps, ancient cartographers used to draw dragons. They symbolized the unknown, something most people were perfectly willing to leave to the dragons.

When you move toward becoming a freelance writer—free, especially, of both the security and confines of a "regular" job—you move toward the edge of the map, the outer limits of the comfort zone, the lair of the dragons. Never mind that without the unknown there would be no discoveries; this is Scary Stuff! Being your own boss, putting your talents to the test, and making the leap, however swiftly or slowly, toward self-employment—this is the stuff of sleepless nights and, for most writers, of endless daydreams.

The true "eccentricity" inherent in being a freelance writer, in fact, is not so much a behavioral oddity or emotional imbalance. It is a function of stepping outside the "system," the status quo, the cultural mandate of Monday-to-Friday, nine-to-five. Eccentric means being outside the center, and once there, you must begin to transform your relationship to the world of work and business, even to the world itself, and certainly to yourself.

You Are Not in Kansas Anymore

Just as traveling to a foreign country demands of you a new language, a new measure of awareness and resourcefulness that wasn't required of you at home, so, too, will leaving employment for self-employment. As you leave the nine-to-five world behind to pursue a writing business, you quickly discover that you are not in Kansas anymore:

• There is no punching out at five, no fixed point where work leaves off and life begins. This is both a blessing (almost everything under the sun is deductible) and a curse (even your vacations turn into assignments—though it's almost impossible to get sympathy for this). Still, you experience less of the rift between work and play that so many people do. You will never sport bumper stickers on your car that say "I'd rather be sailing" or "The worst day fishing is better than the best day working." What you do is what you'd rather be doing.

• You begin to see that business is no longer a place you commute an hour to each morning, but a lifestyle; and success not so much a thing you achieve as a way you feel. As for the commute, you get to avoid it, along with the six months of life that the average commuter will spend just waiting at red lights.

• You set your own goals, not just work to realize someone else's. But though there may no longer be a boss leaving hot, condensed breath on the back of your neck, if you have clients, you still have bosses, and there is always a bit of genuflecting you must do. The beauty of having many bosses, though, is that there is safety in numbers. You can better afford to drive hard bargains, disagree, or even refuse work altogether, because if you lose one client, you still have others.

• You make all the decisions and abide by all the consequences, a notion that, not without reason, scares the hell out of most people. Decision making is stressful; the status quo is not (unless you're trying to escape it).

• You decide when to work and when not to, and you begin to realize that it can be every bit as hard to stop as to start, that discipline also means knowing when to knock off. You find that having your nose to the grindstone, your ear to the ground, your shoulder to the wheel, and your back to the wall is, for long stretches of time, not the most comfortable position in which to work. Sometimes lying in the bathtub is.

• You discover that freelance writers have really boring annual company picnics.

• You have to work to get work, and well over half your time in the first few years may be spent just getting assignments, in many cases selling first and then writing. This percentage diminishes, though, in direct proportion to how quickly you learn to narrow your sights and target individual clients — to switch, as it were, from buckshot to bullets.

• You find out quickly in freelancing that income is more closely tied to output than in large companies, in which laziness and squandering are still rewarded with paychecks and where there is a bigger buffer between mistakes and failure. When you leave a corporation, you lose the institutional momentum and budget that take up the slack created by any number of individual time-management sins. *You* now pay for extra-long lunches, leaving work early, talking to friends on the phone, hanging around the water cooler, coffee breaks, clock watching, indiscriminate wastes of paper and supplies, and those sick days that were really paid vacations your company didn't know it was giving you, those sick days you returned from with a tan.

Also, without a company to pick up the tab for phone bills, health insurance, disability income, child care, pension or paid vacations, stretching a buck becomes canon law. And with no more automatic, contractual raises, you now have to *ask* for more money from editors and clients when you want it.

• The root of the word corporation is *corpus*, meaning body, and when you're self-employed that body is *you*. You're not just the boss, you're the company, and that means having the fortitude and humility to assume all the attendant responsibilities of running it, to wear all the proverbial hats, from chief executive officer to chief cook and bottle washer.

Writing is no longer a profession for people who only want to write, and the further you get from working for someone who does the business for you — the marketing, promotion, bookkeeping, and so on — the more you have to take the reins yourself. In addition to being the product, you are your own manager, bookkeeper, secretary, sales rep, shipping clerk, stockholder, financial planner, and even collection agency.

• You are more accountable in your own business. After a while, you begin to realize that there is only one character who always seems to be around when things go wrong. You.

• Because you are no longer connected to the office grapevine, with its regular flow of feedback, information, gossip, politics, trends and contacts, you learn to finesse these things from the world at large. You live tentwise, ready to move fast. You find out that a hungry animal has better hunting instincts than a well-fed one. Those who fare best take the time to figure out how the system works and how to work the system: how things get done in the business, where to get help, who pulls the strings and who dances.

Zane Grey Was a Dentist: Supporting Your Writing Habit Until It Supports You

One from the "life is cruel" department: It is excruciating to contemplate how much more writing I could have done over the years if I hadn't had to spend so much time making ends meet. Or for that matter, how much more creativity the world would have if writers, artists and entrepreneurs could spend more time at their crafts and less at their calculators.

I have certainly spent my share of angry days cursing Fate because I felt I wasn't put here to "earn a living" but to *write*! And the landlord couldn't care less.

It's easy to blame Fate, or a job or your kids for not allowing you the time and energy to pursue your writing business, for having to squeeze it into the occasional weekday night when you have the strength. The fact is, that's just the way it is, and it's frustrating. Most writers have to hold down jobs to support their writing, even the talented and "successful" ones who know that *it isn't necessarily the good writers who survive, but the strong ones*, the ones willing to do whatever it takes to give themselves a shot at their writing.

There is absolutely no disgrace in working to support your writing habit or build your writing business. You are no less successful a writer for having to take a job, for not wanting to fall into the abyss of relying on your writing to do something it may not be ready to do: support you. A long line of esteemed writers attests to this fact:

Franz Kafka was an insurance salesman, Wallace Stevens a lawyer, T.S. Eliot a bank clerk, and Zane Grey a dentist. Kurt Vonnegut was a PR man for General Electric, Thomas Pynchon a tech writer for Boeing, and Walt Whitman a secretary for the Department of the Interior.

John Steinbeck and Erma Bombeck were journalists, E.L. Doctorow a manuscript reader for Random House, and William Faulkner the landlord of a brothel. Joseph Heller, Dorothy Parker and Aldous Huxley were all ad copywriters, O. Henry was a bank cashier who fled to South America after being charged with embezzlement, and Agatha Christie was a pharmacist, which explains why she knew so much about poisons.

And many of these writers never pursued their writing full-time. The English novelist Anthony Trollope worked for most of his life as a full-time postal clerk. He got up at five A.M. every day to write for three hours until he was due at work and completed forty-six books in his lifetime. Nowhere is it written that a successful writing career has to support you; only that you have to support it!

Short of being outright subsidized by someone or of quitting your job in a blaze of passion (which I do not advise, in a big way), there are essentially three ways to go:

1. You can work full-time at a regular job and build up your writing business weekday nights, weekends and wee hours. This was my approach: Build up your writing, business know-how, capital and contacts, and slowly shift your energies toward freelancing while leaving just enough to maintain your job without getting fired for sheer lack of interest. Then when the signs are right, batten the hatches and plunge into savings, giving your writing 100 percent until you break into the black or can't afford to do it anymore, whichever comes first.

2. You can work six months of the year and then write six months (or some variation thereof), if you can stand the discontinuity. Pulitzer-winning playwright Marsha Norman once worked three jobs (teaching, newspaper stringing, and scriptwriting for an educational TV series) to finance taking the following year off to write.

3. Or you can work part-time at both writing and a job. Though you will live a bit closer to the edge by taking this route, it reduces much of the friction that naturally builds between the desire to go freelance and the need to make ends meet.

Part-time freelancing is advantageous in the beginning for the same reason that writers sometimes write books first as magazine articles. It allows you to road test the marketability of your ideas, as well as your stamina—a book can take a year or three to write—while keeping your initial investment to a minimum. Part-time freelancing will certainly tell you whether full-time freelancing is for you, giving you the relative luxury of making egregious mistakes without suffering egregious consequences.

A part-time job also offers you the time and, perhaps more importantly, the energy to write. You are less likely to come home from work devoured of your creative energies.

Ideally, you always want to come to your writing when your biorhythms are up, with the fullest possible complement of your creative juices. But this isn't always possible when your peak-performance hours are appropriated by a job, leaving your writing only leftovers or second winds.

More than likely, you will need to build your writing business in snatches of time: evenings, weekends, lunch hours, sick leaves, early mornings, holidays, commutes and vacations. I once spent an entire two-week paid vacation at home, firming up my freelancing in preparation for The Leap.

Generally speaking, the more skilled the job you hold, and the more it involves writing or other critical/creative faculties, the less inclined you may be to want to do more of the same when you get home. Some writers even insist that the best employment for writers is physical labor, which saves the mind for writing. But a job in the writing profession gives you something that more than makes up for this: writing experience.

My stint at the newspapers had everything to do with my success as a freelancer. Not only did I learn to write quickly and accurately, but I made great contacts, polished my interviewing skills, and wrote scores of stories that I later reworked into freelance articles. When I decided I wanted to go freelance as a magazine writer, in fact, one of my first steps was to persuade my editor at the *Enquirer* to let me write part-time for the Sunday *Enquirer Magazine*, to start giving me magazine-writing experience.

I also used my job to help me further research the freelance life by writing stories for the paper on self-employment, job changing, working at home, the fear of failure, decision making, procrastination and even profiles of people who were told they had six months to live—because their message was always the same: Do it now!

Finally, when I left to freelance full-time, I took my former employer, Gannett News Service, as one of my first clients.

Even if the writing you do at a writing job is not the kind you ultimately want to do, keep in mind that no writing is really detrimental. It can always teach. Journalism taught me conciseness in storytelling, research skills, and how to work on deadline. Public relations taught me an eye for drama, brevity, persuasion, and the ability to step into someone else's shoes, if not their head. Copyediting taught me grammar, clarity and the need to read my writing with a reader's ear.

Furthermore, almost anything in the field is good practice for working with editors and for giving you a visceral experience of the publishing world that can't be had any other way.

Jobs in the field might include anything from internships and staff positions with writers' professional organizations to production assistants at TV stations, reporters or copyeditors at newspapers, researchers for magazines or authors, manuscript readers for publishing houses, public-relations assistants, or working in a bookstore.

Even secretarial and clerical workers in the publishing world sometimes work their way into editorial positions. I know of one who became her newspaper's consumer columnist. You might also consider asking your company if you can freelance for some department or division within it, or for a company associated with it. I know writers who, in volunteering to write their company's memos, newsletters and reports, worked into full-time writing without ever quitting their jobs.

Short of taking on part-time work, there are ways to juggle full-time jobs so that they are less at odds with your writing goals and circadian rhythms. Ask your boss about flextime (having the option of coming in early and leaving early, or coming in late and leaving late), four-day workweeks (means three-day weekends, though it also means ten-hour days), job-sharing (two people, one job), and even telecommuting. More and more companies are opening to these options, in an effort to boost morale and productivity as well as decrease absenteeism, turnover and idle time. It's worth asking about.

Just don't take on a job you abhor merely to help you get by. If it is a job from which you eventually hope to jump into freelancing, you will create a lot of negative motivation at the start of your enterprise. You could end up leaping for the wrong reasons or well before you're ready.

Knowing When to Say When: The Importance of Timing

There is nothing so powerful, they say, as an idea whose time has come. But how do you know when an idea's time has come (or not arrived yet, or come and gone, or isn't in the cards at all), especially if that idea is yours, and it's about quitting your job to go freelance?

In these matters, it is harder to find The Perfect Moment than it is The Imperfect Moment. It's a guessing game, and you want your guess to proceed as much from logic as passion and with a firm eye on the signs. Here's how I knew it was time for *me* to jump:

- When the pain of staying became greater than the fear of leaving, the fear of becoming what I already was: unhappy.
- When I had done my homework faithfully and as if my life depended on it—because the life I want for myself *does* depend on it!
- When I had a respectable amount of freelancing up and running, and a half dozen letters of assignment. That is, guaranteed work. (Note: If you begin your transition to full-time freelancing by moonlighting, don't start spending the money you make from that writing. Your lifestyle will just expand to include the income, and since that will then become the income level to which you are accustomed, you will need to earn that much more money as a full-time freelancer. Sock it away instead. Use it to launch your full-time career.)
- When I had two years' worth of savings.
- When there were no more appeals; when I couldn't go any further with only

changes in job description, merit raises, or cosmetic readjustments in my lifestyle.

- When I was finally willing to let go of the security of my regular paycheck and the comfortable dollop of celebrity I had as a good-sized fish in a good-sized pond.
- When my older brother told me that at my age, savings are meant for transitions, not retirement.
- And finally, when the waters parted momentarily and a great voice roared "*Go!*"

The Transitions of a Writer's Life

A dream is an organism, a living entity, with an animus all its own. It exerts a centrifugal force on your life, constantly pushing out from within, or perhaps pulling at you the way a certain character in a novel-in-progress might strain at the leash, demanding to go her own way.

If you are at all faithful to your dreams, they will often lead you to a point of decision. Here you must decide whether to say yes or no, now or later, ready or not. And they will keep coming back until you give them an answer.

You must decide if you are ready for a change, and in a writer's life there are many changes: from employment to freelancing, from unemployment (or school or retirement) to freelancing, from a full-time to a part-time job, from corporate to fiction writing, magazines to books, books to films, even just at the ending of any major project. Or perhaps the transition is simply into the frame of mind of being a writer at all, to say nothing of being a writer in business.

Each requires that you end one thing—a mind-set, a lifestyle, a trade—before beginning another, and as such these transitions involve both fear and elation, terrible anxiety and tremendous freedom, the freedom to make new choices, to redefine your work and your life. But transitions don't necessarily happen fast, and much of the pain of making them occurs as your initial enthusiasm fades inevitably before the mechanics of keeping the fires burning.

My own transition to freelancing took five years, from the first realization that I was emotionally unplugging from my job to that warm, rainy Sunday morning in November when I packed everything I owned into a rental truck and drove west, past 315,000 white lines on the freeway between Cincinnati and San Francisco. And that trip was only the *middle* of the transition.

It took that long partly because I knew there was something trying to come through me, and I was scared to step aside and let it through, afraid of the pain of dissolution. I am always struck by the fierceness with which I cling to the status quo even when it no longer serves me, transfixed by my fears like a deer mesmerized by headlights, unable to move out of the way.

Transition, though, is very much about feeling caught in the middle, between the known and the unknown, and I think it is one of the peculiarities of successful people that they can tolerate prolonged periods of uncertainty and, most importantly, hang onto their faith.

But letting go of what is familiar (a job, for instance) is not something to take lightly. I do not belong to the sink-or-swim school of thought and therefore heartily do *not* recommend that you just up and quit your job, unless the prospect of financial ruin and emotional turmoil is preferable to the psychological death you are experiencing at work. As Henry David Thoreau once said, "The mass of men lead lives of quiet desperation, but it is a characteristic of wisdom not to do desperate things."

There were many times when I came a hairbreadth away from quitting my job as a reporter, out of desperation, and just starting to freelance — and thereby nearly following in the footsteps of the Spanish explorer Cortez, whose first order of business upon reaching the New World was to burn his ships, so he and his men couldn't turn tail and head back to Spain.

Fortunately, my survival instincts prevailed, or I was talked out of it by people who knew better, who knew that if I tried to freelance full-time without preparing for the rigors of that business (as well as starting a new venture in the emotionally shell-shocked aftermath of quitting a job in desperation), I would drown. One friend, an environmental writer, pointed out that in nature, sudden transitions are usually of the catastrophic variety: eruptions, earthquakes, flash floods.

Freelancing is best phased in slowly, not leapt at in a single bound. Give yourself the time to build up momentum and confidence. One writer I know, an accountant, dropped client by client as she added magazine by magazine. I myself built up to freelancing by moonlighting evenings and vacations for several years.

But preparation can easily devolve into procrastination. With any major transition, there is no end to the rehearsals you can make, the questions you can ask yourself, the experts you can consult. And it is depressingly easy to get stuck in the kind of chronic vacillation that reduces your determination to a monotonous recitation of yes-no-yes-no-yes-no, the very anthem of the indecisive. At some point you simply have to make a leap of at least some distance. You cannot cross a chasm in two small jumps, as the British statesman David Lloyd George once said.

But you also have to be gentle with yourself. Big transitions are by their very nature dramatic and effortful, and growth always in some sense violent and disruptive. Treat yourself as if you were in a cocoon, not a padded cell.

I think of the times, when I was growing up, that my family went on vacations. For the few weeks preceding our departure, my mother would take the dogs to the kennel several times, for longer and longer stretches of time, to get them used to it, so they wouldn't be frightened when we finally left.

On the other hand, do not be so easy on yourself that you cheat yourself out of changes you may really need to make. When I first became aware that I wanted to move on from my job, I almost completely ignored any soul-searching that might tell me why I wanted to move on, or where to, or what I really wanted to do next. I just started sending resumes and clips to newspapers around the country, hoping to land a similar job elsewhere, just to get out.

But I was fooling myself, thinking that switching positions was really making a change. Moving laterally is not moving forward, and it is no coincidence that nothing came of it, despite some concerted effort on my part. The fact is, I was leaving completely untouched the deeper changes that needed to take place: greater challenge, more freedom, the chance to do my own writing.

To make transitions easier on yourself, though, it helps to be familiar with your own relationship to change, especially to endings, and to the style in which you typically deal with them. Perspective is power.

During periods of upheaval, I often reread my journals, in particular those sections that pertain to turning points in my life. The patterns I rediscover— the by-now predictable things that take place in my moods, my body, my work and my relationships—help me remember that anxieties, fears, and omens of burnout are not necessarily signs that something is wrong, but that something is changing.

I also realize that I always survive transitions, that when one door closes, another inevitably opens. And just as a doctor can look at a set of symptoms and tell you what's wrong, knowing what your instinctive responses to change are can help you manage it better.

Some observations from veteran writers on the challenge of balancing employment and self-employment:

I have a sign above my desk that says: "Nobody told you not to be a plumber." And there are times when a pipe wrench looks pretty good, when I've lived on beans for weeks at a time. It's always feast or famine, but as long as you can live with yourself, you do what you have to do to survive as a writer, including taking on jobs to bring in money, and facing up to the business side of writing.

My students respond with everything from derision to horror at the prospect of doing business. They think of themselves as artists with a capital *A*. But what happens to artists with a capital *A* is that they starve.

Just never hold a job in which you can't tell the boss to take this job and shove it, where you can't write novels during your lunch hour, even though they think they're buying all your talents. Work part-time at something that won't compete too much with your writing. Physical work, computer work, being a short order cook. Early on I waited on tables, and did telephone suicide prevention. I also put myself through college writing schlock, bad romances.

MARION ZIMMER BRADLEY
AUTHOR, *THE MISTS OF AVALON*

I took part-time jobs on and off for six years until I could afford to just write. I worked in a bookstore, did canvassing door-to-door, phone sales, was a production assistant. But I left my daytimes free, since I'm most productive and focused then.

All my jobs had value from a business standpoint. I learned sales techniques, making good presentations, how to use my voice. These helped me in pitch meetings, and in talking to production executives. But a job also leaves you tired. A job is by definition work. It's hard to shift gears to writing. The bookstore was easiest that way. It didn't tax my brain.

I also had mixed feelings about myself during this period. Am I really a professional if I have to work part-time? Does anyone care what I write? But you just have to persevere, if writing is what you really want to do. It takes sheer doggedness. My latest film has been a ten-year process. But if the quality is there, you eventually attract attention.

BRUCE SINGER
SCREENWRITER, TV SERIES "MOONLIGHTING," "PAPER CHASE" MINISERIES, "YEAR IN THE LIFE"

I jumped into freelancing from an editorial job at *InfoWorld*, where my next step was either onto the managerial track or out. I was a little impatient, so I did it sink-or-swim, though the magazine became one of my first large clients, and at a significantly higher hourly rate. In the beginning, I took a part-time job as a bank teller, but eventually concluded that the time could be better spent writing.

Start building a client base while you're still at a full-time job. Prove there's really work out there, and that you can really do it. And though you might take on anything in the beginning just for the skills and contacts, narrow it down until you're doing what you like best, because that will be your best work, and you'll get paid for it. It works that way.

Also, when people talk about recession, I always say, "I refuse to participate." I nearly doubled my income during one recession. There are always opportunities in cutbacks. Often staff publications people are the first to go, and since many don't want to be outside consultants for their old companies, or they're busy trying to find other jobs, or they're off balance from just being laid off, companies with emergency projects often use freelancers. Everything's insecure anyway, so why not gamble on yourself?

CAROL A. RANALLI
PUBLICATIONS CONSULTANT
CORPORATE WRITER FOR IBM, HEWLETT-PACKARD, HITACHI

I didn't plan on being a freelance writer. I lost my job at the local CBS radio station. But since I had wanted more creative satisfaction and to get out from behind the scenes, once I was thrown into it, it appealed to me. Still, I strongly recommend part-time jobs. They give you financial stability and help you stay in touch with the world. It's also much easier to go home and write after a part-time job than a full-time job. Especially a job in broadcast journalism, which is wipeout stuff, and always more than eight-hour days.

You have to make financial sacrifices. Just trust in the reasons that led you to believe in your writing to begin with, and don't be too influenced by American consumerism.

DIANE KEATON
FREELANCE AGRICULTURAL WRITER

I have taken on a lot of different assignments in order to support my habit, which is fiction. Sometimes a week of magazine work can buy me a month of fiction writing. So is that a compromise, or an opportunity too good to pass up? With nonfiction, it's often easier to make money that pays for the time you invest. I also do writers' conferences, lectures, panels and readings.

From time to time I also teach a university writing workshop, which keeps me fairly close to what I like to be thinking about. Academia has become a major patron of writers. It's work that usually leaves you time to write. When I taught freshman composition at a community college, though, even part-time, it stole away my language energy. In those days, making my living as a musician was more workable. It used up nervous, physical energy, but never depleted my desire to write.

JIM HOUSTON
AUTHOR, *LOVE LIFE, CONTINENTAL DRIFT, CALIFORNIANS, RETURN TO MANZANAR*

Sign Language: How to Use the Clues

There are South Pacific Islanders who can sail for a thousand miles under cloud cover, with no sun, moon or stars to usher them from island to island, and know exactly where they are by the kinds of waves beneath their rafts.

This quality of mindfulness is essential to anyone who runs his own ship. Success demands that you *pay attention to the signs*. If you don't, you can waste years of your life following bum directions, or trajectories that once worked, but don't anymore.

Put another way, nature favors the most adaptive creatures, those who best accommodate to and utilize changes in their surroundings. It is thus indispensable to stay tuned.

It may seem contradictory, but although you want goals that are concrete, you don't want them set in stone. They must be reevaluated regularly. What were once be-alls and end-alls can lose their intoxication after five years, put you completely on automatic pilot after ten, and become a prison after fifteen. Your interests, aspirations and circumstances are fluid, not solid. When they change, so must the objectives that grew out of them; otherwise they not only cease to serve you, they hold you back.

It doesn't take long for any of us to become disgruntled with the status quo, a condition that, depending on how easily you bore, can set in faster than a sunburn at high noon. What you once yearned for can burn you out when you attain it. It can do so even if you do *not* attain it. Perhaps especially so. Nothing breeds success like success, they say, but nothing breeds failure like failure. If you consistently fail to reach an objective, take another look at it.

I personally take time out for palm readings every few months. I take a tape deck upstairs to the rocking chair that looks out onto the mountains and dictate something of a quarterly report from management to the CEO: What have I accomplished in the past quarter, where am I still blocked, what skills need polishing, how do the finances look, and how do I *feel*?

After such a report, it is not uncommon for me, for instance, to drop an editor a note requesting a deadline extension when it becomes obvious that a story demands more attention than I anticipated. Not only am I always granted the reprieve—assuming I didn't request it at the eleventh hour—but I avoid unnecessary anxiety. I have also reexamined my timetables and expectations, rearranged deadlines and work habits, pitched to easier or more challenging clients, studied the market more closely, upgraded my skills, and even quit jobs.

Throughout your writing career, you need to listen carefully to the voices inside your head, the signals that blip across the screen of your business, and to feedback and guidance no matter what forms they take, whether failures, physical symptoms, or dreams. You need to observe patterns, recognize important moments when they happen, and ask of every mistake, "What are you trying to tell me?" And then you need the courage to change course when the weight of evidence demands it. Don't ignore signs of change, any more than you would ignore symptoms of illness.

It isn't always easy, of course, to know what the signs *mean*, and what you're supposed to do about them. If your book proposal is rejected by twenty publishers in a row, is that telling you to give up, to keep going, to change tactics, to reevaluate your work or your talents? It depends on many things, perhaps most of all your ability to listen. There is, at any given moment, a subtle breeze blowing through each of our lives, and we need to learn how to be still enough to make out which way that breeze is blowing.

Let me offer some examples of signs that have helped point me toward important changes in my writing business, messages that were hieroglyphic until I apprehended what they meant:

• In the year or two before I left my job, I experienced a persistent pain in my lower back whenever I sat down. Nothing seemed to explain it, until a chiropractor suggested that "perhaps you don't like where you're sitting." The day I decided to leave my job—not the day I actually left, but the day I simply *decided* to leave—the pain disappeared.

Talents become needs, and if those needs are not met, I believe, they become symptoms.

• For a long time in the beginning of my freelance career, I convinced myself that I wasn't good enough to get essays published in the Big Magazines. That is, until I got one into *The New York Times Sunday Magazine*. Suddenly I had to completely rethink my sense of self. Which I did. Shortly thereafter, I had essays accepted by *Psychology Today*, *Glamour* and *The Christian Science Monitor*.

Sometimes it's important to follow your beliefs instead of the evidence. But sometimes, as in this case, it is more important to follow the evidence than your beliefs.

• After five years of building up my science and health freelancing to the point when I was earning enough to give me something worth stealing, I started losing my stamina for the concentration this kind of research demands. I found the articles themselves harder and harder to write. And worst of all, I didn't even enjoy reading them anymore when they hit print. When I finally braved a look in the mirror, I no longer saw the writer I had been even a year before. What I saw was someone who now wanted to write more essays, not more articles.

Don't stand in your own way. Admit when something isn't working for you anymore.

• In the weeks prior to losing a reporting job early in my career, one I was hanging onto primarily for security, my dreams were absolutely splitting at the seams with portents of how I really felt about trading off integrity for material comfort. And though I faithfully recorded them in my journal, I mostly tried to ignore them. In one dream, I was handed a stack of hundred dollar bills and later discovered that only the top bill was a hundred dollars; the rest were ones. In another, I found a golden calf, deformed and chained to the ground. In still another, I lost my wallet with all my identification cards in it.

Because I had my head in the sand, the loss of that job came as a complete shock to me, when it shouldn't have.

Granted, facing facts can be like suddenly standing up in a canoe. Your life immediately becomes unsteady, and a voice inside your head booms, "Sit down! You're rocking the boat."

Stand up anyway. You will get a much better view of the approaching rapids.

To get the most out of any of the oracular arts, I think, requires a Grand-Scheme approach to looking at your life, one that is suffused with a sense of meaning, a sense that things happen for a reason and that lessons come in a myriad of disguises, some of them distressing.

With such an outlook, though, all lessons, all "failures," occur within a context of purpose. It becomes easier to find meaning in everything that happens to you, whether in the form of job changes, illnesses, sudden opportunities, a book that mysteriously makes its way to you, or a compelling accumulation of "coincidences."

Such as: The Monday following my Friday dismissal from the aforementioned job, I was supposed to interview the author of a book called *Starting Over: How to Survive the Loss of a Job*. Even more astonishingly, I had the book sitting on my night table at home, since I planned to read it over the weekend. Needless to say I did, and its impact on a very painful transition was profound.

In my own Grand Scheme of Things, this was not a coincidence to shrug off. It was a synchronicity to embrace, a sign that, awful as it felt, there was a quality of rightness to losing that job which was as difficult to explain as to deny.

Hell and High Water: The Power of Persistence

The cartoonist Gary Larson, creator of *The Far Side*, once related in an interview that on the morning of his second day of kindergarten, when his mother came in to wake him up, he rolled over and groaned, "What, again?"

Of all the characteristics that might mark a writer for success, none, I think, is as important as endurance, the willingness to stick with it, to go to your desk day after day as if it mattered, as if the writing you do in the world made a difference. And it does.

Endurance is the knowledge that success takes time. It will, in fact, take every bit as long to become a successful writer as to become a successful brain surgeon. Success is achieved by the slow, incremental adding on of one day's labor to another's.

Sometimes endurance will pay off quickly, as it did when Voltaire cranked out *Candide* in three days. Other times, you will pay for a single piece of work with a third of your life, as James Joyce did, spending over seventeen years writing *Finnegans Wake*. One of my own articles took five years to finally get published; I rewrote it half a dozen times for three different magazines, each of which paid me for it and then canned it.

Either way, what is required of you is the discipline and devotion to pursue your writing wherever it takes you. You must follow it from the first illuminations, through all revisions to the final execution, and then out into the world. "Everyone has talent," Erica Jong once remarked. "What is rare is the courage to follow the talent to the dark place where it leads."

Compared to talent, persistence is a modest, even lowly virtue. But it is an essential one. It is the beast of burden on whose shoulders your craft is not only carried to completion but carried to market. Without it, your talents will never see the light of day.

However, persistence can make up for only some of the multitude of our sins. Nor is talent alone sufficient. Putting it to work is the thing. Unfortunately, as Sylvia Plath observed, most writers would rather "have written" than write. Writing is hard work, and sticking with it even harder. The pen is not only mightier than the sword, but heavier.

The discipline to carry it, though, does not arise solely from grim willpower, from holding yourself to your work by the scruff of the neck, and certainly not from fear—though there will be days when you pull yourself through only on that part of your brain that is pure survival.

Discipline grows primarily out of the compulsion to communicate, the need to understand and be understood, the addiction to the truth. It is also a natural by-product of your commitment to yourself. Simply put, all the deadlines, unpaid bills, and fears of starvation and bankruptcy will not inspire in you nearly the resolve that ascends from doing work you love.

Unfortunately, discipline has a bad name. When I think of it, I think of spankings, trips to the principal's office, and staying after school to write one hundred times on the blackboard, "I will not carve dirty limericks onto the desks." I think of punishment.

But discipline is nothing more than the concentrated effort necessary to get work done. It is by *not* being disciplined that we truly punish ourselves, because without it we drift endlessly, and our dreams recede from us.

We also rob ourselves of the emotional stability that comes from establishing a daily work routine, *and sticking to it*. That means that if you lose a morning here or an afternoon there to some social engagement, or just because you don't feel like working, you make up for it somewhere down the line, even if it takes a Friday night or a Sunday morning.

It means taking yourself seriously, so that others will. Like family. They need to know that busy means busy, and that interrupting you while you're writing is like walking into a photographer's darkroom when the red light is on. They expose delicate material to the light of intrusion and risk ruining it.

For that matter, if your family and friends don't occasionally complain that they don't get to see you enough, and that you seem distracted when they *do* get to see you, it is entirely possible that you may not be working hard enough to make it as a full-time freelance writer.

After Michelangelo died, a piece of paper was found in his studio on which the old master had written a note to his apprentice, a message that speaks eloquently of endurance: "Draw Antonio, draw Antonio, draw and do not waste time."

Power Lounging: In Praise of Idleness

When people think of Sisyphus, they think of a man condemned to push a giant stone up a mountain, only to watch it roll back into the valley just as he nears the top, and to do it all over again—the curse being not so much the fruitless labor as knowledge of the inevitable end result of his labor.

But the true instruction of Sisyphus's life is overlooked, I think. It is that each time his great grindstone rolls to the bottom of the mountain, Sisyphus is granted a rest while he walks back down to retrieve it. Though he must work for all time, according to the curse, he does not work all the time.

Nor should we.

Freelance writing is a heavy stone, and it demands a steady labor to keep it rolling. But one of the tasks of perseverance is knowing when to stop persevering, to simply drop everything and take a break. It is a discipline all its own. Just as the "rest" in music provides the ear with brief repose, and the paragraph gives the reader's eye momentary release, so are idleness and leisure integral to work.

Writing is a profession dominated by the intellect, and writers are the kind of people who have been told all their lives, "You think too much." Sometimes it's true. Sometimes we don't know when or even how to stop, to climb down out of our heads and into our bodies, spirits and glands.

Also, because there is often such a fine line between life and work, and simply to be a writer is to always be at work, it is difficult to punch out. In a way, existence is our occupation, and to be is to do.

Still, we need deliberate, if not scheduled, escapes into physical adventure, sport, lovemaking, nature, good friends, good music, and even just pure and wholesome inactivity—what an acquaintance of mine calls "power lounging."

Contrary to what Plato has said, the unexamined life is a terrific relief once in a while, and leading just such a life occasionally is vital to your productivity, just as letting fields go fallow helps the land build strength. The novelist Octavio Paz cites the example of a French poet who hung the inscription "The poet is working" from his door while he slept. And Agatha Christie, the top-selling woman author in the world, once said that "The best time for planning a book is while you're doing the dishes."

Still, when we're not working, when we allow ourselves to drift and dream, we often feel as though we're overindulging ourselves, wasting time. But we're not, any more than winter is a waste of time just because seeds aren't flying around. Besides, this is your life in addition to being your business. It has to be fun, too. And since you are your only employee, you have to be good to yourself. You have to honor the creator, not just the creation.

Unfortunately, droning away in the boiler room of our culture is a juggernaut of a machine, one that heaves out a message strong enough to pump cement through your veins: *Work!* We are valued less for who we are than for what we produce, for how closely we can come to approximating a Dewar's Profile. So we're constantly *doing*. And when you're busy doing, you don't have to be busy feeling—feeling that maybe you're not enjoying your work, or you're working too hard, or you're avoiding something by working so hard.

Work is a great way to feel in control, but when you overwork, when you ignore the need for change or rest or introspection, your life becomes more a parody of being in control. You're like someone frantically making the bed while the house is burning down.

And it is often when you need it most, when you're the most anxious and overworked, that you are least inclined to give yourself time off. I know this firsthand. I often act as if the only solution to panic, especially about money, is to work *harder*, not to stop, even if doing so is for the curative purposes of gaining perspective, reevaluating my approach, and unplugging from the immediate stress.

Sometimes the best solution is a breather, and the single most salutary and replenishing variety I know of is the retreat (or what a friend of mine prefers to call advances), particularly when you're in the middle or at the end of an all-consuming project like a book or in the transition to a new business. It is an opportunity to get away and take in the big picture, to step outside the store and look back through the window.

In these cases, though, be aware that big projects build up big momentums, and they don't necessarily end for you just because the work itself ends. It's a bit like a head-on collision: The car stops suddenly, but the passengers don't. So break it to yourself slowly, perhaps by designing large projects so that there are smaller and smaller tasks toward the end.

In any case, my criteria for the consummate retreat include:

- A trip *away from home*. That is the only way I really get away from work.
- A trip of at least three days. It takes me that long to unwind.
- Time alone. I needn't actually go alone, but I must take some time during which I can talk out loud to myself, be absolved of all accountability and, I hope, find quietude so penetrating that the faintest murmur of the mind sounds like a cannon going off.
- An inspiring place. For me, that means anywhere that I can take in huge chunks of the world at a glance, possibly even the curvature of the earth, anywhere I am soothed by the benediction of rivers, mountains, ocean or forest. I need a place where I am reminded of my relative size, reminded that great beauty goes to waste every day in the world, and that there is too much to do in a single lifetime, so I have to choose my battles carefully.
- And finally, a great book, one that speaks directly to where I am at that particular juncture in my life.

Solitude and the Writer

In any enterprise, there is always the unforeseen. And of all the unforeseen elements in my own freelance career, few have taken me as much by surprise as the isolation, the amount of solitude involved, how lonesome the writing profession can be.

Furthermore, I have found that isolation usually increases as you:

- Move from part-time to full-time freelancing.
- Start writing books.
- Write less for local publications and more for national ones, since your interviewing takes place more over the phone, and your contact with editors becomes less physical and more epistolary.
- Shift from corporate or nonfiction writing to more "literary" writing, since your research moves closer to home.

The solitude of writing is, of course, a mixed blessing. On one hand, there is great freedom in solitude: Anything we do within it is normal; we are the most ourselves when alone.

Also, ironically, solitude gives us our best connection to the world, since writing *is* the way we connect, and writing, for most writers, only happens in solitude.

It is, in fact, the fountainhead of a writer's creativity, the silence out of which the art is born. This is why it is so important, as the poet Rainer Rilke said, to learn to love your loneliness, not just endure it. "Love your solitude and try to sing out with the pain it causes you."

Anthony Storr, in his book *Solitude*, adds that "for creative people, their most significant moments are those in which they attain some new insight, or make some new discovery, and these moments are chiefly, if not invariably, those in which they are alone." Some writers have even found that prison provided just the sort of aloneness they needed to get some work done. Sir Walter Raleigh, while imprisoned on charges of treason for twelve years in the Tower of London, managed to write a little treatise he called *The History of the World*.

The beneficence of solitude, however, can easily go bad. You can simply get too much of it, causing you to feel marooned, cleft from community, and isolated from feedback. This is one of the reasons why I teach. It is a wonderful antidote to the isolation of writing, a way to keep in contact with other writers, and a good parallel income. I get paid to monopolize the conversation, something that cursed social grace otherwise prevents me from doing.

But it isn't necessarily only the writer who suffers from solitude. It can also be the writing. Because writing is communication, the circuit is not complete until you give it to someone. It does no one any good to keep it to yourself for too long. Especially if you are not being published yet, it is important, I think, to give audience to your writing, some outside recognition that it, and you, both exist and are progressing.

Publication is obviously one of the more desirable ways of getting feedback on your writing, though even then you cannot really count on editors to critique and validate your work. Best to get this from friends, family, colleagues, consultants and other writers.

Short of this, you can give *yourself* feedback by sticking your writing in a drawer for a week before sending it out. When you come back to it, with renewed objectivity, you can really see where it leaks.

Feedback is so important that, while working at a former job, I once made the following proposal to my boss: I would be willing to take a $1,000-a-year cut in pay if he would agree to give me a fifteen-minute feedback session every two weeks. He, however, declined, even when I presented him with studies showing that people perform better with regular feedback.

Mostly I have sought out the communion of other writers, sometimes individually, sometimes in groups and classes. I do this occasionally for feedback on my writing, but primarily because I want congress with people who under-

This Business of Writing

stand my lifestyle and speak my language; people with whom to commiserate; people who know that etymology is not the study of bugs.

An old Hebrew proverb says that God created people because He loves stories, and perhaps it can also be said that He created support groups because some of those stories can't be told to just anyone. Writers' support groups, or even just self-employment support groups, are valuable in providing a "been-there" factor, people who empathize, as well as a place to belong, a place to "swap juices," as Mark Twain put it. Just be vigilant that your writing remains your own and doesn't become a committee function.

Fear Is a Tool of the Trade

What holds most writers back is not so much lack of know-how or talent but fear. Fear of what failure may say about you, or what success may demand of you. Fear of letting go of your writing and of the public exposure that invites rejection, criticism and book reviews. Fear of closing doors without knowing whether they can ever be opened again. Fear of putting blood, sweat and tears into something that isn't a sure thing.

The minute you take up oars in pursuit of something you don't currently possess, you set off into the unknown. And fear is a natural response. When you want something, you're afraid of not getting it, or of losing it once you do get it, or even of getting it to begin with.

Because the writing profession involves taking risks, and thereby kindling fear, you must possess the ability—but more importantly the willingness—to *have a relationship with your fears*, to examine the experience of fear when it arises.

Don't ignore it. Whatever is suppressed not only has power over you, but will help create obstacles to continually remind you of what you're hiding from, where you feel you don't measure up, and where you don't have faith in yourself.

Success often has as much to do with finding what is standing in your way as with talent or persistence. Marcel Proust, for instance, couldn't finish his epic *Remembrance of Things Past* until after his mother died. He was too inhibited by the fear that his material might hurt her feelings.

Just as you cannot acquire immunity to a disease without first coming into contact with it, you will never move through your fears until you move *through* them, not around them. A fear of the dark will not be ameliorated by turning on night-lights. Light does not eliminate the fear of the dark; it only eliminates the dark. Similarly, not sending your writing out into the world does not stop your fear of rejection. It only stops the rejection.

Think of how you feel when someone else takes your fear and pain to heart, when you feel heard. The pain begins to dissolve. Well, you can do the same for yourself. "Believe your pain," said the poet W.H. Auden. Take it seriously, know that it has meaning and utility, and that out of it grows a powerful kind of writing.

Unfortunately, we have become conditioned to avoiding what is fearful. The logic is impeccable at an emotional level: If we don't try, then we don't have to be afraid, and we can console ourselves that even if none of our dreams come true, then at least neither will our nightmares. The avoidance becomes its own reward.

So what's wrong with avoiding what you're afraid of?

Nothing—unless you fear ants and like picnics, fear elevators and work on the thirtieth floor, fear rejection and like selling your writing, fear failure and enjoy success.

The fight-or-flight mechanism was never meant to be stuck in the "on" position. Fears are supposed to be real, not imaginary. They were designed to warn you of large, dark shadows in long, narrow caves, of stepping outside of your car at the safari park, of breathing underwater.

They are actually there at your service, though it may not often feel that way. For one thing, when fears begin to surface, especially after a deep sleep, they do not do so quietly. Pain is not subtle when anesthesia wears off. But where there is fear, there is power. So use your fears. Don't let them use you.

One of the great fears, of course, is the one attached, like a barnacle to a rock, to the idea of failure. And though we try to pep ourselves up by affirming that "It's OK to fail" and "Those who succeed the most fail the most," most of us have also found out that failure is much scarier in person than in theory. Yes, it's OK to fail, but it's quite a different matter to actually live with failure or with someone who is failing regularly. Especially if they're out there failing with family money.

Still, success is as much a matter of making mistakes as making headway, and the worst mistake in life—certainly in business—is to be in constant fear of making one. "If you are not failing regularly," I was once told, "you are living so far below your potential that you're failing anyway."

Failures are not only natural in the course of ambition, they're vital. In Chinese, the word *crisis* is composed of two characters: one means danger; the other, opportunity. Failure is opportunity in disguise.

When I look back at incidents that, at the time, I thought of as disasters and defeats, I see that they often became some of the most colossal opportunities in my career, the biggest turning points in my life. If I hadn't hated the first college I attended, I would never have transferred to a school where I took a course called "How to Run a College Newspaper," which was my initiation into journalism.

If I hadn't left my job in journalism, Writer's Digest Books would never have approached me to write a book about freelancing.

Mythologist Joseph Campbell has called these experiences "directive crises," and author Gail Sheehy refers to them as "falling up." They are failures that set you up for ultimately life-enhancing changes. As in a Dickens novel, accidental encounters and happenstances turn out to be formative events. But you have no idea at the time; only in retrospect. So when failures occur, ask what they might be showing you, how they might be plot twists that you won't understand for another two hundred pages.

As meditation students often learn, whatever interruptions occur while "sitting" are not distractions from the meditation; they *are* the meditation. Similarly, failures are not obstacles in your path; they *are* your path. Don't fight them. To borrow a bit of folk wisdom: If it starts to rain, let it!

Also, if life is an experiment in which there are no failures, only results, then how you interpret the results of your own experiment will determine how successful you feel. If, for instance, after a publisher rejects your novel, you conclude "wrong publisher," that is very different from concluding "lousy book," though it may well be that your book needs more work. Either way, it will greatly affect your next step.

Fear of failure, though, is only one side of a particular coin, the flip side of which is the fear of success. This might be your fear that exposure brings with it criticism and judgment, or that the more you have, whether of fortune or fame, the more you have to lose. Perhaps you worry that your good news might be someone else's bad news, or that as business picks up, so will the demands on your time.

Success is also intimidating because in order to achieve it, you must push beyond limitations you perceive in yourself—your bad back, not enough time, the kids, your typing skills, the ghost of your high school English teacher who wondered aloud to you one afternoon if perhaps you had ever thought of a career in engineering instead. Success demands that you let go of these familiar, maybe comfortable, constraints.

And then there is the fear of trying to top your own successes. The effect of receiving a major prize like the Pulitzer demonstrates this ably. There have been more than a few writers who, having received this coveted honor, felt thereafter that it was the worst thing that ever happened to them. From then on, they could barely scribble a note on a matchbook cover without wondering if it was Pulitzer material.

Pulitzer-winning columnist Ellen Goodman, perhaps attempting to cultivate a protective detachment, simply said of her prize: "All it means is that I now know the first line of my obituary."

Fall Down Seven Times, Stand Up Eight: How to Handle Rejection

The single most abominable rejection I have ever heard of a writer receiving was this: "Dear Mr. Andrews: We cannot use the paper you sent us. You wrote on it."

With editors like that, who needs enemies? It is no wonder writers are often reluctant to send their work out. Mr. Andrews probably went on to become a Writer's Block poster child.

Fortunately, there are mercifully few editors so short on generosity, or so short on paper. But they do exist, and they are there to show us that rejection sometimes says more about the critic than about the writer. Sometimes what you learn from rejection is just to keep trusting your own instincts.

And then sometimes you'll get a nugget of valuable feedback along with your rejection, and it is important to recognize the good news amidst the bad. Here are some examples of the advice editors have passed along to me in rejection slips:

- "We'd prefer you not pitch us features as an unknown writer (to us). Try one of our columns first." (*In Health Magazine*)
- "A great story idea. So good we did it ourselves recently. Send more." (*Seventeen*)
- "Please read our guidelines before querying again." (*Good Housekeeping*)
- "All our money pieces are done in-house." (*McCall's*)
- "Not new enough." (*New Woman*)
- "The piece doesn't seem as funny as when you queried it." (*Las Vegas Journal Review*)
- "We just ran this piece. But call with more ideas." (*Newsday*)
- "Not sexy enough." (*Gentlemen's Quarterly*)
- "Our profiles lean more toward the truly well-known." (*Vis a Vis*)
- "Too specialized for us." (*Glamour*)
- "Too controversial for us." (*Ford Times*)

Whether you receive form rejections or first-person rejections, though, rejection itself is 100 percent guaranteed in the writing profession, as predictable as eyestrain to a programmer and headaches to a politician. The only way to avoid it is to not send your writing out at all, though by doing so you avoid rejection but not failure.

Although in most cases rejection slips are simply people saying no-thank-you, and writers are instructed not to take it personally, I think this is specious advice. It *is* personal. It's your writing, your ideas and visions, your delicate filaments of hope extended to what often feels like an ungrateful world. And when editors hide behind standard rejection forms (which they do, understandably, for the sake of expediency), it somehow takes from us the right to face our accusers, if not the opportunity to find out *why* our writing was rejected, though we may not necessarily want to know.

To say that rejection is nothing personal, that editors are rejecting your writing, not you, is unconvincing. Most writers believe that their writing *is* them and do not wish to cultivate the kind of emotional detachment that, say, doctors maintain regarding patients, lest they anguish over every relapse.

It's OK to grieve. To curse. To mutter about the indignity of it all. If rejection doesn't hurt, there's something fishy. Let it hurt. And then let it go. Get your writing right back out there. Rejection by its very nature robs you momentarily of control, and the best thing to do is to regain that control by sending your work right out again to the next client on your list, preferably the same day. Follow the simple recipe for success described in an old Japanese proverb: Fall down seven times, stand up eight.

Several years ago, I pitched a newspaper editor the idea of doing a profile of one Kevin Ryerson, Shirley MacLaine's personal medium, someone whom the spirits seem to use as a human telephone. I received the following rejection note: "Dear Gregg—Thanks for the query, but I just can't bring myself to give these quacks publicity. Just because people are dead doesn't mean they're any smarter."

The same goes for editors. Just because people are editors doesn't necessarily make them admirable judges of writing, though many are. They have their opinions—and they are just that: opinions, not verdicts—and you have yours. If your opinion is that your writing is good enough for publication, then don't stop until you find that place.

And take solace from history. It is full of the indiscretions of editors who thought they were being smart. Here is a smattering of examples from an inspiring little book called *Rotten Rejections*:

- *The Diary of Anne Frank*: "The girl doesn't, it seems to me, have a special perception or feeling which would lift the book above the curiosity level."
- *Catch-22*, Joseph Heller: "A continual and unmitigated bore."
- *Lady Chatterly's Lover*, D.H. Lawrence: "For your own good, do not publish this book."
- *Lord of the Flies*, William Golding: "It does not seem to us that you have been wholly successful in working out an admittedly promising idea."
- *A Portrait of the Artist as a Young Man*, James Joyce: "It is not possible to get hold of an intelligent audience in wartime."
- *The Fountainhead*, Ayn Rand: "It is too intellectual for a novel. It won't sell."
- *Mankind in the Making*, H.G. Wells: "Only a minor writer of no large promise."
- *Animal Farm*, George Orwell: "It is impossible to sell animal stories in the U.S.A."

Now, where would these writers have been—where would literature be—if they had listened to these editors?

Listen to a few more firsthand ruminations on the qualities important to being a freelance writer:

It may be an old-fashioned, unpopular idea, but I think success in writing takes primarily talent, and some business acumen, taking notice of what the public's mind is preoccupied with at the moment. But there's a real danger in that. Too much business can be damaging to the product, though writing is really a by-product. Of living.

Beginners often think of writing as something with jackpots in it, and sometimes it is. But if you start hunting for jackpots, you become a jackpot hunter, instead of a writer. Writing should make its own market.

And if you're going to work to support your writing, it shouldn't be too close to writing itself. I don't think you can write for an advertising agency all day and then come home at night and write anything very responsible. You just wear out those nerve endings. Writing is intensely concentrated work. There's only a certain amount of it you can do every day.

WALLACE STEGNER
AUTHOR, *ANGLE OF REPOSE, THE BIG ROCK CANDY MOUNTAIN*

Older writers often suggest that success is mostly about talent. Perhaps that's the way it *was*. But there are fewer highbrow readers today, those who would help make a writer's reputation, and fewer editors and publishing houses willing to nurture young writers along.

You certainly need more than talent today. Publishers want a product that will sell, and the harder your work is to sell, the more it will serve you to become involved in the business end of writing. Writers need to promote themselves, understand writer-editor relationships, and consider who their audience is and if there is an audience available for their work. Writing to please yourself alone is a path full of painful disappointments.

It becomes almost an existential question: What is meaningful to you? To get your work out, what are you willing to do? If a publisher said to you, "If you put in a kidnapping, we can sell your book," would you do it? For me, it was both a compromise and a strategy to begin writing nonfiction along with my fiction. It was too painful to continue writing the sort of fiction that could garner only a very small audience.

There are no easy answers. These are real human dilemmas.

ERIC MAISEL
THERAPIST/AUTHOR, *STAYING SANE IN THE ARTS*

I took a good hard look one day at the writing I was doing for Hewlett-Packard, and it was boring compared to when I write my fiction. I'm a hack, and I have respect for hacks. I can always use these skills, and writing is a great skill to have. I can always get work. But when I find my job so in opposition to myself, I can't do it anymore.

I'm transitioning out of work here, but I have no illusions. I know what the worst that could happen is: I send out resumes again. There are a ton of companies I could work for. But you look for ways to do it, not ways to talk yourself out of doing it. I figure I've got twenty to twenty-five years left to me, so what the heck. I'm going for it. At some point you just ask yourself, "Where is my soul? And when do I come face to face with it?"

MICHAEL SLACK
MANAGER OF PUBLICATIONS, HEWLETT-PACKARD
FICTION WRITER/PLAYWRIGHT

Self-discipline is the most important quality. Without it, talent goes nowhere. Writers also have to get over their fear of editors, publishers and rejection. Remember: you're the product. Publishers are marketers, and editors are teammates.

DOROTHY DOWDELL
AUTHOR, HISTORICAL ROMANCES FOR RANDOM HOUSE
THE WOMAN'S EMPIRE, SEAFARING WOMAN

Without talent, nothing will happen. But even with talent, nothing may still happen. Just as important is perseverance and attunement with one's generation, an ear for what's going on. I write about my own obsessions, but I'm not naive. I frame my proposals so that what I care about will also sell. I think about audience, and come up with an accessible angle.

I'm also very determined. Sterling Lord, a big New York agent who has handled Jack Kerouac and Gloria Steinem, took a risk with me because I was able to communicate that determination to him. But I figure writing is the only thing I've been able to do, so I've *got* to succeed at it.

ELIZABETH FISHEL
AUTHOR, *SISTERS, FAMILY MIRRORS, THE MEN IN OUR LIVES*

CHAPTER TWO

Goals: Setting Your Course for Success

The first article I ever sold was a feature for *The Cincinnati Enquirer*, for which they gave me $75 and, I thought at the time, immortality.

I stayed up until 2:30 A.M. the morning it was to hit the streets, because I was too excited to sleep, and because the morning paper comes out in the middle of the night.

I took my copy to the all-night diner around the corner from my house, sat down at a booth, opened it to the People Today section, and had the first shock of my young career: They spelled my name wrong! "Gregg Lewis" isn't even close.

I was so mad I slammed my fist down on the table, clattering dishes and silverware. The waitress walked over and said, "Hey, if you want a cup of coffee, all you have to do is ask."

Disappointments have occurred with an unmistakable regularity throughout my writing career, and they will occur throughout yours, as well. But what has kept me going in spite of them is that, from the very beginning, I have been 1) doing what I love, 2) setting goals that lead me back to what I love, and 3) using every resource at my disposal to reach those goals.

Combined, these factors have helped me answer the questions continually posed by setbacks, such as "Now what?" and "Where is this all heading?"

When you have spent a day battling the long arm of the law—Murphy's Law—you need answers to these questions that satisfy even the cynic in you, or else you won't be able to go the distance. Dreaming is not enough. You must articulate your dreams, get them in writing, turn them into goals. *Success is the achievement of a goal, and without goals there can be no successes.* Ships don't come in. You build them and take them *out.*

Besides, if you have identifiable milestones for your business, you'll know when you hit them and know that you're progressing. Goals will also give you clarity, and clarity will give you a cussed determination to outlast all the obstacles fate puts in your way to test your resolve, the "failures" that turn out to be merely the Muse in disguise:

- A magazine or account folding and taking half your rent money with it.
- A month's work down the drain when new editors stake out their claim to authority by canning everything the previous editors had assigned.
- Payments-on-acceptance that aren't.
- Rejections that would depress a panhandler.

- Fear that is deeper than you thought.
- A climb that is steeper than you expected.

It is to your passions and your intentions that you will return again and again for solace, encouragement and guidance when you hit setbacks. They must be on firm footing, so that they can support your dreams and your business, and help you become the kind of writer you aspire to be: a busy one.

Goal setting is based on the notion that, if you know what you're looking for, it is easier to find. It is not unlike the "hidden pictures" in children's magazines: In what appears to be an ordinary scene with a lake and woods and farmhouse are "hidden" a pitchfork, a toothbrush and a lightbulb. Once you know what to look for, they are plainly there. You wonder how you missed them before.

Procrastination: Cholesterol in the Arteries of Success

In her travels through Wonderland, Alice asked the Cheshire Cat, "Would you tell me, please, which way I ought to go from here?" To which the Cat replied, "That depends a good deal on where you want to get to."

"I don't much care where," said Alice.

"Then," said the Cat, "it doesn't matter which way you go."

There is more than a passing analogy here to the way many writers navigate their careers. They refuse to acknowledge where they want to be, by when, how they want to get there, and what they want to do once they arrive. They simply fail to set the goals that will get them what they want.

Understandably, perhaps. Goal setting is intimidating because we suspect that whatever we come up with might not be what we are presently doing with our lives. We're afraid to change, to set in motion, even just by our desires, a storm that will undoubtedly rock the boat. And change often demands hard work in undoing a status quo we may have worked very hard to create.

Furthermore, writers are often stricken with the notion that goal setting will bring the spontaneity of writing crashing down to earth. It's so . . . businesslike.

One result of this is the Mañana Syndrome, procrastination—a waiting game that is a form of resistance to making changes, sending your writing out into the marketplace, approaching new clients, dealing with fear, and clarifying the goals that will help you overcome obstacles.

It is not, however, a form of laziness. Procrastination, in fact, often takes the shape of quite frantic activity, in which you feel as though you're shoveling coal into a furnace that's burning it up faster and faster. And it affects writers at all levels. At every new level of achievement, with increasingly more demanding audiences, and with every new goal, you are, to varying degrees, going to feel like a beginner again. There is risk, fear, and the opportunity for growth at every stage.

Procrastination is also a practice at which writers are fairly cunning. This is not just because we're clever and good at rationalizing, but because procrastination can masquerade as perfectly legitimate business tasks, such as studying the market, making phone calls, researching and networking. The trick is to know when you are avoiding something and when you are not. And it is tricky. Sometimes you're genuinely gathering your forces, marinating in your own juices, or waiting for the writing to come. And then sometimes you're just screwing off. They can often look a lot alike.

Do any of these common put-offs sound familiar?

- Hiding behind research: reading just one more book, interviewing just one more source, avoiding writing the damn thing for just one more day.
- Telling yourself you don't have enough time, as in "I only have an hour today. I can't get anything started."
- Talking about writing, not writing.
- Cleaning and organizing the office for the third time in a month.
- Going back to school, and letting school get in the way of your education.
- Catching up on your magazines or watching television, claiming that it is, of course, all part of a shrewd strategy for market analysis.
- Taking any writing work that comes along, convincing yourself that, after all, a writer must pay dues.
- Continuing to write what you've been writing for years because it's what you know, and not taking a leap into whatever you've been hankering to write because it's risky.

Whatever you do by way of procrastination, it can fairly safely be said that all the energy you have bound up in resisting your own potential is more than you will ever need to actually reach that potential. Failure takes at least as much energy as success.

A lesson from physics might also be instructive here: The amount of energy needed to get something moving is more than that needed to keep it moving. The hardest part is simply getting yourself started.

Here are a few observations from veteran writers about the task of getting yourself started:

Don't think in absolutes. It's easy to become paralyzed by thinking all-or-nothing; that you have to be writing your book full-time or nothing-at-all; that you have to commit yourself to freelancing full-time or nothing-at-all; or that once you make up your mind or go in some direction, there's no turning back.
DAVID BUMILLER
MAGAZINE WRITER, HARPER'S, GQ, PSYCHOLOGY TODAY

Sometimes I feel as if I'm poised with the key to my Pandora's Box, afraid to reach down and open it, to let loose the chaos my art is partly made of. What really helps are my "Creative Plans." These are my yearly goal statements, which include writing and financial goals, strategies, personality inventories, even obstacles. When they're written down, goals can turn from fantasies into something real, and I can see what's standing in my way. They're a real beacon for the year; a yellow-brick road that gets me moving.

REBECCA BRUNS
TRAVEL WRITER/AUTHOR, *HIDDEN MEXICO*

Because I didn't have a clear picture of what I wanted in the beginning, I succeeded only in fits and starts, and lived from job to job, often ending up somewhere by default. I also procrastinated a lot. But because I found myself often competing with ad agencies, I had to be more businesslike. So in my second year, I set some goals and did a business plan. I started advertising my services, cold calling, reading the business section of the paper every day, and introducing myself to startup businesses. That year my income jumped to $15,000, and in my third year, to $30,000.

CEIL GOLDBERG
AD COPYWRITER, MACY'S, AT&T, ACLU

Getting in Focus: The Power of Clarity

If there is one fact that haunts even the most ardent and sophisticated goal-setter, it is that there will never be enough time to do everything you want in this or any other lifetime.

I am reminded of this every time I walk into a bookstore. I become over-whelmed with the desire to sell my soul to the devil in exchange for a hundred extra years—just to read! For this reason alone, *it is imperative to focus your sights.* As comedian Lily Tomlin once said, "Ever since I was a little girl, I always wanted to be somebody. Now I see I should have been more specific."

This is a lesson I learned the hard way. Here is a cautionary tale:

During my third year at *The Cincinnati Enquirer*, I began to get itchy. In my fourth year, smoke began coming out from under my collar. By the fifth year, I was climbing the walls. I wanted out. I wanted new challenges, a bigger audience, a city by the sea.

Unfortunately, all I gave myself was a wishy-washy goal: I want out. The fact that I said it repeatedly and adamantly didn't make it any stronger. And because I didn't clarify it any more than that, I drifted for the next two years and didn't get one inch closer to getting out. Instead, I became stifled and learned how to climb walls.

It took a crisis for me to start setting clearer goals.

The Gannett newspaper chain, which owns the *Enquirer*, was starting up their new national daily, *USA Today*, and invited me and a hundred other Gannett reporters from all over the country to be journalists in Washington, D.C. I jumped at the chance!

The deal was this: You came for a four-month trial period. If the paper flew and you fit, you stayed. If it didn't fly or you didn't fit, you were guaranteed your job back at whatever paper you came from.

It never entered my mind that it wouldn't work. I considered it purely a technicality that I kept my apartment in Cincinnati by subletting it. I assumed that when the four months in D.C. were up, I would simply fly back, grab a few things, and flick off the lights.

Well, it didn't work. I turned out to be too much of a feature writer, a "stylist" as my editor there put it. And because she was the person who had hired me at the *Enquirer* years before and claimed a certain appreciation for my talents, she insisted *USA Today* wasn't the place for me. So she sent me back to Cincinnati, with apologies and with my tail between my legs.

It was wrenching, and I embarked on what I refer to as my Blue Period, triggered by what I would only later come to see as a benevolent crisis.

But now I *really* wanted out, only this time I began plotting *exactly* how I would do that. No more wishful thinking. I began setting goals, and it was precisely by doing so that one-and-a-half years later I ended up in San Francisco as a full-time freelance writer, doing exactly what I wanted.

What I learned was that *vague goals are powerless*. Like sunlight through a magnifying glass, the more focused your energy, the more firepower you have. And the purpose of goals is to help focus your energy and attention. You must know, for example, what you're selling. Beginners have a tendency to write anything for anybody who is willing to pay them for it, and though you can accrue valuable experience this way, you can also pull yourself apart at the seams, scatter your energies, and dissipate your morale.

An effective goal, therefore, is not "I want out," but: "I want to write creative nonfiction articles and essays on the subjects of health, science, psychology and travel. I want to emphasize innovation, cooperation, creativity and human potential. I want to write for *Omni*, *American Health*, *The New Yorker* and any other magazines that can afford to send me to exotic places and rent me cars with electric windows. I want to freelance full-time and live in San Francisco within two years, start teaching writing classes within two years of full-time freelancing, and earn at least $15,000 from my writing in my first year. Unquote!

Write It Down: Making Simple Maps of the Territory

Carpenters don't build houses without having pictures of them first. Football coaches don't plan elaborate plays before diagramming them on the blackboard. Stone sculptors don't begin chiseling until they have a clay model to work from.

All achievements begin as pictures in someone's mind, and the more clearly they are held there, the more easily they can be hewn onto paper, stone, playing field.

Businesses are no different. They work better when you have a picture to work from. If you can hold solidly in your mind the picture of what you want your writing business to become, without losing it in the static of a million competing impulses, all the better; and I envy you. Otherwise, write it down.

A business plan is nothing more than a picture in words of your intentions as a writer. And you don't need a complex architectural rendering to capture it. A simple line drawing will do, something that fits on a napkin, something you can pull out of a drawer from time to time to remember what your vision looks like.

This business plan is not a sales pitch to venture capitalists or prospective stockholders. Rather, it is a private articulation of your purpose, a complete story of your writing business in half a page. You might even consider it an informed letter to a friend, describing your objectives.

In Journalism 101, I learned that in writing news stories you try to get all the five Ws—who, when, why, what and where—into the first couple of paragraphs. That's all a business plan is: a couple of sentences about each of the five Ws, so you know exactly what you're doing and where you're going.

It is a simple way to organize your thoughts about such things as why you're in business, what your hours of operation will be, what your niche looks like, how you'll promote yourself, what tasks you'll hire out, what skills you'll need to brush up on, and how much money you'll need to get going. At the least, it should answer the following questions:

- What kind of writing do you want to do?
- What do you want to write about?
- For whom?
- By when?
- For how much?

But just as important as mapping out your goals and expectations is realizing that the map isn't the territory, and nothing turns out as you plan.

As part of my original business plan, which was based on the experience of roughly a year's worth of part-time freelancing, I made some conservative projections about my start-up costs, as well as my full-time freelance income and expenditures. I was way off, though fortunately in the direction of black, not red. I turned out to be both thriftier and more workaholic than I imagined myself, so my start-up costs weren't the four grand I braced for, but only three (new computer, office furniture and promo budget); I earned more and spent less than I thought I would.

If your life ends up conforming perfectly to your business plan, you are lucky, not clever. It is nearly impossible to really plan a career. Life is too unpredictable. And though businesses that are thought-out ahead of time generally do better than those that are not, they are all subject to the vagaries of life: miscalculations, setbacks, windfalls, acts of God and the tendency of people to never show up on time.

Goals cannot account for everything. They will help you plan for the future but not predict it. So make some room among your anticipations for the unexpected. There will be both serendipity (the editor of *Mademoiselle* caught your essay in *Psychology Today* and wants you to write for her) and setbacks (Braniff goes belly-up and takes its in-flight magazine, for which you were writing, with it).

This book itself didn't figure at all into my plans. But the opportunity presented itself one day, and it was like a subway door opening: You make up your mind fast. There is little time for diddling. You make a decision and it changes everything.

Sometimes it is changed for you. I know a man who owned a gallery representing a single artist's work; when the artist suddenly died, so did the gallery owner's entire business. There is a natural entropy that operates in the universe, and it affects all the best-laid plans of mice and men.

It is therefore wise to factor into your schemes a fallback plan or two, so you know what you'll do if your main event gets rained out. In risky professions, one must design a few fail-safes, the same way that cliff-dwelling birds lay pear-shaped eggs that roll in circles and not over the cliff's edge.

Business plans are generally too enamored of success. Optimism is fine, essential. But know your worst-case scenarios as well as your best. Don't start out with a "failure is not in my vocabulary" attitude. Not only can and does failure happen, it *will* happen, in one form or another. Fear of failure is healthy. Be on speaking terms with it.

If you were to take your business plan to venture capitalists for a loan, they would be the most impressed by a plan that gives a tip of the hat not only to the prospect of success, but the prospect of failure. It would demonstrate that you know what you're getting yourself—and their money—into.

Divide and Conquer: Making Molehills Out of Mountains

I always try to begin my writing day with the easiest task I can find, one that will provide me with a small success first thing in the morning and thereby start my day off in a good mood.

The journey toward long-range goals should also begin with, and be sustained by, short-range goals that you can easily dispatch. Going after huge, distant goals—being a best-selling novelist, designing a Clio Award-winning ad campaign, becoming the country's next Poet Laureate—is like trying to drink orange juice right out of the frozen-concentrate can. It's too much. You need to break them down into small, manageable tasks, bring them closer to home, and minimize the risk of giving up out of sheer intimidation. If, for example, you were going to write for a publication on-spec (if they like it, they buy it), you would want to start small, with a newsbrief or column-length piece, not with a full feature.

So, once you have identified your biggest goals, *work backward* from each of them—asking yourself over and over: "What would I need in order to get that? And then what would I need in order to get *that*? and so on—until you come to the shortest-term goal there is: tomorrow's to-do list!

The shortest-term goals have all the power, because they are the only ones you can get your hands on immediately. The big ones are, in a very real sense, out of your control. You can't become a famous novelist or the hottest speechwriter in town overnight, contrary to reports of overnight success. But you can write two pages of a short story, make five cold calls to potential clients, query an editor, study a magazine, sign up for a class, or even just practice a creative visualization.

Don't tell yourself, "I've got to get some work done today." Give yourself a specific list of exactly what you will do. It's the best way to close the gap between your long-range goals and the present moment and to give yourself small successes all along the way. (The Goal Breakdown Chart on page 40 illustrates how a goal breakdown might look.)

Are You Having Fun Yet?
Rewarding Yourself Along the Way

Not only must you give yourself small successes as you go, but rewards as well.

Anyone who has ever dieted knows that a respectable figure is always months away, and chocolate cake is always right under your nose. So when striving for your goals, make certain that all the advantages are not long-term and all the problems short-term. Give yourself plenty of gratification throughout the journey. Since you may not even reach your goals, or they may change radically before you arrive at them, it is crucial to enjoy the process, the getting-there.

Particularly after reaching short- and medium-range goals, treat yourself to dinner out, take in some live music, go away for a weekend. And if you are self-employed, leave on a Friday morning, just because you can.

Sometimes, half of success is simply noticing it!

Whose Idea Is It Anyway? An Aviso

Whatever goals you choose, make sure they are *your* goals—not those of your parents, your partner, your teachers, mentors, colleagues, friends or the fellow next door, who always seems to know what you should write about, even when you don't. They must be yours!

In fact, if you are listening closely enough to the song of yourself, an inappropriate goal, a false move, should bring about a response not unlike that of a body rejecting foreign tissue.

Goal Breakdown Chart
Turning Long-Range Goals Into Tomorrow's To-Do List

Long-Range Goals 2–5 years	Medium-Range Goals 1 month–2 years	Short-Range Goals 1 day–1 month	Tomorrow's To-Do List
Freelance Full-time	Build editor relationships Sell magazine/ newspaper pieces Study the profession Build business skills Identify areas of interest	Sell 1 piece to local weekly newspaper Devote 1 night per week to freelancing Query 1 story per week Take a writing/business/ typing class Check out professional writers' organizations Talk to freelancers	Call for name of editor at local paper Call 1 freelancer for lunch Buy *Writer's Market* Call 3 writers' organizations Buy correspondence ledger Sign up for a class Write tomorrow's to-do list
Save $10,000 Financial Cushion	Save money Cut costs Work overtime Invest at higher interest rates	Put $300 per month into savings Reevaluate budget Talk to 3 financial counselors Read 2 money-management books	Ask boss about overtime or raise Find 10 ways to cut costs Call 1 financial counselor Buy 1 money-management book Bring lunch to work
Write Health & Science Articles	Bone up on these subjects Study health/science magazines Subscribe to newsletters in the field Read books on science and medical writing	Make list of potential story ideas Get on medical school news service mailing lists for their research bulletins Study *Writer's Digest* magazine articles on science writing Take class in an area of interest	Go to library and study magazines Call Harvard and Stanford news services Sign up for a class Buy 1 book on science writing
Teach Continuing Ed Courses	Build credentials and experience Improve public speaking skills Identify what you teach Put together curriculum	Create a "class" file Study curriculum design Study college catalogs to find niche	Begin outlining class curriculum Call local colleges for applications Type up resume and gather clips Sign up for public speaking class

The 80 Percent Solution: Choosing Attainable Goals

I have a poster above my desk to remind me that "The trouble with trying to change the world is that *weeks* can go by and nothing happens."

It reminds me that things take time, my goals sometimes exceed my reach, and trying to change the world can be like trying to stop the tide.

Indeed, I long ago discovered a sobering fact: When I publish an article, governments do not topple, tectonic plates do not shift, public opinion does not veer noticeably left or right, and no one awakens the president. Friends, however, do sometimes call, and occasionally a letter to the editor appears several months later.

When choosing goals, particularly the longer-term ones, make sure they are goals you feel you can realistically attain, and within a time period that won't see the coming of the next ice age.

Is your writing slick enough to get into *Esquire* or *The New Yorker*, or would you be better off starting with the local weekly? And if it is the latter, can you allow yourself to aspire to that without judging yourself harshly?

Is your technical-writing portfolio ready to impress Fortune 500 companies, or should you bolster it with a few Fortune 1000 companies first?

Can you really make the transition from your current job to full-time freelancing within a year, or would your family heave a sigh of relief if you settled for part-time freelancing?

Is your speech writing hot enough for the local Senator? Your children's books childlike enough to win the hearts of the adults over at Random House? And do you really know the publishing business well enough to give your book a fair shake without an agent or lawyer?

Only you can be the judge of these things, and you must be an honest one. You must also ask not just if you are worthy of your goals, but if they are worthy of you. Your verdicts will determine whether you overestimate or underestimate yourself—both of which are surefire recipes for disappointment and frustration—or choose goals that will bring out the best in you.

The goals you choose, though, should challenge you and push your limits, not so hard that you shrink from the task, but not so little that you suffer what psychologists call "miasmus," the failure to thrive. It helps to have a sense of your own optimum level of challenge and stimulation, the level of activity below which you're bored and above which you're anxious. This is very individual. One person could be bored at an amusement park, and another could keep perfectly busy in a straitjacket.

Try choosing goals that you can attain with what the late psychologist Nicholas Hobbs called "just manageable difficulty." These are goals, he suggested, that will tap roughly 80 percent of your capacity but leave a reserve for special demands. He argued for goals that maintain self-esteem, yet avoid the worst kind of writer's block—boredom, especially through goals that are too easy.

Determine what level of risk is comfortable for you, and go just a bit beyond that. Not into the realm of stark terror, but beyond comfortable. Again, this is a very personal assessment. Can you easily toss off risks like leaving a regular-paying job or writing an entire novel on-spec? Or would you rather jump out of an airplane?

Though studies have shown that people who are assigned difficult goals perform better than those given easy ones, and people with specific, challenging goals outperform those with vague goals such as "do your best," it is important to give yourself a good chance to succeed. Don't stack the deck against yourself, expecting to crack top national magazines, syndicate a column, bust into prime time with a hot new TV script, or land IBM as a tech-writing client in your first month. That would be like moving from Florida to Minnesota in the winter. You just wouldn't give yourself half a chance.

Some more observations about pushing your limits:

Every piece you do must go beyond the one before it. You should be continually making your writing and photos better, your story angles more unique, your audiences bigger, and your goals more challenging. And know not only where you want to go, but by what route.

Also, every time you sell something, ask that editor "Who else might be interested in this? What else can I do with it?" By pushing yourself a little each time, you *will* get better. It's a very palpable process. It does grow.

LONNIE SHAVELSON
PHOTOJOURNALIST, MOTHER JONES, IN HEALTH, PSYCHOLOGY TODAY
CO-AUTHOR, THE POISONING OF AMERICA

There is a time-honored trajectory for many writers, in the Hemingway tradition: from newspapers to magazines to nonfiction books to fiction books. If you go this route, use each step to move up to the next. Really design your career.

PERRY GARFINKEL
AUTHOR OF TRAVEL WRITING FOR PROFIT AND PLEASURE, IN A MAN'S WORLD

A note about deadlines: If it is important to push your limits, it is also important to set a few, and that means deadlines. Deadlines (again, when they are attainable) are really lifelines to your goals because, as editors have long known, they get the job done. They tell you how to pace yourself and what's expected of you.

So set target dates and finish lines. Don't say, "I'm going to be a writer someday." Pick a day. "I'm going to write a short story by the first of the month!"

"The health of the eye demands a horizon," wrote Ralph Waldo Emerson. So does the health of your goals.

Clearing the Decks: Making Room for New Goals

By setting new goals, you effectively add more work to your life: new commitments, expectations and deadlines. To avoid unnecessary stress and conflict of interest, *do not try to squeeze this added work into your schedule; you must make room for it.* And that means readjusting your priorities.

Unfortunately, whatever or whomever you decide to spend less time with (in order to spend more time writing) will probably protest in some form or another—people will complain, abandoned projects will make you feel guilty, habits will die hard—and you will have to deal with it.

When I began this book, I committed myself to getting a chapter done a month. But in order to do that, I had to put a few things on the back burner. For the first time in seventeen years, for example, I gave up my daily journal writing because it consumed forty-five minutes a day I felt I could put to better use. I also gave up most of my magazine subscriptions, ate out less often, stopped writing everything longhand and editing as I wrote (two lifelong habits!), and perhaps most difficult of all, cut back on socializing with friends. I did, however, forewarn them.

Making room for new goals involves making trade-offs. Excellence, says Tom Peters, author of *In Search of Excellence*, is a high-cost item. You must give up things to achieve it. So start by asking yourself what you're willing to give up to achieve your goals. Would you sacrifice weekend time, let your garden go, see your friends less often, work overtime?

In setting new priorities, also remember that you will not make any headway pushing against an immovable object. If you have too many fixed commitments in your life, you won't have the time or stamina to pursue your writing.

The Priority Chart on page 44 may help you fit new goals into your in-basket. It has three columns into which you should enter all your current activities and involvements: 1) Cut Out, 2) Cut Down, and 3) Keep or Increase. What you fill in, of course, will depend on what your individual goals are. But here is one possible scenario; it is taken from my own experience in reprioritizing for this book.

Count Your Chickens: How to Get All the Help You Can Get

I am descended from a family of writers. My grandfather wrote mysteries for the old Ellery Queen radio show in the 1940s, my mother is a published poet and former ad copywriter, my father wrote for trade journals, and his brother, my uncle Bob, is the author of several business books for Prentice-Hall.

As a writer, this makes me feel that I belong to a tradition, that writing is not just some career I picked out of an occupational handbook but something

Priority Chart
Making Room for Your Writing

Cut Out	Cut Down	Keep or Increase
Magazine subscriptions (for 1 year)	Housecleaning (twice a month)	Exercising
Journal writing (for 1 year)	Socializing	Time to write (at least 2 hrs. per day)
Writing longhand	Buying books (use more library books)	Time alone with partner
Editing as I write	Sleeping (set alarm ½ hr. earlier)	Maintenance chores (e.g., shopping, etc.)
Socializing out of guilt	Recreational reading	Well-planned breaks and rewards
People who don't support me	Volunteer work	Teaching writing
Driving during rush hours	Health club (do exercises on own)	Word processing skills
	Long lunches (keep to under 1 hr.)	
	Yardwork	
	Movies (more videos)	
	Long phone conversations (esp. during peak-rate hrs.)	
	Letter writing	
	TV	
	Taking classes	
	Attending professional organization functions	

compelled from within, something murmured to me from my blood. In any case, it helps me feel less lonely.

I mention this because, in order to reach our goals as writers, we need all the help we can get. We need to draw upon every single thing that can give us power and motivation, every resource at our disposal, every well on the property. We need to turn the potential energy in our lives into kinetic energy. We need to be inspired by the German novelist Goethe, about whom Henry Miller once said, "Both the past and the present nourished him. *Everything* nourished him!"

Therefore, as you move into your writing career, and especially as you move toward relying on it for livelihood, make what the Alcoholics Anonymous folks call a "searching and fearless inventory," of all the tactical support and supplies available to you, as well as all the skills and passions you possess. And use them!

Assess what incomes you have within reach, what monies you can lean on: savings and loans, grants, Social Security, pensions, royalties, investment interest, job incomes, your partner's paycheck and anything in your house you can sell.

Figure out where you can lay your hands on equipment and supplies without having to lay hands on your bank account: a typewriter in your parents' basement, a friend's old computer. Ask everybody you know if they have any gear you can use or services you can tap.

Dig up any writing you've previously done that can be resold.

Pore over old letters, performance reviews, journals, anything that will remind you of what talents and strengths others have praised you for, just because it is important to remember yourself and what you have to offer.

Know the things that inspire you and draw succor from them routinely: music, museums, friendships, great writings and great teachings, the elemental forces. I personally am drawn to places where power is unleashed: the surf after a storm, giant waterfalls, building demolitions, horse races, airport runways, the Olympics, any great book, my own dreams.

Invoke whatever fourth-dimensional graces help you get by (and make no apologies to anyone): gods, guardian angels, spiritual guides, Lady Luck, fairy godmothers, the spirits of your ancestors, the souls of the dead.

And the souls of the living as well. Draw abundantly on the strengths of as many people as possible: friends who run their own businesses, consultants whose mistakes you can profit from, old college professors and former bosses who might have leads for you, a family member who's an accountant, freelancers whose brains you can pick, anyone who owes you a favor, but most importantly, anyone who really thinks you can do it!

Businesses with large "founder teams" typically fare better than those with smaller ones, or those with only one person at the helm. So don't rely too heavily on your rugged individualism. There will be plenty of opportunity for that in the day-to-day labor of keeping the wheels turning. Plug in regularly to a community of people who are both realistic and optimistic, and who are busy with passions of their own. "Do not surround yourself with people who do not have dreams," says the poet Nikki Giovanni.

You might even consider forming your own Board of Directors, an on-call assembly of friends or colleagues who can help you monitor and evaluate your progress, give you feedback and advice on your product, finances or management, and tell you when you appear off-course. Call them together every six months. Feed them dinner. Take notes.

Especially among those closest to you, you need people who *actively* support you. You don't want people who only give lip service to the idea of support: "Hey, go for it. I'm behind you all the way. And if you ever need to talk, you can call anytime and talk to my answering machine as long as you like."

Getting support sometimes means asking for it. It means asking your loved ones—especially partners—to make sacrifices that are real and inconvenient (and, of course, returning the favor). It may mean cooking dinner for you for a week while you're on deadline; spending less time with you than they'd prefer, in order to give you the time to write; not griping when you spend vacation time in bookstores; even picking up your part of the rent for a month or two while you get your business started up, because this time you feel like you really mean it.

Support is a verb. It's going to your poetry readings, book signings and lectures; clipping magazine articles out for you; reading your work with a keen and compassionate eye; paying attention to what you love and regularly asking you about it.

But perhaps most of all, it's working *hard* on their own reactions to your work, your commitment to it, and your absence, and knowing that it's better to have a happy partner you don't see as much than an unhappy one who's around all the time.

Several years ago, I wrote an essay for *The New York Times Sunday Magazine*, the first paragraph of which was a not altogether flattering portrait of my stepfather. When it appeared, I penitently called my mother in New York to ask if she still liked me. There was a long pause. Then an audible sigh. And then she said, "Gregg . . . a writer's gotta write."

Finding Your Passions: There's Goals in Them Thar Hills

Most heart attacks, according to the American Medical Association, occur on Mondays. I would venture to guess that this has something to do with what most people do on Mondays, which is go back to work. Or perhaps more to the point, back to work they don't like.

My own father was one of these people, and though he died of a heart attack on a Tuesday, he still spent most of his Mondays as a businessman who should have been a scientist, whose true passion was literally relegated to the basement, where he had a chemistry lab of Frankensteinian proportions.

My fondest memories of my father coincide with those times when he was doing what he loved most; when, for example, he would come to school with me in the morning, before driving to work, and be my Show-and-Tell. He would draw the blinds, lay a sheet of aluminum foil on a table, and from an old apothecary jar pour out a cone of green powder a foot high. Then, with a huddle of spellbound fourth-graders peering over each others' shoulders to get a look, he lit a long wooden match, waved it under his chin for ghoulish effect, and lit the top of the cone to simulate a volcano. Right there in the middle of Mrs. Doer's elementary school classroom.

A career based on work you do not love, on goals that are not your own, is like a car running on empty: You may get it started, but eventually you end up having to push it, and the only place it drives you is nuts. All that pushing is also bad for the heart.

The most successful people have goals that grow out of their passions, work that is meaningful to them. They have found a match between who they are and what they do. A simple business axiom is at work here: *Success is much easier when you're doing what you love.*

Furthermore, writing clients—whether editors, corporate executives or colleges through which you offer writing classes—prefer to work with your passions, because they know that the best work grows out of those enthusiasms.

The assignments editors have given me over the years have proven countless times that passions lead directly to paychecks. During a recent trip to visit my magazine editors in New York City, I was reminded once again how true this is. Rather than field a mad flurry of story proposals from me over lunch, they were just as likely to engage me in general conversation, and whenever I began waxing rhapsodic about any particular subject, gesturing wildly and flaring at the nostrils, they would say, "Write *that* story for me."

To help you choose your goals, therefore, you need to discover what motivates and inspires you, what has value to you, what puts a fire in your belly. And then you need to design goals that will give you at least *some* of it now, not just five years from now.

You need to find what Barbara Sher, co-author (with Annie Gottlieb) of *Wishcraft*, calls your "touchstones": the emotional cores of your goals, the *needs* your goals will satisfy, what you want your writing to bring you.

If, for example, independence is your highest priority, you will need goals that steer you clear of staff-writing positions (which, of course, will also steer you clear of salaried writing positions).

If creative expression is your raison d'etre, your goals must lead you toward fiction, creative nonfiction, essays, book reviews, and sometimes ad writing.

If recognition is important to you, commercial writing such as corporate brochures, public relations and direct mail will probably not satisfy you. They don't give you a by-line.

If control is your thing, stay clear of Hollywood.

Some examples of "touchstones":

• *Creative fulfillment*: The exhilaration that comes with using your talents in creative ways, giving words to your innermost voice—the one you hear when you talk to yourself; the feeling that poet Anne Sexton was referring to when she said, "When I'm writing, I know I'm doing the thing I was born to do."

• *Recognition*: To be acknowledged for the quality of your work; to be taken seriously, counted among the creative, glamorized, anthologized and paid handsomely; to have major publishing houses call you and ask, "Got any books you want to write?" A variation on this might be the satisfaction of seeing the look of astonishment on your family's faces when they realize you actually had it in you.

• *Independence*: The freedom to choose your own work and schedule, go to work in your pajamas, and not be told what to write; having the choice also to live in a place that has climate and not just weather.

• *Status*: Being regarded as an expert in your field.

• *Variety*: Having work in which change is a regular component.

• *Security*: Having work in which paychecks are a regular component.

• *Influence*: Being in a position to change people's attitudes and affect the course of events; being able to use your writing to express your sense of outrage, injustice, hope or love; contributing another honest voice to the world's debate.

The potential for influence, for "making a difference," for saying something through their writing that the world needs to hear, is what drives many people toward the writing profession. But the difficulty with this desire is that the impact of your individual endeavors is impossible to measure. It is like throwing a rock into a lake. You know that, because the rock is sitting on the bottom, the level of the lake must have risen, but you have to take it on faith. Your personal effect in the world will be more like the ripples moving out from where the rock hits the water that continue to move even after the rock has sunk.

As far as feedback goes, you will only discover how much of a difference you have made when people tell you or write letters to the editor, occasions that are relatively rare. But positively memorable. Several years ago I received a phone call from a woman who told me that an article I had written about the will to live had literally saved a man's life. He was someone she worked with at the local hospice, someone who had given up trying—until she pulled up a chair and read him my story word for word. She said it completely changed his mind, and in so doing completely changed my sense of my own work in the world.

For the most part, though, you must generate your own sense of mission, so it helps to quantify this touchstone. What *kind* of difference do you want to make, how directly do you want to affect the world, whom do you want to make a difference to, and what will satisfy you?

Ferreting out your passions is a bit like reading a Rorschach inkblot, trying to pull out something recognizable from the jumble of images in your head about what your life should be like, what's important to do or believe in, and in what direction to go.

Here, then, are four exercises that may help you get in touch with your touchstones:

Values Checklist

Make a list of all the important activities and involvements in your life, past and present. Include jobs, hobbies, careers, projects, travel, creative pursuits, recreation, achievements, etc.

Under each activity, briefly list what was of value to you about it, what made it enjoyable, what the qualities were/are about it that make it worthwhile to you. When you're finished, circle those values that keep cropping up. (You might refer to the "touchstone" list for ideas.)

Example:

- *Working at the newspaper*: recognition, creativity, variety, working with people, influence.
- *Reading*: the challenge of new ideas, introspection, variety, using my mind, relaxation.
- *Running the poetry workshop*: community, creativity, recognition, influence, aesthetics, personal challenge.
- *Playing the piano*: creativity, feeling accomplished, relaxation, aesthetics, recognition.

Interview Yourself

Pretend you have an assignment from *Esquire*. Write out a list of questions designed to find out what makes you tick.

Twenty questions you might ask:

1. Where did you get your passion for writing?
2. If you could interview any writer in history, who would it be?
3. What kind of writers should be drawn and quartered?
4. What would your obituary say?
5. If you won a million-dollar lottery, would you keep writing? Would you change what you write?
6. What's your worst nightmare as a writer?
7. If you could change something about the world through your writing, what would it be?
8. What do you receive the most compliments or praise for?
9. If you weren't concerned with humiliating your family or yourself, or having an ayatollah put a price on your head, what story would you love to tell?
10. What activities do you most look forward to?

11. What is your single worst memory?
12. What is the best thing you ever wrote?
13. What do you procrastinate the most about?
14. Name three things you constantly tell yourself.
15. If you could teach any class, what would it be?
16. If you were to start your own magazine, what would it be about?
17. What book would you love to write?
18. What skill do you wish you possessed?
19. If you could take any writer's job in the world, who would you relieve of duty?
20. Finish this sentence: "If I died tomorrow morning, I would regret . . ."

Dialogue With Your Writing

Writers are often engaged in looking for their writing "voice." So why not take a moment and actually give your writing a voice, and then talk to it.

In dialoguing with your writing, you may discover, as novelists often do in developing a character, that it takes on a life of its own and has a very clear sense of direction.

Just as you would write dialogue for a play, allow both you and your writing to speak to one another, taking a moment first to identify with each.

You might also try dialoguing with your favorite writer, the Muse, your parents, your future, your dreams, your current job if you have one, emotions like fear or joy, your talents, a personal spiritual guide, even your bank account.

As the playwright Henrik Ibsen once declared, to be of any help to the public in clarifying and deciphering the world, a writer must first be "in dialogue with himself." Or herself.

Slipping in Under the Radar

At the moment of waking or of dropping off to sleep—when you are the most receptive, when your conscious mind isn't on full alert—ask yourself, "What do I really want?" Listen carefully.

Also, consult your dreams. They never lie! They also never cease pouring forth story ideas. Robert Louis Stevenson's "Dr. Jekyll and Mr. Hyde" was born of a nightmare.

Another way of tapping into the dreams you have for yourself is by writing a brief fairy tale or fable, a myth, about your life. A myth, like a dream, is simply a story in symbolic form, in images. It is like going down into a well and tapping into the life that is taking place under the surface, beneath the day-to-day, living on Mulberry Street life that each of us has: jobs, commuting, relationships, worrying about money, trying to cut down on sugar.

Your myth should include:
- The hero/heroine (you, in the guise of a king, queen, prince, princess, space traveller, monk, fisherman, farmgirl).

- A goal (the Emerald City, the Hand of the Princess, a ring of power, a treasure).
- Obstacles (lions, tigers and bears; monsters; warlords; powers that must be mastered; masters that must be overpowered).
- Allies (oracles, animals, wizards, witches, magic, supernatural forces).
- Landscape (desert, mountains, forest).

You might first write a brief outline of your setting and cast of characters, or you can just start writing. Either way, do not worry about everything making sense or remaining in perfect chronological order. Characters can suddenly appear; things can suddenly happen. And don't worry whether it's good or bad. This is just for you. The point is to let your subconscious go on a roll and tell you a story about your life that you are sure to find illuminating. Simply begin with "Once upon a time . . ."

Whatever values and passions continually surface when you are doing these exercises, make sure you highlight them with a bright fluorescent marker. Like dreams, they have a tendency to disappear the moment your feet hit the floor, unless you get them in writing.

The values you unearth through these exercises will be the core of whatever goals you set, and they will direct you toward goals that have meaning for you. As Friedrich Nietzsche once said, "He who has a why to live can bear almost any how" — and the whys, furthermore, will show you the way to the hows.

Skillful Means: Finding Salable Skills

I never thought of being single as one of my skills. A talent, unfortunately, but not a skill. Yet I turned being single into a salable skill when I convinced *The Cincinnati Enquirer* to hire me as their singles columnist.

Since then, I have taken a microscopic look at my assets, with an eye toward flushing out overlooked skills that might translate themselves into writing jobs.

I have also met more than a few writers who have done likewise. One parlayed her counseling background — particularly the skill of listening — into a specialty writing profiles. Another's college linguistics training makes her a quick study as a technical writer, picking up and translating computer languages. Still another turned his knowledge of erotica into a lucrative business writing telephone-sex scripts.

Here are three exercises that might help you identify skills that might apply to writing — and jobs that might accrue from them. The more skills you can come up with and bring to bear upon your writing career, the more doors will open to you.

Life Skills

This is a variation on the Values Checklist exercise, except this time you will substitute "skills" for "values" and generate a list of the skills you have picked up through your life's various enterprises. Examples:

• Working at the newspaper.

Skills: reporting, researching, analyzing data, conducting interviews, writing fast, editing, working amidst commotion, translating technical material into English, and otherwise bringing the dead to life.

Possible jobs: reporter; magazine writer; researcher for authors or publishers; opinion research interviewer; obit writer; media columnist; publicist; celebrity profiler; freelance editor; science, technical or corporate writer doing magazine articles, brochures, company histories, financial reports or product literature.

• Giving poetry readings.

Skills: speaking before groups, bringing drama to the language, writing tight, developing an ear for the best material and leaving the rest at home, knowing when to quit.

Possible jobs: teaching everything from college and adult education classes to elementary schoolchildren, or being a Writer or Poet in Residence; ad copywriter; manuscript reader for a publishing house.

• Managing a coffeehouse.

Skills: generating publicity and promotion, bookkeeping, booking entertainment, writing ad copy, food preparation, doing detail work.

Possible jobs: public relations writer, publicist or events promoter; restaurant or music reviewer; writing annual or financial reports; writing consultant to businesses; business or entertainment writer.

Also, don't overlook what are called "trade skills," those gut-level business smarts you picked up by osmosis from doing the paper route as a kid, working as a counselor in a summer camp, flipping burgers at McDonald's, or bellhopping at the local hotel. These include skills at making contacts and allies, customer relations, reading the marketplace, and being personable.

For example, an early stint as a waiter in a college-town restaurant provided me with a trade skill that I put to good use years later doing some promotional writing: persuasiveness.

College boys on dates do not like being "carded" when they order wine. It embarrasses them, and they take it out on the waiter, usually by leaving no tip. But if I didn't ask for IDs, I risked losing my job and bringing the law down upon the establishment. My solution: When a young man ordered wine, I would graciously say, "Ah, a man who knows his wine. That's one of our best house labels. However, I'm a man who wants to keep his job and not get my boss into a heap of trouble, so I have to honor our house policy of requesting IDs of anyone lucky enough to look under twenty-one years old. Will you help me humor them?"

Personality Skills

Obsessive-compulsive behavior, such as correcting people's grammar or sitting through tedious movies and boring books because you can't tolerate stopping in the middle, might drive most people crazy. But it might also fit certain job descriptions to a tee—movie critic, manuscript reader for a publishing house, editor.

Personality traits are often skills in disguise. Examples:

- *Skill*: being persuasive enough to sell somebody their own shoes.

    Possible jobs: ad copywriter, speech writer, resume writer, direct-mail writer.
- *Skill*: being bullheaded.

    Possible jobs: investigative reporter, scriptwriter in Hollywood.
- *Skill*: being methodical and attentive to detail.

    Possible jobs: proofreader, researcher, indexer, technical writer.

Also, don't overlook the traits and skills your friends, family, colleagues or mentors consider your shining qualities, even if you don't.

Do people tell you you should be a comedian? You might consider comedy writing.

Do your friends complain about your being a loner because you enjoy holing up for the weekend with books instead of company? Take advantage of it and write book reviews.

Does your family back East rave about your letters? Businesses could use just such a skill in putting together the form letters they use to improve customer relations.

Finally, here's what a few skillful writers say about putting your skills and passions to use:

When you first start out, don't send queries and manuscripts to *Esquire* and *Atlantic* just because they're *Esquire* and *Atlantic*. You'll get rejected, more than likely, and then you'll quit. When I first began, I went for *Yankee Magazine* because I could really *see* myself in *Yankee*, I read it religiously, and I once lived in New England. If you haven't sold yourself on why you're doing what you're doing, you won't be able to sell editors either.

STEPHEN ALTSCHULER
ENVIRONMENTAL WRITER
AUTHOR, *HIDDEN WALKS IN THE BAY AREA*

If you have a passion for fame, a note of caution: writers do not get mobbed at restaurants, and flashbulbs do not pop when they step out of cars. That is, unless you're Stephen King, and that's only because he stars in his own movies and does American Express commercials. Also, find your own voice. It's OK to go through an imitative phase. Most writers do. But by imitating, you'll always be second-best. Be first-best. Do it *your* way.

CHELSEA QUINN YARBRO
AUTHOR/PRESIDENT, HORROR WRITERS OF AMERICA

Most people flop into their careers, by accident or restlessness or being laid off. They don't choose them, and this is dangerous. Especially if you're self-employed, you're not in a good position to make mistakes, to stick it out without winding up going back to a job.

Make a list of what it takes to be a writer in your field — the skills, knowledge and personality traits. Then make a list of those you possess, and subtract that from the first list, to find out what you'll need to acquire to succeed. Then either develop it or hook up with someone who has it. Even if it's a personality trait like discipline, you can still hire that out in some sense. Find someone willing to call you regularly to keep you on track. Find writers who have succeeded without that trait, and ask how they did it. It takes some doing, but you can always find someone who has done what you want to do, or solved the unique problems that you face.

The only trait without which you'll die on the vine is the willingness to turn to others for help. Self-employed does not mean you're all by yourself.

RICHARD BOLLES
AUTHOR, *WHAT COLOR IS YOUR PARACHUTE?*

Just as your writing can be a vehicle for your voice, your voice is but a vehicle for a larger voice that wants to speak through you. The truer you are to yourself, the more you may find that eventually your voice and that larger voice — God's, if you will — become indistinguishable.

M. SCOTT PECK
AUTHOR, *THE ROAD LESS TRAVELED, PEOPLE OF THE LIE, THE DIFFERENT DRUM*

CHAPTER THREE

Market Research:
Looking Before You Leap

Writers spend far too much time worrying about the ravages of writer's block, when the malady far more likely to strike them down is agoraphobia. According to its original definition, it means "fear of the marketplace."

By refusing to not only encounter but *study* the market in which you will be plying your trade, as well as the customers who will be buying your wares, you effectively end up diving in before finding out if there's water in the pool.

You then risk becoming part of the statistics: Two-thirds of all new businesses fail within the first five years, and a major reason for this is lack of market research.

A market is just a demand backed up by money, and it is far easier to sell your writing when you know what that demand is and who'll pay what. Besides, you will eventually need to convince clients that your product or skill can help them tap deeper into their own markets: who's going to buy your book if it is published, who does your TV pilot appeal to, how is a particular company newsworthy enough to generate local media publicity?

Whether you want to write children's books from a minority perspective, develop a new sitcom based on an interracial couple, or create promotional material for environmental groups, *study the market before you plunge in.*

Don't be blinded by the brilliance of your own ideas to the point where you fool yourself into believing that the world is anxiously awaiting your arrival. Plan your reception; don't just assume it will happen. Too many writers presuppose that the public or the publishers are hungry for their (yet another) advice column, family sitcom, or hardboiled-female-detective novel, without bothering to check it out.

It would be a demoralizing waste of time, for instance, to try to syndicate a computer column without getting a line on what's already out there and what, if any, niches remain to be filled (by getting hold of the annual *Editor & Publisher Syndicate Directory*, for starters).

If you were trying to convince investors to put up their hard-earned money to launch your start-up company, they would want to know the answers to precisely these questions. You are the sole investor in your own company; do no less for yourself.

Stiff Chairs and Stiff Drinks:
Market Research in Action

Doing thorough market research means becoming a student of your field, an archivist of its details. It means studying not just the market but the potential customers within it, and learning what is music to their ears. It means hitting the books and hitting the street, reading about the writing business and talking to people in it.

When I decided to leave employment for the brave new world of freelancing, I made the following commitment: I would pick one evening a week and for a full year use that time to do my homework, to prepare for full-time freelancing. I elected Thursday nights, so every Thursday at five I knocked off work at the *Enquirer*, and instead of taking the bus back uptown, I stayed and took myself out to dinner (part of my incentive plan). Then I went to the public library from six to ten, when it closed, and there studied and practiced magazine freelance writing. I wanted to know:

- How big a demand is there for magazine articles and essays?
- Can I make a decent living with the kind and quality of writing I do—and exactly who would buy it?
- What is the life cycle of a story—how does it hit print, how does it get from here to there (and how long does it take a check to get from there to here)?
- How does my writing compare to what's in the magazines?
- What trends are affecting magazine publishing?
- What are the advantages and disadvantages of becoming a specialist or a generalist?
- What is the best and worst that could happen? What are the glories and the horror stories?
- What do people in the business say about the business?

To find the answers to these questions, I immersed myself in:

- Occupational handbooks.
- Books on freelance writing.
- Magazines.
- Trade associations and trade journals (virtually every writing field has at least one of each).
- Magazine readership surveys and publishing-industry surveys.
- Publishing resource books like *Writer's Market* and *Literary Market Place*, as well as city and state media directories.
- Demographics from the Census Bureau and the Bureau of Labor Statistics.
- Writing classes.
- Any and all magazine writing I could lay my hands on.

In addition to my "academic" research, I also tapped into what I consider the most indispensable part of any kind of research: first person. That is, *talking to people in the business*.

When it comes to gathering inside information, the difference between library research and first-person research is the difference between carob and chocolate. There is simply no substitute for finding out what a field looks like from the inside out. Talk to writers, editors, former editors who are now writers, and former writers who gave it up for something else.

While preparing for the rigors of full-time freelancing, I plied a lot of writers and editors with drinks and victuals, beseeching them for the lowdown. And again, when I was deciding whether to take on this book, I talked specifically to a half dozen *Writer's Digest* authors to find out what their experiences were. The insights and advice I picked up during all these interviews have been essential to my success.

For example, one person I talked to while interviewing for the jump to freelancing was an editor at one of the major newspaper syndicates that regularly buys "one-shot" features from writers. She informed me that when syndicates send out a weekly packet of a dozen or so one-shots to client newspapers, there is a point-of-entry person responsible for distributing those pieces among various section editors.

That's how it's *supposed* to work.

The way it often does is that this point-of-entry person fails to connect all the stories with the editors who would be most interested in seeing them, so writers don't ring up sales when they might have, had the sentry been more conscientious.

This editor then suggested that if I ever feel there might have been a sale I should follow up by sending the piece right back to a specific section editor, under my own logo, just to cover my bases. And indeed, I have made many sales just this way, to the very newspapers that ostensibly rejected my pieces when they came through syndicates.

This was information I probably couldn't have unearthed any other way than by talking with someone in the business, and wouldn't have thought to inquire about to begin with.

The upshot of my year spent market researching was that it turned into almost two years, but because I wanted to be able to quit my job *and not regret it*, I settled for the delayed gratification caused by being exhaustively thorough. It's always a bit of a challenge figuring out when you still have more preparation to do and when you're just being chicken.

The fact is, that two-year period was exactly the running jump I needed to make my freelance career take off. It was the cumulative effect of those Thursday nights that gave me the courage and know-how to make it work.

Most Likely to Succeed: Positioning Yourself to Win

Successful businesspeople position themselves to succeed, the same way spiders build their webs near porch lights because that's where the action is.

For this reason, it was of primary interest to me in studying the marketplace to determine where I would have the greatest chance to succeed; with what magazines, what kinds of stories, which of my skills, even in what city (I was prepared to move). "Literature," said George Bernard Shaw, "is like any other trade. You will never sell anything unless you go to the right shop."

In addition, I wanted to position myself to succeed quickly. *It is crucial to have successes early in the game. This is a make-or-break difference.* The sooner you have a sense of accomplishment — primarily by being published — the easier it will be to keep going.

There are, of course, writers who tunnel away for years without being published and then suddenly break into the light — and in the beginning just *doing* the writing is one of the most important successes you can have. But you would need either enormous patience or self-deception to endure years of trying to sell your writing with no successes, not even small ones.

You needn't turn a profit in your first quarter, though, or bring down a big client with your first shot. You just need small and fairly immediate successes, in areas where there is a match between what you love, what your most advanced skill is, and where the market is most receptive to you.

For example, if you love storytelling, have a way with words, and work in a corporation, choose the path of least resistance: Start by writing something for your company newsletter.

If you're a department store ad copywriter and want to go freelance, begin by writing what you know best: retail ads and newspaper inserts, perhaps for small local or start-up companies.

If you have any consuming interest, consider copyediting books in that area.

If you want to write short radio comedy that DJs can drop into their monologues, and your brother-in-law is a DJ, call him first.

When I first began studying magazines, I noticed that most shared a similar construction: the shortest pieces — the newsbriefs — are up front, followed by columns and then features. It immediately suggested a strategy. Since the newsbrief sections usually consist of at least a half dozen 100 to 300-word items, and there are often several such sections in a magazine, the need for material is far greater than for columns and features, and so, proportionately, was my chance of getting in as an unknown writer. Editors would just as soon not take feature-length chances with unknowns if they can start with News-McNugget-length chances.

So I chose to begin pitching magazines with newsbriefs, sometimes queried six at a time. Within a year, I had broken into an admirable number of major magazines that would have been far tougher to crack otherwise.

To ensure successes not just early on but *throughout* the game, though, you must also *keep up with market research*. Keep an eye out especially for mergers, buyouts, resignations, new laws and new players on the field. Whenever any of these arises, ask what it means to you as a writer. Knowledge is power, but only if you use it. When lawyers were first allowed to advertise, for instance, a new market suddenly opened up for those promotional writers who knew an opportunity when they saw one.

When it was first rumored that *Psychology Today* was to be bought up by the company that owned *American Health* magazine, I asked my *PT* editor what she thought that would mean for its editorial content. She said they would probably be looking for more health-related stories, while *American Health*, which I was also writing for, would probably be scouting for more psychologically oriented pieces.

When the merger went through, I used this information to start pitching them more of what they each wanted. I first sold a piece to *PT* on "The Biochemistry of Tears" (we feel better after a good cry in part because emotional tears rid the body of chemicals that build up during stress).

Then I sold a piece to *AH* called "Roommate Recovery," based on studies showing that preoperative patients who room with postoperative patients experience a much better recovery rate than those who room with other pre-ops.

In other words, more health for *Psychology Today*, more psychology for *American Health*, and more exposure and money for me.

Closing In on the Customer

The average newsstand carries about 2 percent of the magazines in the United States — 250 or so titles out of 12,000! Trying to advance a magazine freelance business without knowing this fact is like trying to take in the Grand Canyon by looking through a knothole.

In order to know where you are most likely to succeed — whether you write for magazines, motion pictures or multinationals — you need to know what your full range of choices is, and then, just as in goal setting, you need to narrow them down.

You start with a long view of the publishing field, then zoom in for close-ups of individual magazines, publishers, companies, producers, agencies or even people.

There are several levels of market research, and at each you are generating more and more specific information.

First: Market research should give you the big picture, a bird's-eye view of the publishing world as a whole, with details such as the following:
- Good writing is needed wherever communicating with others is vital, from customer relations and political lobbying to advertising and consumer magazines.
- There are 550,000 writers in America: 82,000 authors, 130,000 journalists, 58,000 technical writers, 151,000 public relations writers, and more, and all tribes are growing.

- Nonfiction comprises the vast majority of published writing and is far easier to sell than fiction. There's simply much greater demand. It is also harder to market your way into fiction; it demands that you master your way in. In fiction, the writing itself counts more; you're selling craft as much as concept. Also, fiction editors often don't want proposals — a primary marketing tool — but finished manuscripts, especially from unknown writers.
- Commercial writing — that done in the service of advertising, technical manuals, corporate videos and public relations — pays far more handsomely on average than magazine and book writing.
- There are over 2,000 "alternative" publications in the country, for which most libraries don't even carry indexes.

Second: You want information about the general field of writing you are interested in (magazine writing, novels, songwriting, advertising). For example:
- Half of those doing technical writing are English majors.
- Most publishing houses specializing in books by psychologists and doctors need good writers to collaborate with them, because "experts" often can't write.
- As much as 40 percent of the news you read in the daily paper is generated by public relations specialists.
- Each major newspaper syndicate receives over 300 submissions of column and comic ideas a week, and buys ten a year. *Redbook Magazine* receives 30,000 fiction submissions a year, and publishes fifteen. Ninety percent of all magazine submissions are rejected.
- Television producers of new shows generally don't buy scripts from unknown writers in the first year. Scripts are staff-written or otherwise already committed to get the show through that first year.
- The opportunities for writing cable television scripts are better in communities with lousy regular TV reception.
- Big ad agencies generally don't take on small assignments like sales letters and in-store ads, for the same reason literary agents don't handle short stories: The 15 to 20 percent commissions don't make it worth their time. But they'll often farm these out to freelancers.

Third: You need familiarity with the specific genre you want to pursue within that writing field (*health* articles, *romance* novels, *Country/Western* songs, *Direct-mail* advertising):
- The hottest new forms of direct-mail advertising are videos and computer disks.
- Science fiction/fantasy books in the midlist range (those selling roughly thirty to forty thousand copies) stay on bookstore shelves for only one to three months on average.
- One annual report for a high-tech company can earn you up to $10,000 for half that many words.

- Most newspaper travel editors have six or twelve month calendars of the geographical areas they plan on covering—free for the asking.

Fourth: You want intimate details about your most-likely-to-succeed clients.

The first step is generating a list of potential clients, the second is turning those clients inside out to see what makes them tick. The Marketing Chart on pages 62-63 is an illustration of how I generate my own client lists, which vary depending on the project.

First I describe whatever story I'm interested in tackling in one short, fat sentence, packing in as many details as I can. The story illustrated on the next two pages revolves around a profile I have sold many times over the years: Percy Ross, a Minneapolis millionaire who gives away his money through a newspaper column called "Thanks a Million," syndicated in over 140 newspapers. People write to him with their tales of need or greed, and he responds, when suitably moved, with a check—a sociable version of the reclusive philanthropist in the 1950s TV show "The Millionaire."

I encapsulated the story thusly: "A 75-year-old, Jewish, Minneapolis, MN, millionaire who gives away his money through a syndicated newspaper column." Then I break the sentence into component parts (i.e., story angles) and list as many magazines as I can find in the resource guides that might be interested in the story from each angle. Generally speaking, my criteria for most-likelihood include publications that:
- I have written for previously.
- Regularly run the kind of stories I am pitching.
- Feature a style of writing similar to my own.
- Have voracious appetites for material, such as newspapers, syndicates, and the "newsbriefs" sections of magazines.
- Just began publication and are likely hungry to develop a stable of writers.
- Don't generally appear on the newsstands.
- Are in my own backyard, geographically or professionally.
- State in *Writer's Market* that they are "eager to work with new and unpublished writers."
- Are owned by relatives.

Casing the Joint: Getting the Details Details

My final semester of college was spent as an intern at *Writer's Digest* magazine. As an editorial assistant, one of my responsibilities was being the moat around the castle, someone writers had to get through to get into the magazine. I read query letters and sent personalized rejections. If someone sent haiku, my rejection note would be in haiku. Eventually my boss intervened, for the sake of expediency, and I had to start sending form rejections.

As part of the long-distance job interview process for that internship, I

Marketing Chart

Describe your story in one sentence. Break it down into topic segments.
List publications under each section that might be interested in the story from that angle.
Circle best-bets and study them in depth.

75 year old	Jewish	Minneapolis, MN, millionaire
Senior mags:	Ethnic & minority mags:	Local & Regional mags:
Modern Maturity	*The Jewish Monthly*	*Minneapolis Star*
Mature Outlook	*Jewish News*	*St. Paul Pioneer Press*
Prime Times	*B'nai B'rith Jewish Monthly*	*Minneapolis Magazine*
Senior Edition	*Hadassah Magazine*	*Minnesota Monthly*
New Age for Seniors	*Inside*	*Twin Citian*
New Choices	*Present Tense*	*City Pages*
		The Corporate Report/Minnesota
		The Skyway News
		Minneapolis Business Week
		Utne Reader

who gives away his money	through a syndicated newspaper column
Business & corporate mags:	Trade mags:
Business Week	*Columbia Journalism Review*
Fortune	*Editor & Publisher*
In-flight mags	*Writer's Digest* magazine
Religious mags	Newspapers that carry the column and regional magazines in those states
Fraternal mags:	
Kiwanis	
Elks	
Men's mags	
Women's mags	
General Interest mags:	
Parade	
Reader's Digest	
Saturday Evening Post	
Ford Times	
Time/Newsweek	
Christian Science Monitor	
Syndicates	

received from then-editor John Brady two issues of the magazine, with a brief note: "Study these and critique them in the margins. Then return. Neatness doesn't count, but energy does."

I learned early on that studying magazines is the way to break into them!

Not studying magazines — or companies, or TV shows, or publishers — is probably the main reason most writers don't break into publication. They don't bother to find out who gets in and why, what approaches work and don't work, whether there is already somebody on staff or on retainer who does what they want to do, and whether they're just plain good enough to get in.

This is a symptom of laziness or impatience, or perhaps insecurity. We don't always want to find out the truth, that our writing may not be up to par, that reaching our goals is going to take a lot more work than we're in the mood for, and it's easier to blame someone else for our failures than to take responsibility for them ourselves.

I hear it fairly often in my classes: "Publishers don't know what they're doing," "Hollywood is totally closed to outsiders," or "I don't understand what the hell editors are thinking."

Having been among editors myself during my stint at *Writer's Digest* magazine, I can offer this: When they're not thinking about lunch, editors think about which one of the next fifty proposals in their in-basket might actually give them something they can use.

To find out what editors can use, look at what they *have* used, and give them more of that, if it's within your ability. And to find out whether there is a fit between your abilities and your clients' needs, *study the client in detail!* It will be well worth the time invested.

Editors have an ability to sense, in parts per million, when writers have taken the time to acquaint themselves with their publications or operations, and do not look kindly on those who try to bluff their way in.

Sometimes it shows in the smallest details. *American Way* magazine, for example, the in-flight of American Airlines, used to have a stylistic imperative that all quotes be in paragraphs unto themselves, something you would only have discovered by reading the magazine carefully or its writers' guidelines, which clearly spelled out the decree and which they were happy to send you for a stamp. If your proposals and manuscripts evidenced that you were familiar with the magazine's peculiar quirk about quotations, the editors knew you were a writer who had done his homework. Professionals pay attention to details — the kind of details you can't see from a distance.

But it's the big blunders that really give writers dead-away: sending stories about woodworking to *Tables Magazine*, when it's a trade publication for the restaurant industry; writing a speech filled with one-liners for a company executive with not a comic bone in his body; sending an off-color, homoerotic play to a dinner theater.

Writers tend to be somewhat insular by nature, and often have little contact with their customers. You must offset this by finding out as much as you can about the person who will be reading your writing at the other end. If you were putting your kid up for adoption, you would want to know who was on the receiving end.

If you're interested in writing for a particular television show, for instance, become a devotee. Don't miss an episode. Get to know the characters, situations, locale, format, themes, audience, politics. Tape it with a VCR and pick it apart. Watch the credits roll and pick out the producer; that's who you send your queries and scripts to, not the network (unless you go through an agent).

If you're casing a company, study the industry it's in. Read in-house publications, articles about it in the media, and product literature. Take factory tours, make on-site visits, and talk to customers, employees and competitors. Don't make cold calls. Make hot ones. Know something about your prospects first.

Find out the most common customer complaints, the scuttlebutt at professional conventions, what problems the company faces, especially those of the person who could give you work. Pore through annual reports (for information about personnel, budget, products, events and operations) and stock reports (for insight into a company's growth and stability). Even check *Who's Who* for individuals within the company.

Plan an article on corporate communications or a profile of a certain executive for whom you'd like to write. Then call up the company or person and say you're writing an article for your corporate newsletter, a magazine, a trade journal or a school report, and could you solicit their expert opinions?

The writing profession is unparalleled in its ability to get you access to otherwise inaccessible people, and even get you free advice that would cost somebody else $100 an hour. You might as well take advantage of it. Whenever I need answers to things professional or personal, I often write articles about the subject and thereby get free legal, financial, psychological and career advice.

If you're setting your sights on a magazine, study that magazine! And not a sample copy either, but a year's worth, if you can. Bring a brown-bag lunch to the public library and spend an afternoon finding out whether there's a fit between your writing and that in the magazine, by way of style, voice, research and writing skill. And don't pull any punches. Give yourself an honest assessment.

Study the magazine front to back, from what's splashed across the cover (those are the stories editors most want) to the ads (so you know who not to offend) to the little classifieds in the back for nose-hair removers and bunion remedies. Take notes. Staple them to the sample copies of each magazine you keep at home. Neatness doesn't count, but energy does.

Find out if the magazine runs the kind of stories you intend to pitch, and whether they've just run one like the one you're *about* to pitch. Is the magazine's style hip and irreverent like that of *Rolling Stone* and *Spy*, or homey like the *Saturday Evening Post*'s? Are there certain departments or columns where your work would feel most at home? No matter how good it is, if your writing doesn't fit into an existing slot, editors generally won't create one.

On the other hand, look for what's missing. Is there a column they could use, a story angle they seem to have missed? If you want to get really ambitious, study a decade's worth of a magazine's table of contents and see if there are stories or subject areas they've overlooked.

Here are some tips on studying the marketplace from veteran students:

It's crucial to watch the shows and see what works and what doesn't, but the hardest truth for writers to swallow is that most of their scripts are generally not good enough. According to one agent I know, a good script occurs once in every 300 to 400. Too many writers approach writing scripts with a condescending "Hell, I can do that" attitude.

KERRY COX
EDITOR, *HOLLYWOOD SCRIPTWRITER*

To write a speech for middle- and upper-management businesspeople, I interview them, and people they work with. I have to intuit what someone is capable of saying, and what they *want* to say. I read anything they've written, or get copies or videos of previous speeches they've delivered. I also get annual reports, and study the company and the industry. The more a company gets to know you, the more access you get. You can sit in on internal meetings, get internal documents.

I also read a lot of speeches, particularly from a publication called *Vital Speeches*, which consists of reprints of speeches made by politicans, businesspeople and educators.

HARVEY STONE
CORPORATE SPEECHWRITER, AT&T, APPLE, VISA

I can tell when a writer knows the magazine. It's something almost spiritual. Something in their approach. You just have it or you don't. It's a certain familiarity. At least a third of all submissions are inappropriate because writers lack that familiarity.

What gets my attention is a story that fits, knowledge of your subject, and enthusiasm. There's more than enough room for writers who have unusual ideas, stories others haven't found yet, and can deliver!

DON WEBSTER
SENIOR EDITOR, *OUTSIDE MAGAZINE*

Inside scoop? You'll get rewritten and disemboweled a lot in this business. Also, the word "whore" comes up often . . . the stuff you've got to write. And the idea is to beat the competition, not necessarily to inform the public.

Nonetheless, every network has a temp-list for when staffers go on vacations. Also, they often put insiders on special projects, and bring in temps—freelancers—to take their places. Send a resume and clips.

VINCE FLORES
VIDEO COORDINATOR, KRON-TV SAN FRANCISCO
EMMY AWARD WINNER

Scoping Out the Competition

Market research means not just studying demand, but also supply—that is, the competition.

Competition in the writing field is no more or less fierce, though, than in other professions in which the payoffs are potentially high, and an analysis of it should never talk you out of entering the field if you really want to get in.

Studying the competition—the numbers of people, what's being written, how it could be improved, who is at the top and why—is thus undertaken not so much to make you assess whether to enter the competition, but more to help you gauge what you will need to do in order to *stay* competitive, such as update your business skills, hone your craft, expand your contacts, generate innovation and stay disciplined.

When it comes to competition, there are two types of writers: those who let the competition intimidate them and those who don't. When comparing themselves to the top people in the field, for instance, the latter types use them as inspiration for what *can* be done, not as excuses for what can't. In fact, they often track the careers of the top writers in their field, following how their writing changes and what they write about, and picking the actual writing apart limb from limb to see why it works.

Also, they turn their competitive "shortcomings" into competitive edges. A freelance ad copywriter, for instance, who must compete with ad agencies (when she is not being subcontracted *by* them, that is) uses her small size as an advantage when selling her services to clients. She points out that she is cheaper and faster and can turn on a dime compared to the agencies.

A freelance science and medical writer with no particular science or medical background stresses to his editors that he brings to these technical subjects a refreshing nontechnical perspective. As a nonetheless thorough researcher and interviewer, he takes nothing for granted the way "experts" often do and can therefore translate stories on these subjects for a lay audience, without going over their heads.

You can gain another competitive edge by studying not only the best writing in a field, but also the worst, because that is often where you will find the easiest place to break in. Many writers have their first experience of the competition—and of success—when they begin noticing mediocre writing and say to themselves, "I can write at *least* as badly as that."

Ultimately, you are probably better off not wasting time trying to outsmart the competition. In fact, you're better off concerning yourself less with your own competition and more with your *clients'* competition. If you can help solve their competitive needs, you will not have to worry about your own, because they will give you plenty of business.

An example: All magazine editors want the public to think of their magazine as the place to go for breaking news. Several years ago, I pitched an editor a story idea about what happens economically when cities declare themselves nuclear-free zones, drawing attention to the fact that it was the first comprehensive look at the subject in the national media, and that in buying the piece he would be scooping the competition.

By addressing *his* needs in a competitive market, I was also able to reach one of my own goals: breaking into *Omni* magazine.

Don't think about the competition, unless it helps get you moving. But if you want to become more competitive, get critique of your work. If someone says, "Wow, you're fast!" make that a standout feature of your writing, a selling point.

MERRY SELK
PROMOTIONAL WRITER, MACY'S, PLANNED PARENTHOOD,
PAC BELL, SIERRA CLUB

Ignore what people tell you about the competition. What do they know about *you?* Just trust yourself. Negative people are the worst competition.

JANET ROSEMAN
MAGAZINE PROFILE WRITER, *ELLE, USA TODAY, LIFE, NEW WOMAN*

When I started out, I had the protection of ignorance. I didn't know who the competition was, or what I couldn't do, or that there were people out there with graduate degrees from Harvard and Columbia. Ultimately there is no competition but yourself.

FRED SETTERBERG
CO-AUTHOR, *BEYOND PROFIT*
CO-AUTHOR, *THE POISONING OF AMERICA*

To be competitive, be enthusiastic and easy to work with. It also doesn't hurt to be a large blond who waves her hands a lot.

CATHY WHEATER
AD COPYWRITER

Far From the Madding Crowds: Picking Niches

Writing is a product and products need niches—market positions that make them unique.

Without some distinguishing characteristic that sets you apart from the madding crowds, your editors and clients will think of you as interchangeable with all other writers. When that happens, the only way to compete is to work for less money.

You can see this phenomenon demonstrated at the supermarket. When nothing differentiates one brand of toilet paper or catsup from the next, the customer goes only for price. But if one company suddenly proclaims that its catsup is *thicker*, and you hate runny catsup, you may be willing to pay the higher price.

The same thing goes for writing. This is a lesson I learned the hard way, while negotiating many years ago with an editor who wasn't interested in paying me more money, though I'd written for him for nearly a year. It hit me when he said, "Look, there are plenty of other writers out there who'd be willing to work for less than what I'm paying you *now!*"

I was dumbstruck and beat an embarrassed retreat because I hadn't given any thought to what made me different, or worth more, than all those other writers out there who were also underselling themselves. It hit me that I had no brand loyalty because I had no brand, only a generic product. I needed to convince that editor he would be *getting* something for paying a premium price.

Your position—and future—in the writing marketplace will be strengthened to the degree you develop what is unique not just about your writing (after all, you want to be more than a commodity), but about *you*, whether it is service, specialty, credentials or personality. Do you bring speed-reading skills to manu-script reading, corporate experience to business writing, an artist's background to arts reviewing?

A niche can be not only *what* you write—medical stories, sitcom scripts, educational videos, nonprofit newsletters—but *how* you write—humorously, inspirationally, satirically. Your voice can be your niche.

A niche can be huge (*USA Today* targets "mobile America") or circum-scribed (an acquaintance of mine is a billiards writer).

A niche can even be created from scratch. The word *niche* comes from the Latin "to nest," but nowhere is it written that you have to move into somebody else's nest. You can build your own out of your passions, politics, needs, skills and hobbies. Most syndicated columnists have taken this approach: William Safire (language), Dr. Ruth Westheimer (sex), Sylvia Porter (money), Dave Barry (humor).

You can also build niches out of trends. Example: For the first time in history, Americans now spend more years caring for aging parents than depen-dent children, a consequence of our long-lived society and a trend that will redefine family obligations and caretaking demands for years to come (the nest won't be empty when the kids leave home). This will undoubtedly increase the demand for articles, columns, books, advertisements, videos and eventually a heartwarming made-for-TV movie on this multigenerational dilemma.

Playing Geography

Any retailer knows that the right street corner makes all the difference. So consider *where* you want to carve out your niche. In medieval times, artists weren't considered in the running unless they made the journey to Rome. The study of art meant the study of antiquity, and antiquity meant Rome, so artists of the time were drawn there as if to Mecca.

Writers often feel they must similarly go to whatever city is considered the center of the universe in their field, lest they get locked out of the castle: New York for publishing, art, finance and fashion; Washington, D.C., for politics; Los Angeles for movies; Detroit for automobiles; Nashville for music.

To some degree this is true, depending on what kind of writing you want to do. You aren't going to find loads of corporate writing jobs or cultural events to review in rural communities. The opportunities for writing educational video-scripts will be fairly limited in a town with a one-room schoolhouse. Nothing beats New York City if you want to schmooze with writers, publishers and agents. And try doing thorough research in a town whose library consists of a bookmobile.

I moved to San Francisco, in fact, not just because it was the most beautiful city I could find, but because it is to innovation stories (the kind I wanted to write) what Atlanta is to Delta Airlines.

On the other hand, access to writing jobs may be easier and less fearsome in small and medium-sized ponds. When I was looking for somewhere to go after college, I was cautioned by more than a few professors, as well as friends who had graduated a year or two ahead of me, not to head for New York City, lest I end up just another writer driving a taxicab or working for an exterminating company. So I went to Cincinnati, and it indeed made all the difference. Again, start where you have the greatest chance to succeed.

I am not suggesting that geography is destiny, but it is a factor. And even in this small world of telephones, modems, faxes and computer research — in which no one is really isolated — you should at least plan to make the occasional pilgrimage to whatever city approximates Rome for your writing field, just to plug in, keep up contacts, visit editors, attend trade conventions and soak up the ambience.

Also, consider not just what locales your niche suggests, but what niches your locale suggests. Use your proximity to an area, a tourist attraction or an industry (the Inside Passage, Mardi Gras or Silicon Valley, for instance) to market yourself as an authority on it, providing publications all over the country and abroad with a regular flow of related stories. I know one writer who became the Northern California correspondent for the *Boston Globe*, essentially using his locale as his niche.

Some further field notes about niches from writers who have been there:

As a corporate video-scriptwriter, I've chosen a rather broad niche and have a wide client base, so that if a client or field slows down, I've got other avenues. Corporations tell me there aren't enough corporate scriptwriters around, and one reason is that corporate writing is a contradiction in terms to most writers.

JOANNA RAMEY
CORPORATE SCRIPTWRITER, APPLE, FORD AEROSPACE, WELLS FARGO BANK, CITICORP

My style is my niche. One of my editors described it as "Talking out of the corner of your mouth." My goal is to write with *my* sound, to go to the markets which resonate to that and ignore the others. I had three rejections from *Cosmopolitan* magazine recently, because I was trying to be who I wasn't. It was a big shock. Don't do it.

JOE FLOWER
CO-AUTHOR, *AGE WAVE*

I'm an odd bird: a mechanic who can write and a trucking writer who has hands-on experience. But it's opened up a good niche for me. There are fifty to sixty publications in the field, and several dozen with circulations over 50,000. The advantage to finding a niche is regular customers. The disadvantage is that it's a challenge not getting stale.

TOM HOWE
TRUCKING WRITER

Even though I'm in a rarified niche as it is — pool and billiards writing — I also set myself apart by pointing out to editors that I'm the only woman covering it. I get more personal details out of the guys I profile, bringing a more human angle to my stories. I disarm them because they don't expect me to know so much.

ELIZABETH HOLMES
BILLIARDS WRITER

The Great Debate: To Specialize or Not to Specialize

No discussion of writing niches would be complete without mention of The Great Debate: whether 'tis nobler to be a specialist or a generalist.

Some insist that the world loves an expert and that this is the way to go. Others contend that they would rot on the vine if they had to write about the same subject day in and day out, and therefore choose to be generalists. Finally, there are those, like me, who combine the two, specializing in several areas and trying to do them each excellently.

Here are the facts of the case: Specialists put all or most of their eggs in one basket; generalists spread them around.

A specialty might be fund-raising brochures, financial books or automotive writing; or even more specifically, nonprofit environmental fund-raising brochures, investment books, antique-automobile writing.

There are as many specialties as there are fields of human endeavor and eccentricities of human behavior, and no matter how narrowly you set your sights, you will still be within shouting distance of at least one publication or association catering to that niche. On a recent flight to New York, I sat next to a fellow reading a copy of *Urology Times*.

Specialists are quick to point out, in fact, that the trend in the business world as a whole is toward what advertisers call "micromarketing" — targeting ever more specialized audiences.

If you choose a specialty, though, just be careful that it isn't so narrow that, if one or two clients dry up, so does your career. Some writers do feel that specialists, because of their reliance on fewer clients, are more vulnerable to the whims of the marketplace — publications folding, clients moving, editors being fired, economies and administrations changing — than are those who cast wider nets. Generalists, having a broader client base, may more easily weather such changes.

It is true, though, that the publishing world loves experts, and all things being equal, an editor will go for the writer who has written on a subject before. Also, the more frequently you write for a client, the more dependent that client becomes on your services, and this improves your bargaining power — unless, of course, you develop a bad reputation instead of a good one. In small niches, as in small towns, word gets around (for better and for worse) with blinding speed.

Specialists also find it easier than generalists to keep up with a field, because they've focused on one or two subjects, not five. The more you write in a field, the less research you have to do. Whereas generalists must start from scratch each time they research an assignment in a different subject area, specialists build up a body of research knowledge. It is also easier to land syndicated columns, book contracts, consulting jobs and teaching positions as a specialist.

The flip side, of course, is burnout, the feeling that if you have to write one more sports story, one more ad about ladies' lingerie, one more word about the technical applications of polymorphal framus assemblies, you will go starkers! It is therefore crucial to ask yourself, up front and at regular intervals, how you will feel about your specialty five or ten years hence and to make all necessary arrangements and adjustments.

Since variety is something of an antidote to tedium, generalists are not so prone to flaming-out because they move among different fields. Also, when editors ask for clips, they have an abundance to choose from. When I pitch a science story, I show science clips and stress that I'm a science writer. When I propose a travel piece, I show travel clips and present myself as a travel writer. And so on with business writing, medical writing, etc.

Another burnout issue to consider is your attention span. Do you work best on a steady stream of small assignments (newspaper stories, retail ads, press releases) or on fewer and longer ones (scripts, books, magazine features)? For those constitutionally unable to stand in one place long enough to even leave a decent footprint, being strapped to a long project will be insufferable. And though the paychecks for smaller projects will be smaller, they will also arrive more frequently.

Ultimately, it is best to pick a niche that is not so broad it stretches you too thin, and not so narrow it won't sustain a career. One of my own niches has been science and medical writing—plenty broad—but I have focused on stories of innovation: new products, technologies, applications and ethical dilemmas.

For instance, rather than write a general story about cancer, I will write about the new use of atom-smashers to cure cancer. Or instead of profiling subliminal stimulation, I will focus on new computer software that allows you to program any subliminal message you want to give yourself (lose weight, stop smoking, write faster, take out the dog) and have it flash across your computer screen while you type.

Ultimately, although it is critical to inspect the marketplace before you enter it, it is equally important not to be completely market-driven. Do not attempt to mold and squeeze yourself to fit what you think others want, or write only what will sell; in the process you could become some formless, egoless entity that eventually bores even you.

Your own values, passions and identity combined with a studied approach to the marketplace will sell you most effectively.

CHAPTER FOUR

The Writer's Workshop: Setting Up an Office

M y father had two desks at the factory he owned. One was big, grey, and government-issue, right out on the sprawling shop floor where his factory workers called him by his first name.

The other was a large, ornate oak desk that completely dominated the quiet back office that was his father's and, before that, his grandfather's. Mounted on the wall behind this desk was a shield and two crossed swords.

Whenever I visited my father at the factory, he would lead me into the back office and motion to a green vinyl couch against one wall. He would then position himself across the room, in a high-backed leather chair beneath the crossed swords.

That desk—and everything else in his factory, including that moat in the back office between the desk and couch, that space that was always between us—was sold out of the family when he died recently, because neither I nor my brothers wanted to sit behind it.

This is one of the experiences that has shaped not only the work I do—I wanted my *own* career, not someone else's hand-me-down—but the office in which I dispatch that work. My own desk, for example, sits flush against a wall, not just because that wall is all windows, but because I won't have it between me and anyone else.

An office is not just an office: a roomful of equipment and supplies, a place to get things done, a way to get away from the family. It is also a repository of all the emotions and associations you have about accomplishment, accountability and your position in the heirarchy—and the place where you reenact them.

It is a combination reflecting pool, altar and chopping block, and every day you step up to it you are confronted with the choice to make something happen, propelled by habit and faith, knowing that the only thing scarier than showing up is not showing up.

No matter where you maintain an office, whether in a stately oak-paneled suite with a view of midtown or in a nook under the basement staircase at home, a lot is going to happen in that place. And you will have an emotional, not just a business, relationship with it because, contrary to the unspoken injunction in most offices against mixing emotions and employment, work is just too personal not to get emotional about. The office is a place not just of work, but of worship and sacrifice, and one haunted by ghosts.

In setting up an office, you can't do much about the ghosts, but you can fill it with the spirit of your own intent, as well as with beauty, efficiency and comfort, so that each time you walk into it you are inspired.

You must design it so that just looking at it makes you want to work, the same way that walking into the kitchen makes you hungry, because you're conditioned. You want to trigger a salivary response: *The more it looks, feels, sounds and smells like an office, the more likely you will treat it like one.* You want to build new associations, down at the cellular level, between office and writing, ones that evoke pleasure and not pain.

But an office will contain both. In my own office, I have spilled both champagne and tears, and on one memorable night, I even stood in the middle of the room so paralyzed and frustrated about work that I literally tore the belt loops off my pants.

Sometimes it is a place where I plow into my writing, thrilled at the words that tumble from me, working so furiously that the spit flies and the seat-belt sign flashes on. And then sometimes I pull myself up to my desk as if up to a chin-up bar. On these days I usually just twist slowly back and forth on the chair, pulling anxiously at my lower lip, listening to the blathering traffic of noises in my head, and picking at my work half-heartedly, the way some kids eat vegetables.

Whatever the outcome, though, you need a place (and time) that is inviolable in which to work, and which no one shall put asunder. It need only reflect the level of commitment you are ready to devote to your writing. If you are only testing the waters, a fully furnished office is overkill. But if you have decided to go for it, that you are not willing to leave for kingdom come with all that writing still inside you, then you must give yourself what you need to make it happen, keeping in mind, of course, that lack of a proper office never kept a hell-bent writer from writing.

But whether you build it up slowly over the course of years or decide suddenly one day to take over a guest room and furnish it to the hilt, the ideal office space is not just a physical but a psychological commodity.

It is privacy, refuge from the tyranny of conversation, *your* room. It is the place that will allow you a writer's sort of solitude: the kind of divine and irascible seclusion in which even flies can become intrusive, shadows annoying and distracting. The phone machine goes on. The earplugs go in. You ignore your friends and family. This is business. Nothing personal.

Scouting Locations: Staking Out Office Space

It would be an exaggeration to call my first office an office. It was the kitchen table in a ninety-dollar-a-month studio apartment that I could traverse in exactly six paces and that sported a panoramic view out the window to an alley. My editors complained about spaghetti stains on my manuscripts. If I could have afforded lobster stains, I would have given them lobster stains.

I can think of any number of reasons to avoid using your kitchen table as an office, not the least of which is that you can never really get away from it — *and you must be able to get away from the office*, especially if it's at home. It is important to maintain a boundaried space that is free from any associations other than writing, such as eating, sleeping or entertaining. It is a division of labor that will make it much easier for you to know when you are "at work."

Still, you must also go with what you've got, so when carving out office space, be resourceful. If you plan to be an open-collar worker with an office at home, consider spare rooms, attics, basements, garages, tool sheds, walk-in closets, alcoves, even the spaces under staircases. As long as it is a discrete area unto itself and isn't directly under a tap-dance studio, it's surprising how little you need in order to get work done.

If you have a choice, situate the office to your best possible advantage by way of privacy, comfort, noise level, light and view. Do you need to be in the thick of things, in the center of the house, or does a soundproof trailer at the edge of the property sound more like it? Do you need windows or would you be just as happy working in a walk-in closet, not having to watch the neighborhood children tear up your rose garden?

Whatever your choices, the more distinct your office is from the rest of the house, the easier it will be to "go to work," because you will feel as though you're going somewhere.

Some writers, most notably those who can afford it, take this to what they consider its logical conclusion by leaving home altogether and renting an office. For one thing, the isolation and distraction of working at home drives them daft, and they crave the water-cooler scene and the company of other office workers. For another, they feel the only way to go to work is to go *out* to work.

For them, professional means having a clear division between work and home, which is perhaps the vestige of a culture that does not equate "home-making" activities with being professional, nor grant homemakers much status. Nonetheless, it means getting dressed in the morning and commuting some-where, a ritual embedded in the collective psyche and very hard to override.

Many work-at-homers, too, get dressed in the morning as a way to psyche themselves into work mode. If it works for you, my blessings. You know yourself well enough to know what works for you. To me, it seems a bit like driving around the block and coming back home in order to convince yourself you're commuting to work.

Still, the idea of separating work and home life in some fashion is a good one, and if you cannot do it physically, do it by time management. You must carefully delineate time between the two, staying alert to the fallout from merging the competitive, performance-oriented drive of work with the compar-atively mild-mannered conduct of being "at home." When you work sixty hours a week, as is typical of home-based workers, this is a balance that takes time to achieve.

It may simplify certain matters to rent an office, but it is a luxury few start-up writers can afford. One of the burdens that drag a considerable number of new businesses into the drink is overhead costs such as renting commercial office space. It can be an even more expensive proposition when you add to this cost those of commuting (tolls, parking, wear and tear on your car), eating meals out, a clothing allowance, and possibly even childcare.

And if you put in an hour of commuting every day, you will spend six full forty-hour weeks of your life driving, not writing. I often tell work-at-home writers, in fact, that at five o'clock they should turn on the radio and listen to the traffic reports—just to appreciate.

If you are determined to rent, though, consider an office in nonprofit buildings such as union halls and arts councils. They always need money and often have extra space to rent cheaply. You will probably need a letter confirming your association with a nonprofit, which you can often get if you do any writing for such an organization. It could be the difference between a $50 rent and a $250 rent.

One thing homesteading certainly has in its favor is low overhead, but this advantage is often made up for in domestic distractions. At home, you will work in death-defying proximity to your bed, refrigerator, television, backyard, neighbors and whatever household chores and errands beckon, to say nothing of whatever recreational activities lie outside your door—mountains, beaches, lakes, tennis courts, swimming pools and ice-cream parlors.

An outside office generally has only one major distraction, which happens to double as one of its major advantages: people. When I worked at the newspapers, I never did get used to people being able to hear every word I said, especially when I talked to myself, which I do incessantly and irremediably.

Another thing you must plan for in setting up shop is expansion. The same way you can count on kids outgrowing shoes, you can count on a writing business sprouting paper like weeds. You will never cease accumulating notes, newspaper clippings, magazines, reference books, client files, correspondence, tax documents, sample queries and of course, copies of your own published work. You can't store everything in a computer. Taking on this book, for instance, meant getting an accordion file that expanded as the book progressed.

Also, just as you buy kids shoes a size bigger than their feet so they have room to grow into them, make sure your office has similar leeway: room for an extra file cabinet, shelf space on the walls, a closet. If you have nowhere to put things, they inevitably pile up on your desk, and after a year or so you can drill a hole in the middle of it, take out a core sample, and have a complete geological record of your freelance career, complete with the fossilized remains of the note you once made to yourself reminding you to buy shelves.

Here are some additional viewpoints on finding office space:

Moving from a home office to a rented office made me feel more professional, in a professional setting. I moved from avocation to enterprise. It was a decision to be in business more seriously as a writer, and people now take me more seriously. Our industry could raise its recognition level, and level of remuneration, if people didn't assume we worked out of our homes. It legitimizes us, and in business, PR especially, image and perception are crucial.

Home isn't conducive to seeing clients — I also have two kids — and I'm tired of meeting clients in restaurants, cocktail lounges, even in their offices. A rental office is just one of the costs of doing good business, like equipment, furniture, an accountant and a lawyer. But it definitely costs more. I had to borrow money and rent furniture to get it started.

JOHN KNOX
PR WRITER, HEALTH CARE INDUSTRY

Working at home became increasingly oppressive. I had no contact with other professionals, no separation between private life and work life and my cats were throwing up hair balls on all my material. My office is 8×14 with windows, a twenty-four-hour secretary, candy machine, kitchen, mailroom and free tampons in the restroom. It costs $187.50 a month and is in the Saul Zaentz building (he produced *Amadeus* and *The Incredible Lightness of Being*), so it's filled with screenwriters and filmmakers; people who understand the creative process, being independent and always looking for money. Mostly we talk about fund-raising. But it gives me a framework, an atmosphere of work, not of being casual.

Home, though, is more comfortable when I'm working on a deadline, putting in fifteen-hour days. I can lie down, make dinner, and then go back to work.

CAROLYN MARSHALL
ENVIRONMENTAL WRITER

I went with a home office because I didn't know if the business would work or if I'd like it, and it gave me the freedom to experiment, as well as have no overhead. I also love the lifestyle.

But it takes extra discipline working from home. Part of disciplining myself, for instance, is getting dressed every morning. It sets the tone and helps me make a division between work and not-at-work. I even know a man who leaves his house and comes back in a different entrance.

When business revolves around your home, though, boundaries soften and roles aren't understood the same way by family members. If you have a family, they have to recognize your space and equipment. They must ask to use it, and you must be serious about it yourself. Sit down and talk.

SALLY SHEPARD
PUBLICIST

I use a second bedroom in my home as an office, and I'm thinking about renting, mostly for space. As I'm doing more commercial work — tour planning, photography, designing brochures and newsletters — I'm moving onto a new plateau, and I need the room to expand, to operate more efficiently. It's an investment in my own belief in myself, the same way borrowing money to get a computer was, in the beginning. I had low income and little savings and I took out a $3,000 loan. But it was worth it. I wouldn't be where I am without it. Invest in yourself!

CHRIS BAKER

TRAVEL WRITER, *NEWSWEEK, CHRISTIAN SCIENCE MONITOR, GEO, NATIONAL WILDLIFE*

In Praise of Windows

The University of Minnesota's new engineering building is entirely underground, a concession made to save energy. A system of periscopes is used to project what is going on outside onto office walls below ground.

Whether this strikes you as terrifically innovative or ghastly in the extreme will determine whether you are the type who, like me, needs an office with windows.

Some writers find them a distraction: "Appealing workplaces are to be avoided," argues author Annie Dillard. "One wants a room with no view, so imagination can meet memory in the dark."

I prefer a little less groping myself. Windows aren't merely for light and ventilation, but for visual release, a break in the symbolic repression of a wall, an escape from the severity of enclosed spaces. They also remind me that there is a world out there.

Through my office windows, I watch the shadows of clouds bend in the folds of the hills and across the tops of huge oaks. I watch the neighborhood empty and refill with each day's commute. I watch plum trees blossom in the spring, tomcats stalk birds in the low branches of the fig, hawks and vultures sweep into view on long, slow arcs — and I am momentarily released from being pinned to the ground by the gravity of my endeavors.

Without windows I would certainly suffer from what the National Institute of Occupational Safety and Health calls the "stuffy office syndrome": a slow-growing sense of irritation, claustrophobia, restlessness and apathy toward work. I would also be denied the healthy pleasures of natural light, something that cannot be impersonated by either incandescence or fluorescence.

Hospital studies have even demonstrated the salutary effects of a room with a view, especially a natural view, not of something man-made like a parking lot. Patients spend less time in the hospital, experience less stress, need less medication, and have fewer complications.

If you have no windows, consider murals, posters, photographs, paintings, plants, aquariums or periscopes if you have to — anything to remind you of the natural rhythm of things. Otherwise, learn to swing wide that window in the brain designed for escapism: the imagination.

Confessions of a Longhand Writer: The Benefits of an Electronic Office

In the electronic age, people are not so much writers as typers. Writing by hand is seen as quaint if not archaic, and writers are slowly abandoning their kinship with pen and paper, just as they once forsook pencil and papyrus and, before that, bone and clay tablets.

I have been among the holdouts myself, so I understand the resistance that must accompany such relinquishment. It wasn't until the beginning of the 1990s that I switched, for the sake of efficiency, from longhand to computer (I had used one only for storage and editing before that, not for writing), and a part of me laments the defection. I have watched the callus on the middle finger of my writing hand soften and fade, and I feel the loss as of a personal insignia, literally my trademark.

As it is, I keep a feather-quill pen next to my computer as a reminder that before the 1970s no one wrote on computers, and before the 1870s no one even wrote on typewriters; some mighty good writing was forged in spite of this. It reminds me that *all a writer really needs in order to write is pen and paper and something to say*.

Recently one of my editors even said that he doesn't care if a manuscript is sent on a computer disk or on parchment, whether it comes by fax, Federal Express, or is just slid under the door—he's going to read it. "Just sell me a good idea."

Still, as often happens with transitions from low tech to high tech, I now wonder how I got by writing longhand all those years. It's terribly slow, and a computer keeps up with my synapses much better.

I can say the same of the other electronics in my office—typewriter, answering machine, calculator and tape deck—none of which I couldn't live without, but all of which are tremendously advantageous. They all save time and aggravation, make both my job and my editors' jobs easier, and thereby assist me in earning a better living as a writer. There is a direct correlation.

Furthermore, every professional writer I know has roughly the same equipment I do, and then some (as of this writing, I do not have a fax machine, modem or photocopier). This is, again, largely a function of their level of involvement.

It is fair to say that writers nowadays will have to encounter high technology somewhere along the line. Those who still write longhand, for instance—Norman Mailer, Alice Walker, John Barth, Joseph Heller, Erica Jong and Wendell Berry come to mind—either type it out later or hire someone else to do so. And despite what my rather generous editor says about accepting work sent in on parchment, most editors insist upon a more finished product, though if the writing is exemplary, you could probably write it in crayon and still have it welcomed.

Generally, editors and clients these days assume you have a certain measure of technological prowess. They want material faster than ever before and often on computer disk, not on paper, because it saves them the laborious job of typing it into their systems. If you do send paper, they expect it to be printed with letter-quality legibility. They increasingly anticipate being able to fax documents back and forth. And they are downright incredulous if you don't have an answering machine.

Fortunately, the electronic office is getting cheaper by the day. Every time equipment and prices get smaller, they become more accessible to people, especially if you haunt classifieds, mail-order companies, yard sales and discount or secondhand stores, including Goodwill and Salvation Army.

The amount of time and energy you intend to devote to writing should determine what tools you buy. If you plan on writing only on the odd Sunday, getting a lot of gear is like buying a bicycle for your kid's first birthday.

But if you are determined to write, *invest in yourself*. If you were employed, you wouldn't expect your boss to furnish you with a card table, a stool and a manual typewriter. If you're going to jump in, the devil and all, you should get yourself at least an electric typewriter and/or word processor and an answering machine. It can cost you under $1,000 if you're patient.

If you cannot afford even these basics, you will have to start from wherever you are, and motivation will be your primary tool. It is anyway. The most sophisticated, gleaming equipment is not going to make your business succeed. You are! High-tech gadgets can serve your motivation and creativity, or merely make manifest your lack of them more quickly and legibly.

With this in mind, consider the following primer on the electronic tools-of-the-trade that most frequently show up in writers' offices.

Computers

I walked into a computer store recently to buy floppy disks, and the salesman asked me what kind of computer I have.

"Commodore 64," I said.

There was a long pause, and then he began repeating slowly to himself, "Commodore 64 . . . Commodore 64 . . . ," while stroking his chin and squinting into some middle distance, like a sorcerer trying to remember an ancient spell. Finally he said, "Late Triassic Period?"

Now here is a space-age machine that thinks in nanoseconds, can store on one little box of disks more information than is contained in the Bible, can print out more words in an hour than an entire secretarial pool could in a day, and can connect me instantly with people at the four corners of the planet, and some hotshot is telling me it's obsolete.

Computers come and go like clothing fashions; you could go broke and batty trying to keep up with them. Just figure out what you need a computer for—editing? research? spreadsheets? graphics?—based on your current needs and those you might have when you reach your five-year goals, and get the best computer you can find for the least amount of money. Do not, for example, spend 150 hours learning how to program a computer in order to save yourself three hours on your taxes.

Contrary to popular belief, computers are not like Latin masses; you don't have to know some arcane language in order to understand them. There is nothing cryptic or confusing about computers. Fortunately for people like me, computer manuals nowadays are written with the technophobe in mind. If your excuse for avoiding computers is that they're too complicated, find another excuse.

It will take you one day of earnest concentration to go through the manual in baby steps, a couple of days to get on your feet, and a week to start running circles around your typewriter.

Also, if you're waiting for prices to come down, don't. It's like waiting for movies to come out in video; by the time they do, you've moved on to something else. The prices *will* eventually fall, but the money saved is not worth the momentum lost. If you need it now, get it now.

If you want to keep it mercifully easygoing and keep the bill under $500, a good starter kit that will last for many years is a simple, user-friendly word processor, which you can buy at any good department store. It is a glorified typewriter with a built-in screen, printer and computer editing abilities, essentially those you need to type, edit, store and print. Some market surveys have shown that 80 percent of computer buyers use only the word processing and spreadsheet functions anyway, and personally, I think a computer for bookkeeping is overkill.

I own a computer with word-processing software, and though I don't think it is a compulsory item, I will sing its praises:

• It is essentially an electronic filing cabinet, and you can store great hordes of written material on it so that you don't have piles of paper composting all over your office.

• You can cut-and-paste at the push of a button, editing in such a way that your manuscripts are spotless, not pocked with whiteouts and squeezed-in letters.

• You can change a story (or recast a query letter for a new editor) without having to retype the whole thing. Add or delete words or paragraphs, move entire blocks of print around, correct typos and spelling errors, and then just print out the revised version.

• It allows you to print out an unlimited number of copies, saving you trips to the copy store.

• With computers like the Apple Macintosh, you can create graphics and type layout for desktop publishing of everything from newsletters to books. (IBM PCs and IBM-compatibles are the current favorites for word and data processing and are the most widely used among writers and those in the publishing industry; WordPerfect, Word Star and Microsoft Word are among the most popular software systems.)

• With a modem you can transfer material directly into editors' and clients' computers and can hook yourself into research databases and computer "bulletin boards" worldwide.

One last word about writing on computers, from the school of hard knocks: *Save your material as you go.* Computers are notorious for eating copy alive, usually after you have spent the better part of a day perfecting it.

One afternoon, while I was wrapping up a full day's work on chapter one of this book, the screen suddenly went blank, and the computer froze. I gripped the monitor with both hands and yelled. The thought of having to duplicate the work was sickening, and I pounded the keys furiously, trying to conjure up commands to retrieve the copy, knowing in my gut it was gone. I went through the classic stages of grief all within a few minutes: shock, denial, anger, bargaining with the Almighty, and finally accepting it and trying to resurrect my chapter.

Writing longhand, the worst affliction I have ever encountered is writer's cramp. In writing on a computer, it is heart failure. Saving your copy periodically is a minor inconvenience in light of the consequences of *not* doing so.

From that experience, I now understand why so many computer owners give their computers names, talk to them as if they were pets, and say thank you when they finish a session. It's superstition, and these are the reflexive and improbable rituals we invoke in our attempts to control forces greater than ourselves, and every bit as mysterious. It's a modern-day form of rain-dancing, trying to bring good graces down upon us, hoping to be delivered from power surges and faulty parts.

Superstition or not, I now have a rule of thumb about saving material anytime I work at Lord Byr—, I mean my computer. Whenever I feel a wave of paranoia about losing something, I save it.

For the *truly* paranoid (or smart, depending on how you look at it), I would recommend storing backup copies of all your computer disks in a safety deposit box or at a friend's house. If a fire swept through your home, imagine what would happen to your novel-in-progress, your client files, your Rolodex or your photographs. And imagine how you would feel.

Typewriters

The first two typewriters I owned were a manual and an electric, and for the needs and typing skills I had at the start, they were fine. But now that I have an electronic typewriter, as well as typing skills that I can measure in words-per-minute instead of minutes-per-word, manuals and electrics now strike me as the technological equivalent of speed bumps.

Electronics are the only ones that can keep up with fingers moving at full gallop, without keys snarling with one another.

An electronic typewriter is endowed with semiconductor chips, not moving, grinding parts. Besides making them fast, it makes them perfectly quiet. Electrics, on the other hand, have motors that buzz and rattle, and if you do your writing at the typewriter and are a slow thinker, it's like having someone impatiently drumming their fingers while you work.

I own a typewriter for two reasons. One is immediate gratification. My dinosaur-age computer takes several minutes to boot up, and when I want to dash off a quick letter, I can be licking the stamp before the computer is even ready to begin receiving information. Two, all correspondence goes on my stationery, and I don't want to mess with taking the computer paper out of my printer and trying to stick in letterhead and envelopes.

Electronics come with a multitude of options—some good ones are centering, bold-face and half-space functions—but there is only one that I consider essential: an erase button, preferably one with memory, meaning that you can erase an entire line if you want. The mechanism involves two ribbons. One types and the other lifts it off the page; you are never typing over errors with whiteout. This means you can type on any color paper and erase it cleanly.

Telephones

A writer of my acquaintance has a parrot that once demonstrated to me just how inseparable writers are from their telephones. The parrot, whose cage sits next to the phone, must have noticed that every time the phone rang it got picked up, because the bird eventually taught itself to perfectly imitate the sound of a ringing telephone, assuming, I imagine, that it would receive similar favors.

Anyone who uses a telephone often enough to make others jealous is someone who spends a *lot* of time on the phone. If you fit this description, just make sure your telephone is a touchtone and that you have undivided access to it. Get a separate business line if need be. When it rings, it must only be for you, and when you pick it up, you must have complete right-of-way, able to talk as long as you like without incurring the disdain of family members, housemates or pets. If you make phone calls with any regularity to editors, libraries, interviewees or agents, you don't want return calls to be picked up by toddlers or teenagers, or anyone but you and your answering machine.

Answering Machines

Whenever my telephone rings, it sets off an outbreak of reflexes that would put Pavlov's dogs to shame.

I have a compulsion to answer ringing phones. I have to know who's calling, even if it's someone wanting to sell me storm windows or tickets to the Fireman's Ball. If I'm not bolting for the phone as if it were my only link to the outside world, I'm trying to figure out "Jingle Bells" on the touchtone. Only "Wet Paint" signs have the same kind of allure. Besides, not answering it makes me feel as if I'm defying my elders, who said it was selfish and impolite to not answer when spoken to.

But a ringing telephone is not a subpoena, and this is one of the reasons I own an answering machine. I am trying to deprogram myself from responding in this knee-jerk fashion. Sometimes I want to write without interruption, or finish a book, a hot meal, a bath. Sometimes, the phone can become like junk mail; I just don't want to be bothered.

The answering machine makes a great bodyguard, and I admit to more than occasionally hiding behind it. If I decide to pick up the phone, I can always say 1) I was in the bath, 2) I was eating, 3) I was out getting my mail, 4) I was in the john, or 5) I was just on my way in/out—none of which, I have a feeling, anybody believes. But I am not losing any sleep over it.

I am taking back some of the privacy I have lost to an increasingly insistent world, one that makes me forget how to draw a simple line and then say, "Okay, for the next two hours, I am going to stay on *this* side of the line, and I want everybody else to stay on *that* side."

If it is the ability to discriminate that sets me apart from the lower animals, it is obsessions like answering the telephone that keep me scratching at fleas. I find myself bound by an automatic response to sensation, with no delaying, autonomous control. The answering machine solves that problem, allowing me to control the telephone, not the other way around. It lets me work, and especially if I'm *out* doing work, it helps me avoid losing business in the process, which is another reason I own one.

Here are several others:

• *Memory*: This lets me store oft-used numbers and recall them with the push of a single button. Unfortunately, I don't bother remembering them anymore, and this can be a problem when I need to call one of these numbers from a pay phone or from someone else's house.

• *Auto redial*: I can keep dialing a busy line by pressing only one button. Great for hard-to-reach clients.

• *Speaker phone*: This feature literally gets me off the hook, allowing me two-hour interviews without having to crick my neck the whole time. An alternative to picking up the handset, it allows me to keep both my hands free, pace around the office, even do jumping jacks if I like. Just get a model that doesn't make you sound like you're talking inside a metal drum.

Another way to ameliorate the pain in the neck that comes with long phone conversations is to buy an operator's headset, which fits like headphones and has a speaking apparatus that comes around in front of your mouth. Or at least get a shoulder rest.

• *Record option*: Lets me record conversations and interviews. Because I like to take copious notes of chats with editors (for the sake of negotiation, primarily), this function comes in very handy, especially since those conversations often are impromptu.

• *Remote pickup*: When I'm expecting a call while I'm out of town where I cannot be reached, I tell people to call my home; the remote lets me pick up messages. Another type of remote pickup is the car phone, and if you feel you must get one, at least let it ring several times before picking up, so editors and clients will think you have a bigger car than you do.

• *Unlimited message time*: This lets callers talk as long as they want. The only thing more annoying than talking to a machine is being hung up on by one.

One final reminder: The message on your answering machine must be appropriate for business calls, even if friends will be calling on it. As for criteria, just picture your most conservative clients calling. Therefore, beware of Richard Nixon imitators promising not to erase messages, or clever little songs that sound as if they were recorded underwater.

Fax Machines

The facsimile machine has been about the most rapidly accepted office gizmo in history. Faxes are being used to relay information from space shuttles to ground control, make song requests to radio stations, and order pizza. Teams climbing Mt. Everest use wireless faxes to send and receive messages, and a Bombay swami is reportedly using one to deliver spells and curses. They appeal to our neverending search for a faster way to deliver the goods.

So far, however, few writers find they either need them or can afford them. The extra nanoseconds they save over and above, say, the computer modem don't seem worth the price tag ($500 to $2,500), and faxes don't exactly do much for cutting paper out of the workplace. Furthermore, now there's fax junk mail.

They do, however, allow virtually instantaneous transmission of documents and photos, and writers in some of the more high-tech arenas, such as technical and public relations writing, report that more and more clients aren't merely asking if they're fax-capable—they're assuming!

Fax etiquette, though, demands that writers not use a publisher's or client's fax number to send queries, proposals, writing samples or anything else without authorization.

Photocopying Machines

These gadgets, though they are now as small as computer printers, are still in the same league with fax machines for price and utility for the average writer. I know of no one who owns one.

Another thing to avoid is copy stores, which charge between six and ten cents a copy, compared to post offices, one-hour photo outlets and stationery stores, which if they have a copier, usually charge half that. Sometimes you can even strike a deal with a local business to do photocopying on the premises for a cheap monthly per-copy fee.

Alarm Clock

Alarm clocks have done more than the Communist Manifesto to arouse the working class, but that is not their only use. I have a Braun alarm clock—it has a gentle beep as well as a motion-sensitivity feature that lets me turn it off simply with a wave of my hand—to help me avoid the physical malady most common to our profession: back pain. When it goes off every hour, I get my duff off the chair and stretch for five minutes.

Before I got the clock and began my regimen, I would sit and write for hours, then wonder why my lower back felt like I had been out in the backyard digging trenches all morning. Writing longhand, I was also leaning over the desk, supporting the weight of my head, which a chiropractor once told me is as heavy as a bowling ball—and often just as thick. This compounded my discomfort with additional pains in my upper back and neck. But as soon as I started taking breathers on the hour, the pain stopped. Another direct correlation.

Writing Off Your Office

At the start of my freelance career, when I was conducting business from my kitchen table, I didn't exactly qualify for a home-office deduction. Still, I felt it was more important to be writing than to be writing it off.

But if you have any workspace that isn't shared with other activities or other family members, you are allowed to deduct the cost of running it. That means you will have lower taxes to pay, and this is worth a bundle to you as a writer, even if you write only part-time.

But, as they say in merchandising, certain restrictions apply:

• The office has to be used solely for your writing business. This doesn't mean you can't write the occasional letter home wishing your mother happy birthday, or bring a milkshake into the room while you're working on deadline. It means you can't use your living room as an office unless you cordon off a section with folding screens, bookshelves or barbed wire to stake out some exclusive territory.

If you make a lot of personal calls from the office, though, just keep a log of them and subtract the cost from your deduction.

• The office must be used regularly, even if it's just on regular weekends. The "revenooers" want to know your intent is to run a business and make money, even if it's only eventually.

You can demonstrate this in any number of ways: show them record books, receipts, stationery, business cards, fliers, advertisements, published works, even rejection letters, anything that shows you're consistently putting it out there.

To figure out how much a home-office deduction is worth to you, calculate in square feet what percentage of your home the office represents. Include any space used for storing inventory or records: bookshelves lining a hallway, supplies in an old broom closet, magazines stored in the attic. In sizing up total footage, though, do not include bathrooms, closets or garages, unless you've converted one of these into your workspace.

If your home is, say, 2,500 square feet and your office is 250 square feet, you can deduct 10 percent of your rent, utilities, mortgage interest, real estate taxes, homeowner's insurance, depreciation, even certain home improvements. To say nothing of deducting everything that goes *into* that office: equipment, supplies, books, furniture, decor and repairs.

Example: If you spend $750 a month on rent, $150 a month on utilities and services, and $100 a month on a homeowner's insurance policy, on the twelve grand a year that you put out for those expenses you would save $1,200. That's a lot of spaghetti.

Be aware, though, that you cannot deduct commuting to an outside office, and deducting office items like Belgian rugs, Ming vases and pre-Columbian art will surely raise the fur on an auditor's back.

A home-office deduction itself, though, is not a red flag to the IRS. If there is a higher likelihood of being audited among the self-employed, it is not because of home offices but because 1) the IRS figures the self-employed are more prone to underreporting income, and 2) the Schedule C (self-employment) tax return is simpler than other kinds of returns, and the IRS uses them to train new auditors.

Otherwise, there is little you can do to minimize your chances of being audited. You could lower your figures by half and still be subject to a financial strip-search. But if it's any consolation, only 1 percent of returns are audited on average, 5 percent in a bumper year. And even the cost of being audited (representation) is deductible.

Order in the Court: A Few Words for the Organizationally Impaired

I come from a long line of pragmatists, people who keep their affairs in order, clean up after themselves, invest wisely, and get things done. On his deathbed, my grandfather asked my mother what day it was.

"Tuesday," she said.

"Pay the gardener," he told her.

Being organized is in my blood, and in a profession that runneth over with paperwork, correspondence and information, it's a good thing. Being disorganized is calamitous to a business that generates as much paperwork as writing (and "business management" is nothing more than the art of organizing your business).

In fact, I have an internal alarm that goes off when my desk is piled with paper, when every available surface within arm's reach is plastered with Post-it notes, when I keep pushing the same notes back yet another day on my desk calendar, when I don't say no to new projects, and then don't prioritize those to which I've said yes. In this business, it only takes a few weeks to reach that point, during which there develops a subtle gradient of frustration, a growing anxiety, the gnawing and disruptive sensation of feeling "behind."

I get jittery when I can't see my desk beneath the sediment of paper, and even more so when I finally excavate deep enough to see the surface looking like the inside of a chimney, with ink and graphite smudged into the dents made by ballpoint pens, the scars left by repeatedly dragging my briefcase across it, and the scratches contributed by cutting-and-pasting impatiently with razor blades.

But when paperwork on my desk begins to pile higher than eye level, I literally feel lower in stature. It makes me feel as though I'm not in control, and the fact is, at those times I'm not.

This is bad for business. It is a form of stress, and stress gets in the way of not only efficiency, but enjoyment as well.

Office work is like yardwork and housework: It takes a constant effort to keep the weeds and dustballs at bay, though not a big one if you stay on it. Go through your office, say, monthly—put it on your calendar—and turn piles of paper into files of paper. Catch up on that correspondence you've been ignoring in the hopes that it will take care of itself if you wait long enough. Take "inactive" material either up to the attic or out to the curb (but out of the office). Regain control of the juggernaut of entropy. If you don't, a year or two down the road you will need a forklift and federal disaster aid to do it.

Organization means being willing to make quick decisions, especially on the little things, resisting the temptation to push them onto back burners, where they only nag at you. It means knowing how to immediately lay your hands on anything in your office, even if to others it looks like you would need the help of a private detective. It means having regular to-do lists. It means cleaning up a little before you knock off for the day, so you don't sit down to a mess the next morning, starting your day out already feeling behind.

It means not storing paper when you could store computer disks, not having the most-used supplies stored in the least accessible places, not allowing paper to pile so high that a retaining wall is in order, and not using the floor as a shelf. (Sometimes, though, the floor *is* the best place for things. When I absolutely must remember something, I often write it on a Post-it note and slap it right on the floor beside my desk, between me and the door. It isn't elegant, but it's effective.)

Above all, organization means *giving things names*: This is the idea file, that's the financial file, this is the client file, that's the supply cabinet, and over there is reference. Nearly all forms of organization are a variation on this approach: Give it a name, if not a nametag. In the writing business, information is life-blood, and good files are arteries that keep the blood from spilling about and making a mess.

I even have two different "round files." One is for plastic, the other for paper, which I recycle and which constitutes 90 percent of the trash I generate in my office. My subscription to the daily paper alone creates more than 500 pounds of waste paper every year; recycling a stack of papers three-and-a-half feet high, which takes me barely two months to pile up, keeps one tree alive.

It is important, though, not to allow organization to become an excuse to avoid work; it can be a clever disguise for procrastination. And remember, offices, like homes, are also meant to be lived in, and a little entropy is to be expected. A perfectly clean desk is the sign of a writer with too much time on his hands.

The Low-Tech Tools of the Trade

Pencils have long been an important part of the diet of nervous writers, and chewing on them has provided eons of comfort and catharsis, compromised only by the fear of lead poisoning.

It turns out, though, that writers can graze on them to their heart's content without fear of falling ill. This is because pencils don't really have lead in them, only graphite, which is a kind of carbon and no worse for you than burnt toast. In fact, researchers have determined that you can literally eat a pencil a day and still keep the doctor away, suffering no injurious effects whatsoever to your health. Just watch out for that little brass ferrule that holds the eraser.

There are many misconceptions in the writing profession, and one of them is the notion that the modern office must be an electronic paradigm of efficiency, with primitive accouterments such as pencils reserved for special occasions, like blackouts.

But high-tech tools are not the only ones that contribute to an office that is both workable and livable. So do low-tech provisions, including a comfortable desk and chair, an in-house reference library, personal mementos and even edible pencils.

Here, then, is a simple list of the simpler things:

Desks and Chairs
Mark Twain, Marcel Proust, Rene Descartes and John Lennon all wrote in bed. Thomas Wolfe wrote on top of an icebox. Edmond Rostand wrote *Cyrano de Bergerac* in the bathtub. Ernest Hemingway, Lewis Carroll and Oscar Hammerstein wrote standing up. And Robert Frost was known to take off his shoe and use the sole for a desk.

In other words, desks and chairs are not mandatory items for writers; only a flat surface is required, preferably level. Beyond that, it is strictly a matter of preference.

My desk—of Swedish design, sleek, white and simple—is the size of my outstretched arms. I like big desks because they cut down on profanity, as well as the danger of avalanche. Whatever manages to accumulate on it tends to spread out and not up.

It also has enough space beneath it so I can cross my legs, plenty of file cabinets nearby, and drawers situated to accommodate my left-handedness.

Although writers have the uncanny ability to turn almost any surface into a desk—the tray table on a flight to New York City, the top of a briefcase, the lap—a more permanent fixture, preferably one large enough to play several rounds of golf on, is the most expedient.

But not the cheapest. Office furniture, generally, is pricey, and in fact the second most expensive piece of furniture ever sold at auction was a $12.1 million desk (the first was a $15.8 million Italian baroque cabinet). For slightly cheaper renditions, check the classifieds for companies going out of business or updating their furniture, or check at used office furniture stores. For bargain-basement prices, you can just lay a slab of particle-board or an old door across two filing cabinets. Or, if you can stand the temptation, write in bed or on top of the icebox. Mark Twain didn't do too badly.

As for the chair, all it has to do to make me happy is rock and roll, and be designed with my lower back in mind. Pinching pennies here leads to pinching nerves.

Given that most of us grew up having to sit at those abominable little desk-and-chair units in school—which, I might add, were only made for righties— nothing is too extravagant, in my opinion. Even if you wanted a $12.1 million antique desk, with a $15.8 million matching Italian baroque cabinet, I would not consider it finicky.

Supplies

The best part about going back to school in September was going to the stationery store and stocking up on supplies, especially since someone else usually paid for them. Stationery stores still have a special appeal to me, and I visit them with the intoxication of a kid in a candy store.

That I have to pay for my own supplies now is made more palatable by the fact that it is cheaper to buy in bulk, and in any one visit I therefore get to buy *more* stuff. At a purely irrational level—to the kid in the candy store—this makes a lot of sense.

At another emotional level, to the penny-pincher in me, buying in bulk is a real challenge. Somehow it feels like I'm saving money by doling it out in dribs and drabs, though I'm not, and it is difficult to conceive that paying more at the cash register is saving me money. This is the kind of resistance to long-term thinking that makes tasks like financial planning and goal setting so hard for people, including me.

But unless you need the cash in the short-run and don't want to tie up your money in inventory, *you save money buying in bulk*—a *package* of legal pads, a *box* of pens, a *thousand* business cards instead of five hundred.

Once home, supplies should be positioned so that they are convenient to you. This doesn't mean just stashing them in the office. It means having them within arm's length everywhere you go. I keep pad and pen in the glove compartment of my car, in my wallet, in my belt-bag, in my backpack, and in virtually every room of my house. Thoughts have little staying power against the onslaught of busy lives with constant demands on our attention. Like dreams, if they are not captured quickly, they simply fade away.

Post-Office Box

When I first began freelancing, I found that I unwittingly established a daily cycle of anticipation/disappointment around the arrival of my mailman. Like the telephone, the sound of his truck, which I could distinguish from all other vehicles right down to what key his brakes squealed in, triggered my drool reflex.

Unfortunately, I was generally disappointed. The mail, as a rule, does not bring checks, plum assignments, announcements that I have won the drawing for a free trip to Maui, or letters from people who were just thinking of me. More likely it brings bills, coupons and mail for the woman who used to live in the house.

The almost daily letdown turned into a form of stress.

For this reason I decided to get a post-office box. I visit it only twice a week and thereby both reduce my anxiety and increase my chances of getting "good" mail.

Personal Library

I cannot understand why so many writers have an attitude about the thesaurus. They look on its use with contempt, as if building your vocabulary were somehow cheating, as if it were a literary form of using steroids.

This is horse-puckey! *Thesaurus* means treasure house in Greek, and it is the single most plundered book on my reference shelf.

Whatever books support you in the day-to-day labors of writing should assume positions of prominence and preeminence on that shelf, no apologies. Mine includes:
- *Roget's Thesaurus.*
- *Random House Dictionary.*
- *World Book Encyclopedia.*
- *Writer's Market.*
- *Bartlett's Quotations.*
- *The Elements of Style.* (Strunk and White)
- *Letters to a Young Poet.* (Rainer Maria Rilke's deeply inspiring little book has been a constant consolation to me throughout my writing career. I practically know it by heart.)

For writers who prefer button-pushing to page-turning, several reference books are now available electronically. Quotemaster Plus (Penn Comp Software Development, Houston) is a byte-sized Bartlett's and includes over three thousand quotable quotes. The Ideafisher (Fisher Idea Systems, Irvine, California) contains a massive associational database that acts essentially like a thesaurus.

Personal Touches

During the four-month trial period at the startup of *USA Today*, I was living with a hundred other reporters in an apartment building leased by Gannett to temporarily house the new staff.

Since no one knew if they would be staying on, no one brought much more than the bare essentials, what would fit in a car: their clothes, toilet kit, some bedding, some dishes, a few tapes, maybe a tennis racquet.

I, on the other hand, rented a U-Haul. I brought all of the above items plus paintings and posters, a few stone sculptures, plants, my bicycle, rugs, pottery, lamps, percussion instruments, pictures of friends for the refrigerator door, everything except my piano, and I rented an upright as soon as I got there!

Whenever the other reporters came over to my place, they stood slack-jawed at the door.

"You *brought* all this?" they would ask with amazement.

And I would reply that I had no intention of living out of a suitcase for four months.

I have a need to feel at home wherever I am, to make my own any space more permanent than an overnight hotel room, and that goes for an office as well. I want to feel that I not only work there, but live there. Even my cubicle at *The Cincinnati Enquirer* was a gallery of posters and plants, papered over with fortune-cookie messages, horoscope predictions, cartoons and pithy quotes.

My office at home is no different, only larger. It is filled with personal mementos that help me feel like I belong here, that work is life, yet also that I have a life outside of work.

Along the windowsills I have postcards friends have sent me from all over the world, and along the walls photographs of a few of those places I have been fortunate enough to visit myself. In one corner I have a handful of awards to remind me of some of my accomplishments, and next to them a plaque with a quote from Rilke reminding me that what I have *not* accomplished is really what drives me.

Next to that, there are four playing cards, all queens, in varying stages of decay, one of each suit, and each one found on the street in a different city over the course of ten years. They are the only playing cards I have ever found, and they remind me that there is a great deal I do not understand.

The Captain's Log:
A Filing System for the Professional Pack Rat

In the average lifetime, by certain estimates, some fifteen trillion bits of information pour into our brains through the senses. Storing, indexing and remembering all this is a staggeringly complex task, and it works in mysterious ways: You can't remember your best friend's name when introducing her, but you remember exactly what you had to eat at your senior prom. You would, however, go stark raving mad if you remembered every detail of every day.

This is especially true for writers, who tend anyway to be savers and compilers, an understatement not unlike calling World War II a skirmish. Our offices fill up with newspaper and magazine clippings, story ideas, queries, business cards, financial records, tax receipts, photographs, cartoons, fortune-cookie messages, correspondence and all manner of literary ephemera that we're sure will come in handy some day. We don't just collect; we warehouse.

Our loved ones think of us as pack rats, though we would prefer, of course, the more dignified title of creative conservationist, professional rummager, refuse engineer, perhaps Doctor of Debris.

Needless to say, rather than attempt to remember the deluge of details pouring out of the Age of Information, it is far better to keep good records and ordered file cabinets. You can't carry it all around in your head, no matter how swelled it is, and you can't make good use of it if you don't remember where you put it.

The French novelist Gustave Flaubert once wrote, "Be regular and orderly in your life . . . so that you may be violent and original in your work." The more organized you are in the maintenance chores of the writing profession, the more your writing can soar unencumbered by the demands of rank and file.

But whatever filing system you choose, *keep it simple*. If your files are complicated or confusing—intricate accounting ledgers, unkempt photo files and anything not alphabetized—you will tend to avoid them, for the simple reason that people avoid what is painful, and confusion is painful.

A handful of easy ledgers will help guard against sensory overload and act as a compass for your business, telling you where you are. For example, if I didn't keep a ledger to record the comings and goings of my queries and manuscripts, I would never remember to whom I sent what, if and when they responded, and whether I got my slides back.

The Query and Manuscript Submission Chart on pages 96-97 illustrates how I keep tabs on this part of my business. (This submission log can also be kept on a computer, although if you need quick access to it during a phone conversation with an editor, and your computer is slow, it may not be so advantageous.) Here are the other files that keep me on course:

1. *Story Ideas*. Here I stash ideas for future consideration, currently broken down into two categories: nonfiction articles and essays.

2. *Story Files*. Two shelves contain alphabetized and labeled folders for each article or essay I've written, complete with printouts of the pieces (the originals I store in my computer), outlines, interview notes, research material, contacts' phone numbers, correspondence with editors, rough drafts and revisions, photos, and expense reports such as lists of phone calls made or miles driven in putting pieces together (I keep a phone log near the phone and a mileage log in the car).

3. *Clips*. Above these shelves is one containing copies of all my published pieces.

4. *Contracts*. A small accordion file filled with all my magazine and book contracts, royalty statements, letters of confirmation (which some editors use in lieu of formal contracts), and reprint request forms.

5. *Rolodex*.

6. *Finances*. A homespun, third-grade-simple ledger listing "Money In" and "Money Out," down to the dollar.

As for receipts, I literally use (gasp!) an old shoebox, divided alphabetically into sections for each of my business expenses: Advertising/Publicity, Auto, Books, Education, Entertainment, Equipment/Supplies, Meals, Miscellaneous (accountant's fee, homeowner's insurance, interest payments), Professional Memberships, Photo, Photocopying, Rent/Utilities, Subscriptions and Travel. A *big* shoebox.

7. *Sample Copies*. A box on the floor of my office closet filled with one sample copy of perhaps 250 different magazines (filed alphabetically, of course).

8. *Day Calendar*. Contains all upcoming appointments, interviews, classes, deadline reminders, rent reminders and birthday reminders.

9. *Queries*. Here again I use the computer to store every query I've written, so that if one magazine rejects it, I can simply call it up, make whatever name/angle/style changes are necessary, and print it out for the next magazine on my list.

10. *Class File*. A folder dedicated to the writing classes I teach at a dozen or so local colleges, as well as private consultations: calendars, contracts, promotional material, correspondence, contacts and mailing lists.

And here is a final observation on the fine art of filing and general organization, from someone who ought to know:

We get more information in a month than people in the 1800s got in an entire lifetime, and we run the risk of information anxiety, serious overwhelm. So organization is crucial. Disorganization is often a reaction against authority, like parents, but you're shooting yourself in the foot.

Get paper vertical and into file folders. Put action files in a separate place from historical or research files. Work in zones. A-Zone is within arm's reach (a chair with rollers greatly extends your range), B-Zone is that requiring a stretch, and C-Zone is anything demanding that you stand. Design your office for physical comfort.

Also, color code. Red = action that is a major priority in supporting a goal; orange = modest value; and yellow = maybe it might support a goal. Periodically go through your files and, holding each document in your hand, ask yourself, "Which of my goals is this supporting?" And do the same with your time. If something isn't supporting your goals, it's interfering with them.

CAROLE KANE, PROFESSIONAL ORGANIZER
NATIONAL ASSOCIATION OF PROFESSIONAL ORGANIZERS

Query

Date	Title	Market	Editor	Accept/ Reject- Date	Comment
1/5/89	Twins essay	Psych. Today	Richard Camer	A 2/15	
1/17/89	Nuclear Free Zones	New York Times	Karen Arenson Sun. Biz	R 2/12	"not business enough"
1/14/89	Amazon	Newsday	Marjorie Robbins	⟶	
1/24/89	Hospital Ship	Pursuits magazine	Margaret Leske	R 3/4	"Doing Similar piece
1/27/89	model mugging ― ― ― ― Rich profile	America West	Mike Derr	R 2/12 A 2/18	"too gritty" ― ― ― ―
1/28/89	spontaneous remission	Longevity	Mike Murray	A 2/19	
2/4/89	Prenatal Tests	Health	Bonnie Gordon	R 3/18	"already done"
2/6/89	Amazon	Chicago Tribune	Carolyn McGuire	⟶	
2/12/89	Nuclear Free Zone.	Omni	Mary Glucksman	A 2/20	new ed. Murray Cox
2/18/89	Team Sport Essay	Christian Science Monitor	David Holmstrom	⟶	
2/24/89	Self Help groups	LA Times Syndicate	Karen Hsaio	reprint from Health Mag. ⟶	
2/27/89	Roomate Recovery	American Health	Doug Podolsky	A 3/6	

Manuscript

Date Due	Date Sent	Photos Sent	Photos Ret'd	Accept/Reject-Date	Comment	$
5/1	4/1			4/10		750. 5/10
→	1/14	1/22	2/24	A 1/21	Rums Sunday 2/5	175. photos 2/20 200. story 2/22
4/1	3/20			A 4/15		300. 5/12
5/15	5/10			A 6/4		1766.04 7/1
→	2/6	2/16 6 color slides	4/9	A 2/16		250. 3/3
5/1	4/15			A 5/6		875. story 6/7 373 exp. 6/16
→	2/18			R 3/15	"too many sports stories"	
→	2/26			A 3/21	6 month all rights	100. 4/4
4/15	4/10			A 4/22	mag. money problems. Wait	100. 8/10

CHAPTER FIVE

Promotion:
The Art of Getting Attention

When I was a toddler, I am told, I regularly held my breath until I turned blue and passed out.

It was usually in response to something my twin brother got that I didn't, and a means of signaling my displeasure.

Because of the gales of attention this fearsome little tactic attracted, however, my brother soon adopted it himself, and for a while we were dropping like flies.

Children are geniuses at self-promotion, and none more so than twins, for whom the need to distinguish from the competition takes on Darwinian urgency. It was, in retrospect, good practice for being a self-employed writer.

There are, of course, more elegant approaches to publicizing yourself than feigning suffocation and collapsing into a heap on the floor. But the principle remains the same: *You don't get attention if nobody knows you exist.* Doing business without promotion, as adman David Ogilvy once said, is like winking in the dark—*you* know what you're doing, but nobody else does.

Promotion, though, is not something you set aside an hour a day to do, or something you do, say, once your book is finished. It is a seamless web of actions, a constant planting of seeds. It is everything you do to get the world to pay attention to your writing (accent on the "pay"), to communicate that you have something worth saying, and to build confidence in your product, so that when people have a need that you can fill, they think of you.

For those writers who are disinclined to draw attention to themselves personally, it may help to reframe the objective. Don't think of it as promoting yourself. Think of it as promoting your message, what you want the world to hear. Sometimes it helps to connect to something bigger than yourself.

You promote yourself and your message—or you don't—through your phone manner, listening skills and attention to detail; you make impressions with your handshake, your eye contact and the way you talk about your work; you get your name out there with an uninterrupted flow of proposals, cold calls, advertisements and, of course, good writing, which is the single best promotional tool at your disposal and arguably the hardest to develop. All the marketing and promotion in the world won't persuade customers to buy a lousy product—more than once, anyway.

But you've got to put it out there. Promotion is the fine art of going public, of raising your hand in class and having everyone turn around and look at you. You must be prepared for it, both professionally and emotionally. Don't underestimate this: By sending your writing out, you stand to be judged, and you will be, for better and for worse. It will therefore confront you with whatever fears you have about criticism and rejection, failure and success. Promotion is the act of blowing your cover.

The way people are "discovered" in this business, in fact, is not the way quarks and cave paintings are discovered. No one comes looking for you. You have to go *get* discovered.

Drawing attention to yourself—selling yourself—is excruciating for a lot of writers and can be especially so for women, because they are often brought up with some variation on the theme "Nice girls don't!" Nice girls write scenes, they don't make them.

Authors, for instance, are notorious slouches when it comes to promoting their own books. They expect publishers to do it, then become embittered when they don't, and the books they have spent years writing die in childbirth because of some misguided notion that somebody else is supposed to market it. It's your baby. No one else will give a damn about it like you do. You should no sooner abandon your books after publication than train for the Olympics and then not show up on the day of your event.

Book publishing, in fact, is a bit like horse racing, except that publishers wait to see which books pull ahead and *then* bet on them. Whichever books show the most promise tend to attract advertising dollars; in part what determines such favor is the amount of promotion the author himself or herself does.

Even the *kind* of author you are will determine the amount and resourcefulness of the promotion you have to employ. It depends on how difficult your wares are to sell. Fiction, for example, demands a bigger push than nonfiction.

Take book promotions again. Radio and TV talk shows want news-pegs, concise subjects on which to hang their interviews. Novelists often have a hard time providing this hook. Consider these interviews:

"Nice having you on the show, Mr. Melville. Why don't you tell us a bit about your new book." "Well, it's about this guy who chases after a big fish. . . "

"Our next guest is a Mr. Shakespeare, who's recently written a romance novel. So, Bill—can I call you Bill?—what's this new book of yours about?" "It's the story of a boy and girl who fall in love, even though their families are feuding. They both die in the end, but there's a touching balcony scene. . ."

Needless to say, it loses something in the translation. It's like trying to describe a painting; the power is in the craft of the thing. Still, such books can be more effectively promoted on radio and TV by finding something topical about them. Mr. Melville might pitch his book as a study on revenge; Mr. Shakespeare, as a profile of teen suicide.

Ultimately, the point of promotion is to not have to do it anymore, to have clients promote themselves to *you*, or to be able to afford a full-time publicist. But until then it is strictly a do-it-yourself proposition.

Nevertheless, to the degree that promotion is the task of working to get work, you will find that you need to do less of it as you go along. The bulk of the effort is front-end, in the first couple of years. Getting customers in the tent is the hard part. It costs five times as much to attract a new customer, in fact, as it does to maintain an established one, according to *Success Magazine*.

But as you get better at figuring out what fits where in the marketplace, you waste less promotional energy. You become more adept at the contacts game. You spend less time trying to convince people, because your portfolio begins to speak for you. And as your visibility increases, clients start coming to you.

Getting Good Visibility

One day early in my career at *The Cincinnati Enquirer*, I was in a frame shop matting some photographs of a ski trip to Utah. A woman leaned over my shoulder and asked which ski area I'd gone to.

"Alta."

"Alta?" she repeated excitedly. "I have a very dear friend, Dr. Henry Heimlich [as in Heimlich Maneuver], whose favorite ski area is Alta, and he's got a birthday coming up. Are any of your photographs for sale?"

I said sure, she could have one for $25.

"Wonderful," she said. "I'll write you a check. Who should I make it out to?"

"Gregg Levoy. L . . . e . . . v . . ."

"Oh. Are you the columnist for the *Enquirer*?"

I nodded.

"Then I'll pay you $5 more if you'll sign your name to the photograph."

What I realized in that moment, for the first time, was that name recognition was worth money to me.

That explains why Stephen King and Robert Ludlum do credit card commercials. Why George Plimpton is a video-game spokesman. And why Mickey Spillane does beer commercials. No matter what rung of the ladder you're on, you can never be too visible (Salman Rushdie notwithstanding). Visibility is the bull's-eye of promotion.

Think about what makes *you* do business with people, whether it's employing their consulting services, taking their classes or buying their products. You probably saw their ads, read their books, heard about them through the grapevine, or were referred by a friend or professional organization. (Or perhaps you were simply persuaded by the merits of their product.)

Most people would rather do business with — or vote for, or buy books from, or invite to a party — somebody they've heard of than somebody they haven't. When someone has heard of you before, they trust you more — unless, of course, your reputation comes from having your picture at the post office. Consistency, says Jay Conrad Levinson in his book *Guerrilla Marketing*, equates with familiarity; familiarity equates with confidence; and confidence equates with sales.

Therefore, *get your name out there* in as many places as possible and repeatedly. You want people to remember you, and you want to remember that your potential customers are awash in competing propositions, which appear on their desks in the form of "slush piles" — so named primarily because they're messy and indistinct. You want to distinguish yourself from this anonymous slop of rivalry, and one way to do this is through repetition, by keeping your writing and your name out in front of people.

It has been demonstrated in the advertising world that a typical marketing message has to penetrate roughly ten times before a prospect becomes a customer. Name recognition is a cumulative enterprise, a momentum that you build slowly over years.

Overnight Success Takes Years: How to Build a Reputation

The operative word here is *slowly*. One of the most sobering realizations I have had in my writing career is that it has taken longer than I thought it would. Most of the goals I have set for myself have demanded of me far greater reserves of patience and determination than I ever imagined I needed. Or possessed.

Success is following the dreams you have for your own life — against all the voices pulling at you to abandon them — but success in this or any other business will not happen quickly. "Overnight success" simply refers to people you never heard of before their "big break." But they have been toiling away behind the scenes for years, building their confidence, their craft, their contacts, reputations and portfolios. (When I was in school, I had friends who graduated with Masters in Fine Arts, and I always wondered what it was they were "Masters" of at twenty-one or twenty-two.)

Building a writing career requires that you disengage not only from the expectation that success will happen quickly, but that you will be compensated for your every exertion. In the beginning, *you will give out far more than you get back*, and sometimes you may quite literally give away your writing.

But to get what you want from your first writing projects — to get in the door, to get your writing out there, to start building a reputation — you can't apply to your start-up career a strict cost-benefit, bottom-line approach. Rather, apply what the eminent motivational writer Napoleon Hill calls the Law of Increasing Returns: "Perform more service and better service than that for which you are paid." *In the beginning, clips and contacts, exposure and experience are more important than money, hands down!*

What is important is to get people to try you out and then deliver more goods than they expect to get. A job description is a starting point, not a boundary. In the beginning, I threw in a lot of sidebars with my articles, tracked down a lot of art, burned a lot of midnight oil to get stories in before deadlines, willingly obliged with rewrites even when I thought them redundant, and worked for a pittance—all for the sake of giving more than was expected of me and thereby building goodwill. *But it does come around.* You do get rewarded for it, and not always in ways you expect.

If you can stick with your writing business, especially through the first year, and during that time really put it out there, you've survived the hardest part. And it does build. But you have to personally nail one plank to the next until you have a ship. And then don't abandon it during storms, which there will be. You don't forsake your writing when it backslides any more than you sell your kids at the flea market when they start holding their breath and passing out, though you may be sorely tempted.

The advertisements I put out for my writing consultations present a good case in point. Over the years, I have often felt like heaving them overboard when the phone calls slacken, which they do periodically because of summers or recessions or who-knows-what. But ads need to build up strength, and yanking them prematurely or running them intermittently is like city driving: You don't get good mileage when you're constantly stopping and starting.

Sixteen Ways to Get Discovered

1. Tell Everybody

Word of mouth starts with you. Success is as much a function of what others can do for you as what you can do for yourself, but they have to know about you. Don't miss an opportunity to tell people that you're a writer and you're for hire. I've heard of people using their phone answering machines to let anyone calling know they're looking for writing jobs.

Go through your address books and send people postcards. Ask them if they know anyone who'd be interested in your services. Use recommendations to swing from tree to tree. And build an active mailing list. Especially if you aspire to publish a book, teach, or start your own freelance business, you'll be glad you did. You want people to know you're out there, and you want to know if they, or anybody they know, can help you out.

2. Start Small

To promote yourself, you need something to promote, something you can point to and say, "Look what I've done!" If you start small, you'll have promotable successes more quickly.

Take an example from the magazine world. In an increasingly competitive marketplace, more and more magazines start as one-shots on the newsstands. If they fly, they go quarterly, then monthly, then perhaps international. At each step, they sell themselves to advertisers based on previous successes.

However, don't be too quick to say no to a project if it seems a bit over your head. Take it on and get help, or do extra research. But don't be too quick to say yes either, if it's more than a bit over your head. It's better to admit to your limitations up front than to show a client after you've gotten a go-ahead that you don't really know what they are.

3. *Put Together a Press Kit*

Include resume, published clips, letters of recommendation, reviews, photos, book dust jackets, business card, brochure or whatever you have available that is appropriate to the kind of writing you do and shows you off. Send out as needed. And remember what Will Rogers said: "If you done it, it ain't bragging."

I keep a folder filled with resumes and clips that I send out regularly to new magazines, colleges and writers' conferences that offer my workshops, individuals who call for consultations, and radio stations that need background material on me when I do talk shows about articles I've written or classes I'm teaching.

4. *Sound the Trumpets*

Don't just do a good job; be *noticed* doing a good job. Whenever anything of yours hits print, make clean copies of it and send it out, with the briefest cover letter, to people who might be interested: editors you work with, editors you've pitched but haven't cracked yet, colleagues, agents, hometown and alumni publications (local boy/girl makes good), and professional organization newsletters, which usually have a section for sounding-off about members.

5. *Volunteer*

Don't just join professional organizations; volunteer to serve on a committee, put together a conference, edit a newsletter. You'll make contacts you couldn't make in any other way and get your name on all sorts of literature.

When I first moved to San Francisco to freelance full-time, I volunteered to work every Friday afternoon for six months at the offices of Media Alliance, a local professional organization for media-related people. I answered phones, did publicity, set up seminars, acted as class assistant to MA instructors (and thereby took free classes), had first-come access to the job file, wrote articles for the organization's newspaper, and met a *lot* of people.

Eventually I pitched them my first class, on marketing for freelance writers, and they took me on. It had everything to do with their familiarity with me. Over the years, that stint as a Boy Friday has more than paid for itself. Media Alliance now offers several of my classes, sends me countless consultees, gives me free advertising and exposure, invites me to teach at conferences, and provides me with priceless contacts.

6. *Apprentice*

Another of the most effective ways of trading labor for learning—and in the process getting contacts, visibility, on-the-job training and an inside track that few freelancers possess—is the old Renaissance tradition of apprenticing. The primary qualification is eagerness.

As an apprentice (or intern), you see what a writing field looks like from the inside out, and should you ever decide to make a run for the freelance life, the apprenticeship experience will make your outside-in perspective vastly more insightful.

My internship at *Writer's Digest* magazine paid only twenty dollars a week at the time, but I got to see how a magazine operates, what editors do, and what writers look like from the editorial viewpoint. I did copyediting, proofreading, layout, fact checking and editorial and promotional copywriting. I got a letter of recommendation more valuable than an Ivy League diploma. And the fellow who took me on as the magazine's first intern, John Brady, is the same fellow who fifteen years later referred Writer's Digest Books to me when they were looking for someone to write this book. To say nothing of everything he's done for me in between.

There are scores of internship programs in the writing industry, part-time and full-time, that are open to college students, career changers and even those reentering the workforce. Some examples:

- Television (United Artists/Columbia, Turner Broadcasting, "MacNeil/Lehrer Newshour," Orion).
- Advertising (Ogilvy & Mather, Young & Rubicam).
- Magazines (*Harper's*, *Mother Jones*, *McCall's*, *Rolling Stone*, *Longevity*).
- Book publishing (Simon & Schuster; William Morrow; Little, Brown & Co.; Farrar, Straus & Giroux).
- Journalism (*Los Angeles Times*, *Wall Street Journal*, *Washington Post*, *Newsday*, *Miami Herald*).
- Business writing (Macy's, Aetna, Amway, Bell & Howell, Nabisco).

7. *Be different*

Put a spin on your writing. Offer something unusual, a twist no one's thought of. Editors love novelty. Also, the more unique your product, the less promotion you'll have to do, because word of mouth will take up slack. Tell a story from an uncommon viewpoint, create a TV show produced by kids, write a travel article on the dungeons of Europe.

I always try to throw my magazine editors curve balls. Some examples: millionaires under thirty, outer-space tourism, ten places you can ski in the summer, America's offbeat museums, people who never marry, America's only underwater national park, a professional thief tells you how to crimeproof your home, the link between boredom and cancer, an apartment complex just for people with pets.

8. *Teach*

If you have competence in an area and enjoy teaching, do so. I currently teach four different kinds of one-day writing and creativity workshops through the community-education departments of a dozen universities and colleges in northern California. I earn anywhere from $300 to $1,200 *a day*, depending on enrollment. It's great exposure and supplemental income, an excellent way to add to my mailing list, a place to sell my books, and a terrific antidote to the isolation of writing.

You might also consider offering workshops and lectures to service clubs, trade associations, church/temple groups, high school writing or journalism classes, senior centers, cruise lines, writers' groups and conferences, even through your own home or at a rental space. Or contact the instructors of full-semester college writing courses and offer yourself as a guest lecturer.

One of the best testimonials I ever received about my promotional efforts came from someone at a writers' conference where I was teaching a workshop. "You again?" he said. "Isn't there somewhere you *don't* teach?"

9. *Get Out of the House*

And into the community. As Mickey Rooney once said, put on a show: Gather friends and do an evening of erotic poetry, sponsored by a local bookstore or coffeehouse; organize a chain-story marathon as a benefit for a local charity; host a presentation of works-in-progress. And tell the media about it.

Some years ago I participated in an event called "Solos," an evening at a local art gallery consisting of a half dozen solo performances: a singer, a dancer, a video artist, a musician, a comedian and a writer (me). It was picked up by all the local press and attended by over one hundred people.

A friend of mine whose writing leans toward philosophy used to set up a booth in Harvard Square in Boston with a sign that said, "Philosophical Dialogues: $3 for ten minutes. $4 for existentialists." And boy, did he get press!

10. *Throw in Extras*

Whenever you do an assignment, give your client something extra, the way airlines give away their in-flight magazines, restaurants give free refills, and banks offer free toasters to new accounts. The waiter who throws in a little extra dessert or doesn't charge for the side order of onion rings isn't risking his job; he's doing good business and getting bigger tips.

Give your editors sidebars. Tell them where they can find cheaper artwork. Send business cards specially punched to fit Rolodexes. Include with your story a list of "takeouts"—the best quotes or turns-of-phrase in the piece, which publications often set large and insert into the body of copy.

Enclose with your book proposal a marketing sheet that lists twenty ways you will help promote your own book. Turn around a rewrite in a day instead of the week an editor gave you. Be obsessively punctual; in fact, be ahead of time—get your work in before deadline. Whenever reprints of your work appear with a credit line such as "Originally appeared in *XYZ Magazine*" or "Reprinted permission of *XYZ Magazine*," send *XYZ Magazine* two tearsheets — one for the editor and one for the marketing department.

Whenever you can ferret out personal details about an editor, try addressing them in your stories. This is subtle. For example: I recently wrote a medical piece on what are called wrongful-life lawsuits, the newest form of medical malpractice, in which parents sue on behalf of children who would not have been born except for a physician's negligence in performing genetic counseling, sterilization or abortion.

During the huddle with my editor about the assignment, she mentioned offhandedly that cystic fibrosis ran in her family. So in putting the story together, I featured some discussion of that particular disease to make the piece of extra interest to her.

11. *Don't Overlook the Bio Blurb*

This is the little notice, usually at the end of a piece, that presents biographical information about the writer. It's a free ad. Use it. Mention your book, an upcoming class, any services you offer, your address or just other publications for which you've written.

12. *Think Visually*

When pitching ideas that have dramatic visual/photo possibilities, highlight them in your proposals. Some stories I have thus dramatized: summer skiing, miniature horses, an undersea research habitat, taxidermy, self-defense and sleeping with your pets.

13. *Send Postcards*

Whenever you travel on assignment and stay somewhere more than a day or two, send your editor a postcard advising him or her that the assignment is going well. If your editor is the jealous type, send a postcard with a picture of buildings and not beaches.

Also, keep a stack of blank postcards in your desk and use them liberally to keep your name and your enthusiasm in front of clients. There is great power in the short note sent at the decent interval. You might even consider sending cards with art on the front, so editors will be tempted to tack them up on their bulletin boards and perhaps think of you when they glance up at them.

Whenever a prospect becomes a client, they begin receiving from me a fairly constant flow of postcards, the soul of which is brevity. I send:

- Thank-you notes after trips to visit editors, acknowledging the time they took to see me and confirming that whatever stories they expressed interest in would be in query form, in their hands, within the week.
- Congratulatory notes following promotions.
- FYI (for-your-information) notes on story ideas I think an editor would be interested in but which I don't have the time or inclination to do myself.

- Praise notes complimenting an editor on a particular story in the current issue, especially when it isn't mine.
- Follow-up notes on queries that haven't been responded to within two weeks.
- Wind-up notes to inform editors that I'm finishing a project and that they will have the manuscript within a week.
- Welcome-home notes when I know editors have been on vacation.
- Even "Is-your-kid-out-of-the-hospital?" notes, simply for the sake of good-will.

During a recent lunch with an editor of mine at *Omni* magazine, I was told, "Your notes do not go unappreciated." Or unrewarded.

14. *Advertise*

And if you do, plan to stick with it for at least three months. Otherwise you're pulling fruit off the tree before it ripens.

Advertising, if well placed, works by accrual; you build public trust slowly over time. The ad I run about my consulting services, for instance, has appeared in the same place in the same publication with the same writeup for four years, has doubled my money back, and provided a multitude of names for my mailing list.

Over the years, I have put ads in trade publications, resource directories, newspapers and newsletters, for everything from consulting services, private workshops and college classes to people interested in being interviewed on specific subjects, and even for story ideas. I have discovered that the more I reveal about myself and what I have to offer, the more responses I get.

To wit: I once put a personals ad in a city magazine — for an assignment, of course — and because I wrote a solid four-inch ad packed with specifics and not generalities, I got twenty-seven letters.

You don't necessarily have to pay for advertising, though. I occasionally spin-off an article for a local writers' organization in exchange for free advertising of my consulting services.

Also consider, as a form of advertising, business cards (little brochures), bumper stickers ("Metaphors Be With You!" or "Avoid the Draft — Hire a Writer") and vanity plates. For fifty bucks a year, I have plates that read "Oncepon." I would have preferred "Twasadark," but they only give you seven letters; "Twsadrk" doesn't quite work.

15. *Use Radio*

Whenever you have something published that might be of interest to the general public, especially of a topical nature — even a magazine article or short story — send radio stations a press release about the subject and your availability to discuss it as a talk-show guest.

Also ask about doing a "phoner," an on-air interview conducted over the phone. You don't even have to leave your house. Just make sure all potentially interested parties, such as professional groups related to the subject matter, are advised of the talk show in advance. And don't forget to mention your article on the air.

Radio stations, particularly public radio, are hungry for interesting guests with a modicum of eloquence.

16. *Get Feedback*

Whenever a client comes to *you*, find out by what route. Get a sense of how the net works. Which promotional activities pay off and which don't? When I teach classes, I make it a point to ask how people heard about it, whether from the college catalog, the radio, my flyers, or a friend.

Here are a few more suggestions about the art of getting yourself discovered:

Every writer has a responsibility to a vision, to promoting that vision. It's foolish and irresponsible to expect others to do it for you, or without you. Make yourself available to the cause.

As a first-time novelist, I needed to be aggressive in promoting myself. I took advantage of San Francisco, where I have an audience already, and availed my publisher of those opportunities. Smaller, more cumulative ads in your own backyard, for example, are often better than one big ad in the *New York Times Book Review* section.

If you want your book to have an oral public presence, and gain an audience, work on developing a speaking voice, so you can do readings. Practice reading aloud to wives and friends. Force yourself. What's involved is theatre, without props, costumes or someone else's dialogue.

But it's enormously rewarding when it works. You bring your book to life. It's a completely separate process from writing, but integral to it. And it's a talent that can be cultivated.

FENTON JOHNSON
AUTHOR, *CROSSING THE RIVER*
PROFESSOR, CREATIVE WRITING, SAN FRANCISCO STATE UNIVERSITY

A publisher's interest in your book is about two months in most cases. Your best publicists are people who like your book, and who know you. So go meet your audience in person. If you meet one person, you sell two books.

People go to see authors to see if they're telling the truth, if they're living what they write. If you're authentic, you get the most loyal readers. By doing readings, you not only sell your books, but test and sharpen your ideas with live people, and get feedback.

SAM KEEN
AUTHOR, *TO A DANCING GOD, THE PASSIONATE LIFE, FACES OF THE ENEMY, FIRE IN THE BELLY*

Promotion is a dirty word—bragging—to a lot of people. But it's really just telling the truth about who you are. Writers often consider promotion, marketing and business to be mundane work, compared with writing. But mundane comes from the word *mundi*, meaning the world. By taking care of your worldly tasks, you allow your creativity to be supported. Promotion may require working through some pain and insecurity, but if you want your work out in the world, what other choice do you have?

TERRY MANDEL
MARKETING CONSULTANT

When movies are good, the press credits the director. When they're bad, they blame the script. Writers need better press and promotion. We need to sensitize the media to what we do. When a movie you're working on gets publicized, make sure your bio is in the press kit. Call the publicity department at the studio and say you're available for press.

Having your name around makes a big difference. A fellow whom I went to college with saw me in an alumni magazine and took me on for a movie he was working on. You never know.

You have to keep at it, though—both the writing and the promotion. Your second, third and fourth scripts will be just as hard to sell as your first. Seventy-five percent of the 9,000 members of the Writer's Guild are unemployed, and they all had to sell at least one script to get in. But get to know unemployed writers, at conferences, for instance. Eventually they aren't unemployed anymore, and become valuable contacts.

CARL SAUTTER
STORY EDITOR, "MOONLIGHTING"
SCRIPTWRITER, *JETSONS: THE MOVIE*
AUTHOR, *HOW TO SELL YOUR SCREENPLAY*

I'm accused of being orgiastically involved in self-promotion. I'm a Rolodex humper. I produce my own work and look for financing for it. I developed a theatre, put on solo-performance festivals, organize other artists and produce them. But you have to do it yourself, until you're on Spaulding Gray's level and can hire people.

Value your audience. Be attentive to who they are. A recent play of mine was about baseball, so I pitched it to the baseball audience: sports organizations, bars. You have to lead with the work, though. It doesn't take long for really good work to find its audience. It happens by word of mouth. But meanwhile, don't be afraid to put up 500 posters yourself. Get your bravery from your work.

BILL TALEN
PLAYWRIGHT, MONOLOGIST
ARTISTIC DIRECTOR, LIFE ON THE WATER THEATRE
SAN FRANCISCO

The best promotion establishes you as an authority in your field, and if you specialize, there are fewer people to promote yourself *to*. The idea is to get out there and make people aware of you, to let everyone know what you do. I do a radio show once a month on restaurants. I offer myself as a guest lecturer at food-writing classes. I take leadership roles whenever I can, like chairing a committee in a professional organization, which is a good way to make contacts. All this takes time away from your writing, but it can only help.

JANET FLETCHER
FOOD/WINE WRITER

I'm a real self-promoter, even though I have an agent. You can't expect the publisher to do it. Your books will go absolutely nowhere if you don't promote them. I have a book on music for kids, so I market it to children's bookstores, send circulars to music teachers, belong to organizations which review my book in their national publications, and even bring a boombox to schools to bring the material to life.

I can't write into oblivion. I need an audience and want to be recognized. So I've got to help create that audience. Half the job of being a writer is getting known. It's not my favorite part of it, but I get to be a writer!

JANET NICHOLS
AUTHOR, *AMERICAN MUSIC MAKERS*

More and more authors are promoting themselves, out of necessity. You have to do something to separate yourself from the pack, to acknowledge that your book has been published. But start long before you get an agent or a contract.

If it helps, get some media coaching, especially for TV. Also, get reviews and endorsements, do radio and cable TV talk shows, signings, press releases, a launch party and a local or regional book tour if you can't afford a national one. And ask the publicity director at your publishing house, "What are your intentions? And how can I be of service?" Get what you want.

JUDY HILSINGER
CEO, HILSINGER-MENDELSON, LITERARY PUBLICISTS
AUTHORS: TOM CLANCY, JUDITH KRANTZ, JOSEPH HELLER, TOM ROBBINS, MARGARET ATWOOD, ISAAC ASIMOV

If you're not an entrepreneur, you have no business being in the writing profession. If you're not involved in sales, you don't sell. It's the height of naiveté to separate art from business. Art exists in the commercial world. Don't end up being embittered.

Most writers don't understand book-publishing economics: 65 to 70 percent of trade books lose money. Only 25 to 30 percent break even. And only 5 to 10 percent make money. And no one knows ultimately what will sell. It's a crapshoot. The publishers' business is to identify the big sellers as quickly as possible and throw their marketing efforts at *them*. So you can curse fate or get your butt in front of the buying public.

To sell my books, I've hired national publicists with $5,000 to $6,000 of my own money, who got me on national TV like "Donahue" and the "Today Show" (it's absolutely not true that if you get on "Donahue," your book is a guaranteed bestseller). I've financed fifteen- and twenty-city tours. I've done low-budget book tours by doing "phoner" interviews with radio stations. I sent postcards to radio stations, with a mugshot of my book cover and six reasons why they should book me. Seventeen hundred cards cost $2,000 and netted me 130 talk shows over five months. I've also badgered the guy at Simon & Schuster who sells to the big chains, to make sure my books get there. You have to fight to get in.

All these things have helped me sell books, though one rave review of one of my books in *Playboy* magazine sold 20,000 copies alone.

MICHAEL CASTLEMAN
AUTHOR, *SEXUAL SOLUTIONS*
FORMER EDITOR, *MEDICAL SELF CARE*

First (and Lasting) Impressions: The Power of Proposals

Writers who have a sarcastic attitude toward advertising and "junk mail" might want to reconsider, if for no other reason than that both have a lot to teach about making fast and favorable first impressions, and the first impression is critical to anyone selling anything.

This applies particularly to writers who, like me, do most of their selling through the mail and whose customers generally receive pitches before products (exceptions include short stories, poetry and essays). This is because their foremost promotional tactic—the proposal or query—is essentially a direct-mail advertisement, one that creates (or destroys) a client's first impression of them. (I have heard it said, too, that junk mail is the right proposal sent to the wrong person, and direct mail is the right proposal sent to the right person.)

Your proposal communicates the quality of your writing, the clarity of your ideas, the extent of your homework, and whether you've got a handle on the material or a tiger by the tail. Especially for writers who have no track record, no clips to show a prospective client, your proposal *is* your portfolio. And it's got to sing!

Any profession in which slush piles are a fact of life is full of people who rely heavily on first impressions, and whose snap judgments click into place faster than the wheels of a one-armed bandit. They have elevated the once-over to a professional sport. And they not only rely on first impressions, they stick to them.

This is called the halo effect. If an editor's first impression of you is positive, you can do almost no wrong thereafter. But if it's negative, everything you do subsequently will be tainted with that perception. Even favors or friendly phone calls might be interpreted with suspicion.

Unfortunately, most proposals are suspect before they're even opened, because of the sheer number of them in the writing business that are poorly conceived, written and targeted.

Writers greatly underestimate the power and consequence of proposals. They are in effect job-hunting appeals that ask for an assignment or an appointment, and they can take many forms:

- The letter, with resume and clips, introducing your editing services to a company and describing how you've helped clients similar to them.
- The magazine query synopsizing a story and asking if an editor would like to see it in its entirety.
- The packet that includes a complete rewrite you did of some part of a company's sales literature or of a politician's speech and a note saying that, if they like it better than the original, your further services are for sale.
- The pitch to a television producer, in which you reduce a sitcom or TV movie to a two-minute "commercial" and try to sell it—in person.
- The fiction or nonfiction book proposal, including sample chapter(s) and outline, sent to an agent in hopes of getting representation.
- The phone query to a newspaper (only their Sunday magazines want written queries) asking an editor, in thirty seconds or less, if he or she would be interested in your sending in a particular piece.

The best way to put a halo around your proposals is to include the following ingredients:

Clarity

A product is a solution to a problem. Know exactly what the customer's "problem" is and why your solution will help. And remember that there is a perceived product (information or entertainment) and a hidden product (prestige; power; escape; hope; recipes for success, health and wealth). Every product has an emotional core, and that is what people are really buying.

People don't buy $10,000 Rolex watches to tell time with but to tell the world something about themselves. They're not buying watches. They're buying luxury. Therefore your pitch to write ad copy for Rolex must position you as a writer who understands and can communicate luxury.

Brevity

Curb your dogma. Keep your query under two pages and get right to the point. Take a tip from *Reader's Digest*; their table of contents is right on the cover. It *is* the cover.

Drama

Consider these opening lines:

- "Self-defense and martial-arts classes don't protect women from what happens in real assaults."
- "Boys hold marriages together better than girls."
- "As many as 80 percent of well-known creative writers suffer severe depressive illnesses, compared to 30 percent of other professionals."
- "When the waters of the Amazon River recede during dry season, leaving behind lakes that are cut off from the main channels until the rains come again, the piranha in those lakes get very hungry. It was on just such a lake that I was offered my first opportunity to try out a dugout canoe."

These are opening gambits I've used in some of my recent magazine proposals, and I sold the stories because I observed one of the fundamental laws of publishing: *Grab the reader.* An editor is just a reader with clout, and you want to entertain your readers as well as inform them, to make them laugh and then while their mouths are open feed them. Or as Julius Caesar once put it, "Give the populace bread and circuses."

To put together a high-powered proposal, *you must know the single most compelling thing about your subject and make that line one*, right after the editor's name. Don't stumble in with "Dear Kurt Reply: I've been reading your magazine for years . . . ," or "I'm new in the field and . . . ," or "I'd love to break into your publication . . ."

Step into the ring with a heart-stopping anecdote, a jolting headline, a startling fact, a provocative statement, an incendiary quote, a striking statistic.

When I browse bookstores and libraries for anthologies of short stories or collections of essays, for example, I read the first paragraph of each piece in the book, and if fewer than a third of them grab me, I leave it on the shelf. I make no apologies for this form of impatience, and neither do editors.

The query letter on pages 114-115 is a real-life (and successful) example of a proposal that has this sort of drama.

Authority

What something is worth is not necessarily a function of its intrinsic value, but of what people are willing to pay for it, what the demand is. Consider paintings and pet rocks.

Whenever I design a new class, I send applications out to the community-ed departments at a dozen local universities. As soon as one or two sign me on, I send postcards to the undecideds telling them of the "exciting response." It seldom fails to light a fire under their chairs. The more demand people perceive for a product, the more valuable it becomes.

Therefore, whenever you can, demonstrate to prospective clients that your writing is in some demand. Bring on the witnesses, hoist the testimonials into high relief. Tell them who else you've written for, what awards you've won, who recommended you—anything that lends you authority, implies satisfied customers and insinuates demand.

Even if you're fresh out of school, tell them what creative-writing program

15 Pasadena Ave. San Anselmo, CA 94960

Jan. 15, 1988

Murray Cox
Omni Magazine

Dear Murray Cox:

Takoma Park, Maryland, refuses to buy police squad cars from General Motors.

Amherst, Massachusetts, has canceled a contract for word processors made by the Harris Corporation.

Marin County, California, has divested $20 million of investments in GE, GM, Ford and Westinghouse, out of its $120 million portfolio.

When a city declares itself a Nuclear Free Zone nowadays, it means business! And to those in the nuclear-weapons business, it means a lot more than facing the symbolic and toothless measure that emerged in the earily 1980s, those proverbial mice that roared.

One reason, in fact, that Nuclear Free Zone initiatives have failed in every community in which they have threatened existing nuclear-weapons contractors is that these companies take the initiatives very seriously:

• When Sonoma County, California, launched a NFZ initiative two years ago, Hewlett Packard, General Dynamics, Lockheed and PepsiCo donated nearly $400,000 to defeat the measure.

• Draper Laboratories, a Department of Defense contractor chipped in half the $500,000 necessary to defeat a Cambridge, Massachusetts, proposal to go nuclear-free (which still lost by only a 60-40 margin).

• When Takoma Park sent letters to the top fifty nuclear-weapons contractors, informing them of their ineligibility for city contracts, twelve wrote back—including the chairmen of IBM, Goodyear and Grumman—and AT&T even requested a meeting with Takoma Park officials "to discuss our mutual concerns."

Nuclear-related businesses are beginning to recognize that when a city goes nuclear-free, there is likely to be economic fallout. And municipalities are beginning to appreciate the power of the purse to influence one of the ultimate environmental issues: the arms race.

With over 5,000 cities worldwide having declared themselves nuclear-free (including 161 in the U.S., some as large as Chicago and Oakland), and each carefully considering its purchase of and investment in everything from police walkie-talkies to government T-bills, it is clear that business has important challenges and opportunities to face in addressing those "mutual concerns."

One is the contention that military spending is a bad buy for cities. According to Employment Research Associates, an independent consulting firm in Michigan, far more jobs are generated—six thousand more per billion dollars—if money is spent in the civilian economy instead of the military.

Marin County, for instance, found that after "cleansing" its portfolio of nuclear-related investments, it earned a slightly higher yield.

In one study of nuclear vs. nonnuclear investments, yields were higher for the latter. Over the course of several years, right through the stock market crash of 1987, the nuclear companies achieved an 860 percent rise, whereas the nonnuclear companies a 1,244 percent rise.

I am very interested in putting together for the Earth column a piece exploring what really happens, economically, when an American city declares itself a Nuclear Free Zone.

- What issues face local city managers and businesses?
- How are the choices of public spending and investment made?
- How legally binding and enforceable are these measures?
- What is the response from the business community?
- What are the larger issues, such as the American city's role in foreign policy, into which this issue fits?
- And what lies ahead?

As a freelance writer, I have put together environmental and business pieces for Omni, the New York Times Magazine, Washington Post, Outside and others.

I also live in both a nuclear-free city and county and am well versed in the issues.

Interested in the story?

I look forward to hearing from you.

Cordially,

Gropper

you graduated from, what college newspaper/work-study/internship experience you've had, even what professors you've studied with, if they command some renown.

Include with your proposal clips of published work, letters of reference, articles written about you, even performance reviews—if they relate to the project you're after. And if you have no published work to show off, remember that a good proposal is worth its weight in clips.

Don't say, however, that you're an unpublished writer. Just stress whatever qualifications you do have to tackle the project, and *be resourceful in what you think constitutes authority.* Consider jobs, hobbies, education, personal experience, family background or previous writing.

If you're pitching fund-raising brochures, and you're a publicist, say that. If you're proposing an educational script on family alcoholism, and your father is the town drunk, say that. If you're querying a story on reincarnation, and you've had past lives, list them!

Just don't oversell yourself. No hype: "Put on your asbestos gloves. Here's the hottest script of the season." Or "Been looking for a blockbuster novel? Well, look no more. I'm your man." Or "If you've been waiting for a speech that'll knock 'em dead, your waiting is over."

Some other considerations in putting together proposals:

Propose to the Right Person
Propose to a person, not a title ("Editor" or "Producer"), and make sure it's the person who has power to make decisions.

And don't rely on writers' resource guides or mastheads to pinpoint this person; they're not up-to-date or accurate enough. If you wanted to send a feature query to *Omni*, for example, which of these editors listed on the masthead would you send it to: editor in chief, editor, managing editor, senior editor, editor at large, associate editor, assistant editor, assistant to the editor or editorial assistant?

I would venture that not even *Omni*'s editors know the distinctions between their various editorial roles.

Call and ask for the specific editor of the specific section or department for which you want to write, get the proper spelling of that person's name *and* the proper gender. I've got editors named Mike, Gordon, Lyle, Hank and Jeff—all of whom are women. You don't want to be addressing your correspondence to "Mr. Gordon Bakulis," even if she's used to it.

Generally, I refrain from all salutations anyway. Leave it at "Dear Gordon Bakulis." Keep it safe.

Try, Try Again
If a proposal doesn't fly, consider sending it again a year or two later. Editors change, needs change, times change. I have sold a respectable number of articles just this way, usually because the editor who rejected it the first time

around had left, and the new editor possessed far more exalted sensibilities.

No Loitering

Once a proposal is in the mail, don't sit around waiting on it. It's boring and exasperating. Get busy on something else.

Turnaround time is seldom less than a week, and then only under extenuating circumstances. (The world record for turnaround goes to Bantam Books, which in 1965 took only 66½ hours to not only accept a book proposal but publish the book: *The Pope's Journey in the U.S.* Extremely atypical.)

Usually you wait a month on magazine queries, two to four months on plays, and six months or more on books. If I haven't heard from a magazine within a month, I pop a postcard in the mail reminding them of the proposal and asking for a yea or nay. If they don't respond within two weeks of that, I call. It has never failed to settle the matter one way or another.

Be a Copycat

Make photocopies of all your proposals, and maintain a simple submission log to help you keep track of their comings and goings.

If one customer rejects your overture, you don't want to have to remember all your lines again. Just call it up on the computer, or pull it out of your file, and type it up for round two.

Consider Your Timing

Call it superstition, but I am convinced that there are better times than others to have your proposal land on someone's desk. I base this on a strong intuition, backed up by more than a few national polls, that most people do not enjoy their work.

On Mondays, people are often grouchy because they're back at work, and on Fridays they're psychologically out the door and halfway home. Tuesdays through Thursdays are probably best, but I put my money on Thursdays, because people are over the hump and only have one more day until the weekend.

This is assuming, of course, that editors actually read their mail the day it arrives. Not everybody is like most freelance writers, who tend to rip it open before they even get back to the house from the mailbox.

Keep the Presses Rolling

Keep as continuous a stream of proposals going out as you can manage, with at least several in circulation at any given time. That's when things begin to happen.

In my first year, there were weeks when I did nothing but hatch proposals, cranking out half a dozen or more.

Break the Rules

Some rules are meant to be broken, and the rule regarding self-addressed-stamped envelopes (SASEs) is one of them. Though it is standard operating procedure to include an SASE with all proposals, comply with it only until you break into a publication. Once you have established a working partnership with a client, everybody pays for their own stamps. You appear timid and obsequious by continuing to send SASEs beyond that.

Another such "rule" is that regarding the multiple submission of proposals. That is, sending the same query to several publishers simultaneously, which writers often (and increasingly) do to cut waiting time and boost their chances of getting a go-ahead.

Some editors don't approve of this, especially if you've sent proposals to direct competitors. It undercuts the house advantage. They don't want to spend time reading queries (or manuscripts) unless they feel they're getting the exclusive opportunity to use it.

At the risk of sounding contrary, *tough!* Writers are entitled to get the best deal they can with the least amount of waiting. Life is too short. If you were trying to sell your house, would you settle for offering it to only one customer at a time?

Anyway, we all need to make investments sometimes without absolute surety as to the outcome. Writers do it all the time. But because some editors resent it, and they usually hold more of the cards, writers are either forced to play the waiting game or provoked to commit occasional sins of omission. That is, they simply don't mention in their proposals for articles, plays, TV scripts and books that other editors or agents are considering them simultaneously.

(When you are sending material to noncompeting markets, though—plays to college drama departments, articles to regional magazines—it doesn't hurt to reveal this, because these editors generally don't care.)

In the unlikely event that more than one competing editor gives you a go-ahead on a multiply submitted proposal (I've been in the business almost twenty years, and I can count on one hand how many times this has happened) take whichever gives you the best offer and apologize to the others, and then drop a postcard in the mail to the others and state that you are withdrawing your proposal or manuscript from consideration, thank you. You don't need to explain why.

The trend, actually, is toward increasing consent for multiple proposals, and more writers are recognizing it as a viable tactic in a business that is decidedly a numbers game: The more opportunities you create, the more corridors you open through which success—and even luck—can flow into your life.

Luck, after all, is a force that exists in abundance in the world, like wind—but it only gets into your house if the windows are open.

Pushing the Envelope: How to Package Your Writing

In a culture that seems to operate on the belief that "an ounce of image is worth a pound of performance," packaging has its place. It plays a role, however undeservedly, in the impressions clients form of you and your writing.

Packaging your submissions neatly, simply, and even with a touch of artistry is especially important when you're dealing with proposals, because at this stage there is no product to show a client, only a description of a product. Anything you can do to enhance that description will help.

And when you get around to sending manuscripts themselves, remember that they're products worth $100, $500, $2,000 or $5,000, so treat them with respect and present them professionally. You're being graded.

During my tenure at *Writer's Digest* I was amazed and appalled at some of the "formats" in which writers sent their work. There was pink stationery, giant powder-blue paper clips, and queries handwritten on looseleaf paper, flecked with jelly-donut stains and crossed-out words.

There were manuscripts typed right out to the edges of the paper and sometimes beyond, riddled with typos and little arrows leading to additional notes in the margins, and smeared with correction fluid. They looked more like ransom notes than professional query letters.

Disorderly packaging may not be enough to prevent clients from buying a good product, but it will irritate them, the same way you are annoyed by perfectly good products with unnecessarily troublesome packaging: cassette tapes with no tabs for pulling off the plastic; aspirin bottles that you have to open with your teeth; hand-lotion dispensers that don't allow you to retrieve that last quarter inch of lotion without balancing the bottle on its head.

In the beauty pageant of manuscript submissions, though, don't put too much stock in the bathing-suit competition. Looks count, but content counts more, and you cannot make up for in image what you lack in performance. No amount of tap dancing will distract editors from writing that is mediocre or ideas that are way off the mark. They'll see right through ivory-colored stationery, ornamental typefaces, jazzy business cards with dashing logos, and the fact that you Federal Expressed your proposal. You want to stand out, but for the right reasons.

Only when you have established yourself beyond reproach, have a book on the *New York Times* bestseller list, or play tennis regularly with your clients (and let them win at least half the time) will you be forgiven for sloppy manuscripts. When you're famous, what were once professional slipshods become stylistic eccentricities. But until then, dress for success.

I keep my own packaging rules strikingly simple, though. I don't believe in being infatuated with exact word counts, margins and picas. And neither do my editors. Where they want exactitude is in the writing.

Here, then, are my humble guidelines:

• For letters, proposals, and cover letters accompanying manuscripts: date in the top right. Name, address and phone number in the top left unless you have letterhead. A couple of inches below that, the client's name and company, and below that, the salutation and spiel. Everything is single-spaced. Business card attached.

• For manuscripts: title and by-line centered. Copy is double-spaced. Page numbers in top right corner. No handwriting except my signature. Paper clips, not staples. Anything under four pages is folded into a regular envelope. Anything over that is sent flat in a manila.

Making Contact: How the "Contacts Game" Is Really Won

As much as I would like to think I'm a self-made man, I'm not. I had plenty of help: people who gave me work and guidance, who took chances with me in order to give me a chance, or who were perhaps just returning favors.

Some of them are half my age, others have been dead a hundred years but continue to inspire me, to open doors for me (great teachers, John Barth once said, are the best thing that can happen to a writer). Some of them I have gone after, and some have found me. And though all of them are "contacts," I think of them foremost as relationships. That's all the "contacts game" is: the practice of relating to people, of give-and-take.

To a lot of writers, the contacts game is a contemptible enterprise, a smarmy and manipulative con game based solely on the belief that "It's who you know." The implication is that people are elevated not by virtue of their art, but their artifice, some oily talent for flattery and persuasion, and a certain stealth with small talk (which, for someone who venerates language, is like a leaking canteen in the desert).

But those who complain most bitterly that it's who-you-know are usually those having the most difficulty breaking in; they are angry with themselves for not having the courage to get to know people who could help them.

And to the degree that making contacts involves exposing yourself, asking for what you want, and just being in relationship to people, it does demand courage. Promoting yourself is seldom more intimidating than when making direct contact with people, because it confronts you in the most personal way with how you feel about putting yourself out there and with what you feel your writing is worth. It lays you open to rejection, and the rejection that hurts the most is precisely from those in positions of power over us, people who have something we want, whether it's an old typewriter to get us started, feedback on our writing, or an introduction to an influential film producer.

Few things are as effective in leveling power imbalances as having someone's name to drop. Imagine if someone called you and said that a friend or respected colleague of yours had told them you'd be a great person to talk to. You might think twice about turning this person away cold, if you knew a friend or colleague might hear about it or be embarrassed that they gave someone a bum lead. It makes you a bit more accountable.

Accountability is one reason I also guard my own contacts jealously. It's not that I'm afraid of losing work to other writers. Fear of this sort, I think, betrays a lack of faith in yourself. It is because I need to know someone before I turn him or her loose on my editors or other valued contacts. I don't want a reputation for being indiscriminate, for sending my editors turkeys. If someone is going to drop my name, I want to be proud of it, not embarrassed by my lack of discretion.

The more personal you make the contacts game, though, the better. It is not about cold-bloodedly "working a room." It's not even about making contacts. It's about making *contact*. That is, touching people, offering them a relationship, not just a quickie. We've all been hurt at some point by other people's intentions or been uncertain why we were being befriended, and it is these misgivings that lend the contacts game some of its air of suspicion. But when you develop real relationships, people become willing to open their address books to you.

You can't fake it, though. You either have a genuine interest in people or you're just smiling and saying cheese. People can tell the difference.

You touch people by listening to them, asking about what matters to them, appreciating their struggles, giving of yourself. You do it by realizing that people don't just want good writing, they want what everybody wants: recognition, respect and to feel like they matter. So show them they matter. Compliment them, confide in them, tell them you value their efforts, offer your support or services, put something personal in all your correspondence, thank them for their business or their friendship.

Positive feedback is indispensable, and because of the sheer sparcity of it in most people's lives, it takes on a weight of authority disproportionate to its size. Think of how you feel in the aftermath of a good compliment.

A former editor of mine at *The Cincinnati Enquirer* once told me that a single letter to the editor, pro or con, counted for a hundred readers who felt similarly but wouldn't take the time to write. I've heard politicians say that one letter to a member of Congress reflects the view of a thousand constituents.

Feedback is rare, especially positive feedback. It's one reason professional organizations give out so many awards to their own. It makes up for the lack of applause from the audience.

You also touch people by the sheer force of your own exuberance for your writing and your life. Enthusiasm gives people a "contact high." It generates energy. It tells them that whatever assistance they offer will go toward a worthy cause and be appreciated.

The contacts game is thus as much about who you are as who you know. It is an outgrowth of how you relate to everybody with whom you come into contact. After one of my recent "How to Sell What You Write" classes, during which I mentioned an upcoming trip to New York to visit my editors, a student walked up to me and said she had a brother in New York City whom I might enjoy meeting. "You guys would probably like each other," she said. "Besides, he's an editor at *Savvy* magazine."

A contact like that—of the "I have somebody you should meet" variety—

only grows out of trying to be as authentic to myself as possible, and remembering that what I put out is what I attract. I already know this, because whenever I leave the house in a crummy mood, the whole world becomes a mirror: People cut me off on the road, salespeople ignore me, and I end up on the longest line at the bank.

If you cut a friendly figure in the world, though, you're already winning the game. The rest is being willing to *use* the contacts, to ask for what you want, and to follow through.

One way I use contacts is by gathering occasionally with a group of friends and colleagues for an evening of brainstorming, during which I've gotten inspirations for marketing my writing, story ideas, titles for articles and even more contacts. If you're not using your friends, you're wasting them.

Most people are. They don't appreciate the power contained within even a small circle of friends. This potential was clinically demonstrated some years ago, as a matter of fact, by psychologist Stanley Milgram, in what he called the Small World Experiment. He showed that almost any two strangers in America could be connected with one another through no more than five intermediate acquaintances.

If you don't want to cultivate the relationship part of the profession, though, don't. If you hate networking, it won't work for you. You will just have to work harder at the craft and marketing of your writing. The better your writing, anyway, and the more people see of it, the more they'll start contacting *you*.

But if you're going to invest time in nurturing contacts, do it in a way that suits your personality and skills, as well as your dignity. Know what your limits are.

If you hate calling strangers up out of the blue, or making captive audiences of people over the phone, use the epistolary approach. If you feel more comfortable meeting people in classes and professional seminars than at parties, save yourself the sweat and hangover. If, in making contact with the public, you feel you come across terribly on TV, but have a voice like God on the radio, don't do television; do radio. If you find that meeting your clients face-to-face helps get your enthusiasm across, shine up your shoes.

The Personal Touch:
The Value of Face-to-Face Contact

I, for one, find that face-to-face contact with my editors not only helps get my enthusiasm across, but is an invigorating change of pace from the monasticism of writing. It also gives editors a face to associate with a name and thus greatly personalizes the relationship.

I didn't always feel this way. The thought of meeting my editors in person, even ones I'd been working with for years, scared the daylights out of me, especially since nearly all of them reside in New York City and, in my imagination, held forth from offices with commanding vistas of midtown Manhattan, with secretaries shoulder-padded like quarterbacks, bad attitudes about California, and writers camped out on their doorsteps.

Every time I thought of going, I came down with a case of the jitters. I told myself it was too expensive to fly there, I'm not ready yet, I've got too much to do, and they're probably too busy anyway.

My apprehension kept me from going for years—until one winter day when I got a phone call from John Brady. During our conversation he expressed surprise (with a trace of disappointment) that I hadn't made The Trip yet to visit my New York editors. He said that if I did so I would probably triple my business, and I was so flabbergasted at the prospect that I neglected to ask him if he meant it would triple my income or just my work load.

But I decided that, even if it only doubled my income, it would be worth the temporary discomfort. So I made a declaration to go, and to help cement my conviction I told a few people right away. Going public with your intentions, whether it's to visit your editors in New York or to quit smoking, has a powerfully motivating effect. It makes you more accountable.

So over the next two months, I prepared for The Trip by:

- Calling my cousin in Manhattan and arranging for a place to stay.
- Writing brief letters to ten editors—some I had worked with, some not—telling them of my trip, expressing my enthusiasm to meet them, and asking if they'd like to set up lunch appointments ahead of time. Three did. Five waited until I hit town. And two didn't have time to see me.
- Preparing several story ideas to pitch to each editor and literally rehearsing them using 3×5-inch cards.
- Sending reminder notes two weeks before the trip that included a couple of my best recent clips and mentioned that I was bringing a handful of story ideas they'd want to hear about.
- Interviewing other writers who had taken similar trips, to find out what worked and what didn't.
- Sending last-minute postcards telling the editors that I would give them each a call when I arrived.

A few days before the trip, a friend came over and bestowed upon me a "power tie" that he insisted I take to New York. "This is no ordinary power tie, though," he said with great solemnity. "Imbedded in it is a subliminal message that says, 'Hire this writer!' "

With that I went to New York, met editors at some of the top magazines in the world, and came home with nearly a year's worth of assignments! Triple my business!

Some of it, however, *was* genuinely intimidating, like my meeting with the editor at *Glamour* magazine, who consented to a brief meeting in her office. She was decked out in a flamboyant chartreuse and pink outfit with power-shoulders that could be seen from other galaxies. The moment her secretary led me into the office and sat me down, the editor cast an exaggerated glance at her watch and said, "You have twenty minutes. Go."

Forty-five minutes later, I walked out with two go-aheads.

The highest compliment paid to me on the trip came from the editor of *Health* magazine, who stepped out of a staff meeting to meet with me. Ten minutes later, her managing editor darkened the doorway to inquire whether the rest of the staff should wait for her or reschedule the meeting. The editor paused a moment and then said, "Reschedule it."

Mostly I found the editors to be friendly, gracious and easygoing, and the outcome of The Trip not only boosted my self-esteem but transformed the relationships I had with my editors. They became more friendly and less formal.

I have also discovered that personal contacts in the business have a stabilizing effect on my career. In the publishing world, where mega-mergers, buyouts and natural diebacks are commonplace, it is better to develop relationships with people than with magazines. When someone moves, they take you with them. But when magazines die, which they do with far greater regularity than editors, they take a chunk of your income with them if you have no enduring contacts there.

Some further observations about making contact(s):

If you call networking a game—as in "the contacts game"—then you become a game-player. I prefer to call it circulating, meeting people, conversing and developing the beginnings of the rapport that leads to relationships.

One reason making new contacts is so hard is that we're taught not to talk to strangers. And we feel that small talk is denigrating. But it's an important way we connect, how we begin to reveal ourselves to others, to create the vulnerability that can lead to trust. Writers already have the ability to communicate. They just have to transfer it to another setting. By talking to people, you can also get visual and verbal feedback for your words, which writers don't usually get. Networking is about getting readers, too, since everyone is a potential reader.

If you can afford to hire out your weaknesses, consider an agent or publicist. But also be willing to stretch and grow. Don't hide behind your strengths. And don't promise anything you're not going to do. You're a liar if you say you're going to call someone and then don't. People remember you for it.

SUSAN ROANE
AUTHOR, *HOW TO WORK A ROOM*
BOOK-OF-THE MONTH-CLUB BEST-SELLER

Clients will forget about you if you don't stay in touch. Especially when business is slow, I go back over my old clients and make phone calls and go out to lunch.

When they start talking about projects they're interested in exploring, I spin out a few ideas and we discuss them. I give them a free sample, in other words. You've got to be willing to give it away, to come up with ideas and offer them for nothing. It shows them you're already on the job, and then they feel they owe you something, and you often get work.

TYLER JOHNSON
CORPORATE/BROADCAST VIDEO SCRIPTWRITER, LUCASFILM, ABC, APPLE, GE

The way to impress an editor is, first off, get her name right. I get queries addressed to "Dear Verona Cherry" and "Dear Rona Cheery." They refer to me as the editor in chief, the beauty editor, the new-products editor and don't bother to check these things out.

There's a lot of sloppiness among writers, and it really sabotages them. Typos, lazy fact-checking, inexact titles, misspelled words. They send me poetry, when we don't publish poetry. They don't think about our long lead times, sending September queries for Halloween stories. They see something in the magazine and send us exactly the same idea. And they count out exactly 2,327 words, which really gives them away as beginners.

Writers need to study the magazine, as well as the magazine world, more thoroughly before they pitch us, and unpublished writers especially should start with a short, not a feature.

RONA CHERRY
EDITOR, *LONGEVITY*
FORMER EDITOR, *GLAMOUR*

The best way to meet the right people in Hollywood is to write good scripts, keep writing, and stay in circulation, to show you have stamina. And send queries to agents, not scripts and not phone calls. If you send multiple queries, don't tell them. What the hell? You'll be forgiven. Just make each letter personal. Write a sentence about yourself, a paragraph about your script, and ask permission to send it. Also, if you're from Austin or Murfreesboro, say that. Producers are weary of all stories being set in southern California.

RICHARD WALTER
CHAIRMAN, SCREENWRITING PROGRAM, UCLA FILM SCHOOL

If you want to be well known in your profession, and writing is a very public profession, you can't be invisible. When you first try on being a public person, though, it might feel uncomfortable. But you find ways of dealing with it, of getting through interviews and such. You might make it more palatable by thinking of it as your public persona, some character you're playing.

If you hire promotion out, let the promotion people know all helpful contacts you have, what if any traveling you plan to do so you can make appearances while there, lists of publications interested in what you're writing, or where you've published, where you're known, so that your book can get reviewed there. Make yourself available.

Also, at your publishing house get as many people interested or vested in your book as possible. Don't just be in contact with one editor, who might leave. If he or she does, you need other allies.

CAROL BUTTERFIELD
PRESIDENT, BUTTERFIELD ASSOCIATES, BOOK PUBLICITY FIRM

Sometimes it doesn't hurt to bully your way in. I once called a magazine editor and said, "You need me." He said, "Oh yeah?" I said, "Yeah. You didn't take over the helm of this magazine not to change it. Your magazine has been losing money steadily for over two years. You need fresh blood." So he invited me to come in.

One of the first things I did when I entered his office was to fling open the curtains dramatically and exclaim that there were a million stories in this city . . . but instead of a panoramic vista of the city, we were looking into an alley and an air-conditioning shaft. But I got assignments anyway.

JOE FLOWER
MAGAZINE WRITER
CO-AUTHOR, *AGE WAVE*

CHAPTER SIX

More Than Money: How to (Really) Support Yourself as a Writer

The language we use to describe money is remarkably similar to that which we use to describe our relationships: bonds, shares, trusts, maturity, appreciation, securities, support, advances, even tender.

Money is emotional. Your experience of it will have less to do with the peculiarities of the writing profession—unreliable paychecks, long lags between production and profit, yo-yoing income that makes a mockery of budgets—and more to do with your emotional relationship to money.

It's not just how much you earn, but how you *feel* about what you earn, how you define success, what you think you're worth (self, not net), what you tell yourself about money, and what you're willing to trade off to earn it. (Wealth, it bears recalling, was originally modeled after the word health. It means well-being.)

Furthermore, a writer's career is like a garden: everything eventually gets dug up. And as in any relationship, the deeper you go into it, the more emotions will be exhumed, including those emotional problems that pose as economic ones. This will occur in direct proportion to how much you are 1) in it for money, 2) relying on your writing for income, and 3) steering your course toward more "literary" writing.

By the end of my fifth year of full-time freelancing, for example, I had used up a third of my savings, and the energy I spent worrying about money could have been used to light up a small Midwestern city. A voice inside my head kept telling me I wasn't a successful writer until I supported myself solely by my literary labors, which I, technically, wasn't. But technicalities like these can easily suck the confidence right out of you.

So I began reframing my outlook on failure and success: The difference between feeling like a failure and feeling like a success was the difference between thinking I had "lost" that money and thinking I had "invested" it. I was investing in the start-up of a new business, essentially giving myself a business loan. And though I had less money in the bank than when I began, I also had far greater *earning power* as a writer. In the more expansive light of this new outlook, I realized I was successful not so much *as* a writer, but *because* I was a writer, because I was doing what I love to do.

When the criterion by which I judged myself was money, I felt far less successful than when the criterion was progress, the attainment of my own goals. When I began measuring myself by how far I'd come from where I started and how much less of my savings I used than I thought I would, and considered how few self-employed businesses of *any* kind live past their fifth birthday, it gave me the guts to hold my ground.

"Supporting" yourself as a writer is more than an economic condition. Are you really supporting yourself if you're making princely wages doing writing that bores you? *Supporting yourself is giving yourself what you need.* It means providing yourself with the time, place and permission to write, as well as surrounding yourself with supportive people, trusting your choices, and bearing up under the uncertainty of outcome. With the right criteria, you can be a successful writer and not make a penny, no matter *what* anybody else says.

They don't have to live your life. You do.

Supporting yourself as a writer also means not just keeping the books but acknowledging that the publishing world increasingly belongs to accountants, not publishers (literary superagent Morton Janklow describes book publishing as "a badly managed cottage industry that now needs more Harvard MBAs"), and that for better or worse, the survival of the industry and those in it depends on financial and business savvy.

There is a fine line, though, between focusing too much on fiscal affairs — thereby cutting spontaneity off at the knees — and not paying enough attention, in the process of which you starve yourself out of your writing career. And if you have gone to the extreme and steadfastly refused to distract yourself with pecuniary concerns, when that publisher suddenly accepts your novel, you will be sucked out into the world of finances as assuredly as if your airplane window popped out at 30,000 feet. You will be forced to contend with contracts, advances, royalties, taxes, and a multitude of monetary decisions that you simply cannot hire away.

At some point in your writing career, you're going to have to come to grips with money, so you might as well do it as much as possible on your own terms.

The Dirty Lowdown: What's in It for You?

I have often heard people describe themselves as "frustrated writers." To me, this is something of a redundancy, especially in light of what so many writers earn, which, as Rita Mae Brown once observed, "is not designed to reassure your mother."

Although you can potentially earn more as a freelancer than working for someone else — there's no ceiling on what you can make — it is probably fair to say that as a business you will be more in danger of going bankrupt than of being broken up under the Sherman Antitrust Act.

Beyond that, it is impossible to make predictions about what you can earn. It depends on too many factors, the *least* of which are the statistics. How motivated are you? What kind of writing do you do? How much experience do you have? How good are you? Do you write full-time or part-time? Where do you live? How are your negotiating skills? What kind of person are you?

Earning power depends on all these things, and still there are no assurances. The only writer ever guaranteed sales was chairman Mao Tse Tung, whose little red book of quotations was mandatory reading in every household in China (800 million copies in five years).

In the most grossly general terms, the closer you are to "literary" writing (fiction, essays, plays), the less income you make, and the closer to "commercial" writing (copywriting, technical writing, direct mail), the more you make. As for poetry, they don't call them "little" magazines for nothing.

A 1981 Columbia University study of book/magazine/film/television writers found an average writing income of about $5,000 a year. One-quarter earn less than $1,000, 10 percent earn over $45,000, and 5 percent over $80,000. Half work other jobs full-time.

Money, it seems, is more of a by-product in the arts than in other professions. People don't go into it to make money so much as to make a mark, to do their art, to express themselves. And unfortunately, contrary to legend, penury does not improve the artistic pursuit. More often it undermines it. Fear and anxiety are antithetical to creativity, and the need to make ends meet usually outranks the desire to write, so writers often end up not writing at all.

On the other hand, the fatter the pig, the shorter its life. "The surest way to kill an artist," Henry Miller once said, "is to give him everything he needs."

Those writing for the business world are more likely to meet their financial quotas, typically bringing home between $25,000 to $50,000 a year, with a respectable number pulling in $50,000 to $100,000. The same article that you sell to a newspaper for $250 and to a magazine for $1,000 would probably bring you $2,000 from a corporation. Just as magazines make more money selling ad space than subscriptions, there is bigger money in business than in art.

And still bigger money in writing ransom notes, if you don't mind the risk.

For most writers, whatever money they earn is primarily a means to an end, and that end is freedom — the freedom to write what they *want* to write, though it may not always be what is easiest to sell. But having finally attained, myself, to the position where I am paid enough to write for lengthy stretches of time without much "commercial interruption," I can indisputably say: It was worth the wait!

It doesn't hurt, of course, that I maintain a low-rent lifestyle. The less you need of material possessions and standard of living, the greater your freedom to write what you please and, if you're a freelancer, to stay that way.

Fortunately, the greatest rewards of writing are, for me, intrinsic, not extrinsic. Without interior motives, you won't last more than a few rounds in this business. The rejections will flatten you, the mercurial income drive you to exhaustion, and your conscience give you not a moment's rest.

You have to have something you want to say badly enough, or want to be independent badly enough, to put up with the financial insecurities. This is especially so during the early years, when your income is like a sine wave, pitching up and down, along with your emotions, when some months you earn enough to buy a car (all right, a used one), and other months you barely make enough to throw into a wishing well.

In fact, writing has to be something you're willing to do for nothing, just because you love it. That way, the disappointment of not making money very fast in the beginning won't kill your spirits.

At the other extreme, if money is your only end, your writing turns into merely a means to that end and loses its fascination, its inherent value. It then becomes mean and boring, a thing to get done.

How to Drive a Painter Crazy: Reselling Your Writing

To the degree that money *is* an end, though—and let's face it, it *is*—you can considerably further those ends by recycling (i.e., reselling) your work. I am occasionally reminded how fortunate writers are in this regard by an envious friend of mine who is a painter. She creates a painting and can only sell it once; she doesn't even *see* it again after that.

Writers can not only sell a piece, but resell it, readapt it for different markets, cannibalize it, and make more money with every sale. I make between one-third and one-half of my income this way. And in many cases, reselling my work is nothing more than exchanging a postage stamp for $250, $500 or $1,000.

Recycling can take many forms:
- Reworking a chapter from your novel into a short story.
- Selling one article to three noncompeting magazines among, say, ethnic, religious, regional, or even foreign markets.
- Profiling the same person for different TV stations.
- Reusing parts of speeches.
- Updating material and reselling it as new.
- Rounding up several related articles into a "sampler."
- Using background material from a novel to write nonfiction articles.
- Pulling a column-length story out of a feature, or a newsbrief out of a column.
- Spinning off a profile from a general story.
- Selling a story locally and then nationally (since national markets generally don't consider local stories as competition).
- Writing one general-interest story for five different trade publications, adding interviews with the appropriate professionals to each one.
- Selling to markets that specialize in reprints, such as anthologies, textbooks, syndicates, and magazines like *Reader's Digest* and *Utne Reader* (the "alternative" *Reader's Digest*).

In order to sell or resell something, though, you have to own it. When you sell your writing, what you sell is the right to copy it for publication (copyright), and copyright is just a piece of property like a lawnmower or a house. Once you sell it, you've sold it. It belongs to someone else, and unless you've been promised royalties, you can kiss good-bye any further income from that piece.

This is why you must be entirely careful what rights you sell in your assessment of a work's future earning potential. Rights equal money, and too many writers give them both away for a by-line, only later to discover that they can't make a penny more from their work. You work too hard to cheat yourself out of income because of a shortsighted, hit-and-run attitude toward your writing.

If you intend to resell to a national publication a story you've already sold to a local one, don't sell the locals all rights and don't write on a "work-for-hire" basis. Both mean that they own the full copyright. Sell them first rights. That way, once they run it the first time, the copyright reverts to you.

Hang onto whatever rights apply to the goals you have. The more rights you sell, the more money you should ask for, just as the more extras your car has, the more resale value it has. Also, ask about any new formats your writing might appear in, such as microfiche and computers disks. The more usage, the more it's worth.

The more potential your work has to sell and resell, the more you should keep the rights to do so.

Still, if you decide to sell someone all rights, as you might if the publication opportunity is worth its weight in gold, keep in mind that you're only selling the rights to that piece in that form. You can still rewrite and resell it. But it will have to be a substantial rewrite. No screwing around. New angle, new interviews, new research.

Putting a Price on Your Head

On the open market, the average person is worth about $4.61 in trace minerals.

This is not exactly inspiring, and it doesn't provide much of a reference point in helping you determine what you're worth on the writing market. But it does suggest that what you're worth depends on your viewpoint. Boiled and centrifuged, you're worth barely five bucks to a chemist.

To an editor, you're worth whatever he or she thinks you're worth. Initially, this is based on a perfectly impersonal amalgam of budgetary and market factors—this story is worth $500, that script is worth $1,000, our budget allows $2,000 for the other project—though it can change depending on your ability to alter their perceptions about the value of your work.

What they think you're worth may be just as subjective as what *you* do, which is similarly predicated on an assessment of the value of what you have to offer and whether its availability in the marketplace is more like coal or more like diamonds.

Determining what to charge, or accept, for your services is ultimately situational and therefore demands flexibility. It depends on who's buying, what the budget is, and whether they ask you your rate or tell you what they pay. It depends on what expertise you bring to the job, how badly you want it, and how badly a client wants it done. And it depends on whether you're selling all rights to your work and won't be able to make further income from it.

Perhaps most importantly, it depends on what you need. If you want to live off your writing, this means figuring out how much money you require to live comfortably for a month or a year and then what you'll need to do to generate that.

Keep in mind that what you want is not necessarily what you need, and you don't even have to get everything you need. Money often substitutes for creativity and resourcefulness in the beginning of many businesses. "Companies without money dream and imagine," says Paul Hawken in *Growing a Business*. Hunger speeds the plow.

In order to gross $30,000 a year, though, you would need to crank out $115 projects every weekday, $575 projects every week, or $2,500 projects every month. Needless to say, this precludes your writing for magazines that pay $25 for 3,500 words.

For those already getting paid to write, but who don't set their own rates, it is also not a bad idea—however, occasionally a depressing one—to ascertain how much you're presently earning in an hourly wage. This is a way to get a bead on how cost-effectively you're working. It's easy to be impressed by dollar-a-word rates, but if a 1,500-word piece takes you a month, you're barely making $10 an hour. An outfit paying you ten cents a word can give you a $50 an hour rate if you can dispatch that 1,500-word piece in an afternoon.

A lot depends on how fast you work. When Ray Bradbury was writing *Fahrenheit 451* in the spring of 1950, he did so on an old Remington in the basement of the UCLA library, pumping in a dime for every half hour of typing. Time was literally money ($9.80 in this case), and it still is. The less time you take, without injuring your writing, the more money you make.

You also need to gauge what long-term benefits might accrue from taking it on the chin in the short-term. Cost-effectiveness should by no means be the sole criterion for taking on work. If your first book is 80,000 words on a $1,500 advance, you're being paid two cents a word—but it's also your first book!

If you need to charge day rates for projects, divide the annual income you want by fifty-two (weeks), then by five (days). A $30,000 income would thus necessitate that you charge $115 a day, or roughly $15 an hour—full-time. But because few freelancers who operate by the hour or the day actually work every day, they commonly mark up their rates by 25 to 50 percent to make up for unpaid time marketing themselves, as well as to pay for the benefits they don't get because they're freelancers.

Writers who raise their rates after a period of time often find that business actually picks up. When I first upped my consultation rates, from $35 to $55 an hour, I got *more* clients. People figure that the higher the price, the better the quality.

It may or may not be true, but in your case, make it so. In fact, you should worry less about your price than your quality. The latter will bring you all the customers you need who are willing to pay almost whatever price you ask. You also make yourself worth more by giving whomever you write for more than *their* money's worth.

A caveat: If you charge by the hour, clients often feel you're never working hard enough, and they don't know what you'll end up costing them. But it protects you in the highly likely event that a project runs longer than expected, or a client demands endless rewrites, or the job description suddenly changes in midstream. If you accept a flat fee, push for a contingency clause in your contract that switches the payment schedule to an hourly wage should any of these things occur.

Whatever hourly rate you presently charge, though, translate it into a yearly salary. That's what a corporate editor will assume you consider yourself worth on the hierarchy.

For those who want to get a sense of starting salaries, check an occupational handbook. Find out what a person doing what you do in-house gets paid. One reason companies hire freelancers, something they do more of during lean times, is that they're cheaper than staff writers with all their troublesome and expensive benefits. It keeps overhead down. You can be paid the same salary as a staffer and still be cheaper for a company, because they're not paying you benefits. Your rates, however, should reflect this fact.

The Economics of Sacrifice: How to Avoid Selling Out

Money costs too much!

The price people are willing to pay to have it is far too steep. It is lamentably easy and economical to go the secure route, and to make financial panic decisions that drag you in an undercurrent farther and farther out from the life you intended, so that late in life you find yourself trying to buy your soul back from the devil or striking desperate deals with God.

Furthermore, security-at-all-costs is a lousy way to run a business. Too many writers with such an approach build for themselves a velvet cage: The money's good, but they become only recreational users of their creativity and passion.

The great artistic if not human dilemma of "selling out" involves, I believe, an act of abandonment. It is giving up on yourself, abdicating your integrity, your talents, your dreams, or your growth as a writer. There are any number of ways to do it.

It would have been selling out, for example, for me to take that part-time newspaper job that was offered me in my second year. They wanted to pay me $700 a month for two stories, and though at the time it would have paid half my bills, it was nonetheless siren song, a tempting and dangerous distraction from my intentions. Though the cost was delayed gratification, I felt I could put the time and energy to far better use writing stories of my own choosing, stories I was sure I could get more than $350 a piece for. And I was right. Within a year, I was averaging $700 for *one* story, and within two years, $700 for *expenses* on some stories.

If you're even *worried* about selling out, I have discovered, this is actually a good sign. It means you believe you have something worth protecting, something worth selling. Selling out, however, depends entirely on your aspirations and your values. It is utterly subjective:

- For one writer, taking on a job, any job, is selling out; for another, it's the only way to afford to keep writing.
- For one, it's writing a "popular" book when you'd rather write a scholarly one; for another, it's bending to professional disdain and writing a scholarly work when you'd rather make the material accessible to a wider audience.
- For one, it's trading in your by-line for a heftier paycheck, which is demanded of most corporate writing; for another, it's trading financial security just to see your name in print.
- For one, it's doing public-relations writing for nuclear-weapons contractors; for another, all's fair in love and work.
- For one, it's having children instead of a writing career; for another, it's having a writing career when your children are eating alphabet soup for dinner every night.

Some writers feel that just the act of relying on your writing to generate money puts you on a razor's edge between freedom and wage slavery and tempts a Faustian fate: achieving material and worldly success, but at the cost of your artistic soul.

The Pulitzer Prize-winning playwright Marsha Norman warns that if you start depending on your writing for anything, you begin catering to your audience, trying to figure out what it wants to see, which is a creativity-killer. "You must write out of absolute freedom." If you love something, you must let it evolve, she says. You must constantly be breaking molds.

Indeed, once a writer discovers a formula or a style that sells, there is an almost irresistible urge to encase it, to repeat it over and over. There are romance novels, for instance, that are formulated according to market research done by advertising agencies: the heroine should be nineteen to twenty-seven, the hero recently widowed, the sex steamy but safely within the bounds of matrimony.

Still, you aren't automatically branded with a scarlet letter if you "go commercial." If you want to write movie scripts, writing educational scripts is not selling out if you enjoy it, gain valuable contacts, learn the craft of scriptwriting, and then use all of it to actually write and pitch movie scripts. What you *do* with it makes a big difference. *If you are in the same place you were five years ago, you're selling yourself out, trading growth for security*.

On the other hand, you're not selling out if the decisions you make lead you toward what you really want to do, however circuitously; if they support your goals rather than sabotage them; if they don't make a shambles of your integrity or of others'; and if they are part of a long-term plan and not just a short-term fix.

Though these are seldom simple judgment calls and demand self-awareness, I believe that if they meet these criteria, then whatever circumstances you affect to support yourself—a part-time job, "commercial" writing, a loan, the financial support of your spouse, a sugar daddy—are all honorable.

Only you can decide what price you are willing to pay to bring your writing talents to fruition, and what is a fair trade to assure that when your life flashes before your eyes, it holds your interest.

Are you willing to sacrifice a regular paycheck, time with friends and family, vacations, developing other talents, having children, having weekends off, even health (people do it all the time)?

Most people would naturally prefer to have all of the above, but the dark side of wanting it all is that you then have to *do* it all. It's thrilling to have choices. The agonizing part is that you have to *make* them. The fact is, there are some very real deprivations that may ensue from a writing career, especially one toward the literary end of the spectrum.

However, if you pursue your writing first and money second, you will still have your writing even if money doesn't come through. But if you pursue money at the expense of your writing, you'll never have your writing, and no amount of money will keep your mind off what you gave up. I am reminded of J. Paul Getty, who once remarked toward the end of his life, "I hate and regret the failure of my marriages. I would gladly give all my millions for just one lasting marital success."

I once heard an artist say, "The successful artist is one who continues to make art and is not more than 50 percent bitter about the rest of life." In other words, try to make clear choices and then abide by them, wasting as little emotion as possible on what you gave up to be a writer. Don't consume yourself with bitterness over a choice *you* made and can unmake at any time. Too many writers, for instance, complain that the culture doesn't support the arts. They knew that going in, though. And anyway, plenty of professionals complain of the same thing: teachers, farmers, garbage collectors, social workers.

It boils down to a fairly simple equation: Is the payoff worth the pain? When the payoff is worth it, keep writing. When it's not, stop.

Some thoughts about money from the inside track:

If you're in it for the money, you're badly misinformed. There are no rich, or famous, magazine writers. The money is more in books, and even then you can't assume more than the advance. Don't go by society-page economics, basing your perceptions of the field on million-dollar advances.

I've made an OK living. I'm not hungry. I don't go without essentials. I have some luxuries: travel, medical insurance, kids in college. My Peace Corps experience taught me to live lean and simple. I define success more by having what I write be in line with my values, and having more work than I can do.

Success is when you find something worth devoting thirty years to.

You're damn lucky, though, if you don't have to make some compromises. It's the nature of life. In magazine writing, what's the word we use to describe sending our work to editors? Submitting!

PETER STEINHART
CONTRIBUTING EDITOR, *AUDUBON*
AUTHOR, *TRACKS IN THE SKY, CALIFORNIA'S WILD HERITAGE*

The investment you have to make as a writer is as complete as that for any business, and if you're confident in the value of your work, and you bring that to the bargaining table, you'll be a good businessperson.

You find out the going rate—which is a range, not an absolute—by talking to people doing similar work. Beginners usually get about $25 an hour, though to be taken seriously, ask for more. Don't admit to being too much of a beginner. But when you're asked what your rate is, you'd better have an answer.

As for job security, the closer you are to a company's profit center—the product—the better. All products need documentation.

RAY KRISTOFF
SENIOR INSTRUCTIONAL DESIGNER, APPLE COMPUTERS

In syndicated features (columns, comics and puzzles), thirty newspapers is a success, though at an average of $10 to $12/week per paper, even with a hundred papers, you're only making $1,000 to $1,200/week, which is then split fifty-fifty with the syndicate. Four to five hundred papers is heavy green, but those earning $200,000 and up are household names, maybe ten individuals. Dear Abby, Ann Landers, Miss Manners, Jack Anderson.

There's a tremendous glut in syndication. Everyone wants to be syndicated, but they're usually repeating what's already out there. Because they're writing something, or have a column in their local weekly, they think they should be syndicated. I haven't seen a truly original idea in three years, something that makes my blood pump.

DAVID HENDIN
EDITORIAL DIRECTOR, UNITED FEATURES SYNDICATE

I live on advances, with up to three-fourths of my income from my own books. The rest comes from collaborating and ghosting. I've figured that I need to put out two-and-a-half books a year to keep up my lifestyle. And I have to carefully watch for the disease of spending what I earn. I always put something into savings.

If I had it to do over, I'd look for a job compatible with the kind of writing I want to do—a cash cow—and try to keep my energies for my writing. Generally if you're looking at writing as other than a profession, as just a romance, it's harder to make it.

HAL ZINA BENNETT
CO-AUTHOR, *WELL BODY, WELL EARTH*
AUTHOR, *FOLLOW YOUR BLISS, THE LENS OF PERCEPTION*

I don't have a very optimistic outlook for most writers, especially those on the West Coast who write only for West Coast publications. You have to work nationally, or at least through East Coast magazines. And the discipline it takes is extraordinary.

Early on I won a writing contest sponsored by *Rolling Stone* magazine. The prize was an internship, which I turned into a job. It was the smartest move I ever made. I learned the business, I made contacts, and discovered how to deliver myself and my work. I also learned to stick my nose into the publishing process. I once found out my book was being held up in distribution, so I got involved, and it's now gone through six printings.

You have to educate yourself about how books and films happen, how an article can be spun off into one or both. An *Esquire* article I sold for $3,000 sold as a screenplay for ten times that, for less work.

Finally, I wouldn't survive as a freelancer if I didn't have low material needs. But I'd always choose being poor and having more freedom.

JOE KANE
MAGAZINE WRITER
AUTHOR, *RUNNING THE AMAZON*

Do What You Love; The Money Will Follow — Won't It?

One of the most confounding concepts I have ever run across regarding money is contained in the title of a recent book that has gained almost cult status: *Do What You Love, the Money Will Follow.*

It is confounding because I believe it and I don't, all at once. Or perhaps more precisely, I want to believe it and I'm afraid to. On one hand, it strikes me that it isn't naiveté but the height of wisdom to suppose that this is exactly how the world works, that if you work hard and smart at what you love, you will be rewarded.

The children's book author Margaret Young sums it up convincingly: "Often people attempt to live their lives backward: They try to *have* more things, or more money, in order to *do* more of what they want, so they will *be* happier. The way it actually works is the reverse. You must first *be* who you really are, then *do* what you need to do, in order to *have* what you want."

Money follows, it does not lead, according to *Do What You Love* author Marsha Sinetar. It does not lead to innovation, imagination or initiative. It follows from them. "Money is not important," adds Ray Bradbury. "Getting the work done beautifully and proudly is important. If you do that, strangely enough the money will come as a just reward for work beautifully done."

What makes this so hard to believe is that for many of us it goes against our life's experience; we fear that, if our upbringings are any indication, we won't really be rewarded for being ourselves.

So we refuse to let go all the way, to trust in our writing, in our talents, in the unknown. And just like someone who always keeps the back door open in relationships because he or she doesn't trust the other and wants a ready out, that very lack of trust makes it impossible for the relationship to work. Laws like "Do what you love, the money will follow" similarly rely on and appeal to faith, not logic. You either know it to be true in your gut, or you don't. The hard part is putting your faith to the test.

My uncle, upon hearing me describe the book, said, "But what if you wanted to be a shepherd?" suggesting that there are obvious limits to the belief. I think the limits are not so much in the law but in the laity. If you wanted to be a shepherd badly enough, you would move to New Zealand, where sheep outnumber people exactly twelve to one. *Doing what you love means doing what it takes.*

I am not suggesting that, if what you love to do most is sleep, your mattress will miraculously fill with money. I *am* suggesting that there is always money to be had doing what you love, if the full weight of your intention is behind doing it. (There *are* ways to get paid for sleeping, in fact. Several universities across the country maintain "sleep labs" where sleep patterns, circadian rhythms, insomnia and the like are studied. And they pay for medical volunteers!)

Furthermore, to the degree that plain old hard work contributes to success, you will work harder at something you love than something you don't. The statistics bear this out. The average American worker puts in about 46.8 hours a week on the job. The self-employed worker puts in 58.3.

I am not suggesting that you should focus solely on doing what you love, make no compromises, and let the money part take care of itself. There are no guarantees about how *much* money will follow or *when*, and you have to take care of business while you wait.

So do think about money, do manage it wisely, and do what you need to do to keep it coming in while you build. Just don't make it the operating manual for your life or your writing business.

And don't think about it when you're writing, otherwise you become like a batter concentrating on whether you inhale or exhale when you swing. You become paralyzed. "Money is great stuff to have," writes Stephen King in the introduction to one of his recent books, "but when it comes to the act of creation, the best thing is not to think of money too much. It constipates the whole process."

Hearing Voices:
Listening to What You Tell Yourself About Money

While in college, I took a psychology course during which the students played a midsemester practical joke on the professor based on the concept of classical conditioning, the old Pavlovian experiment in which a dog is taught to salivate at the sound of a bell.

We took advantage of the professor's habit of pacing while delivering his lectures. Whenever he walked toward the window, we subtly, almost imperceptibly, adopted postures of boredom. We would slouch, fidget, doodle, unfocus our eyes and stare vacuously into space. Whenever he walked toward the door, we would just as inconspicuously sit up straight, take copious notes, and fix him with scholarly expressions.

By the end of the day's lecture, we had our professor glued to the door, and I half expected that when the bell rang signaling the end of class, he would start to visibly salivate.

This is one of the images that comes to me when I think of the stimulus-response nature of our relationships to money. That is, the manner in which you relate to money and the effects it has on you are conditioned and can be reconditioned. If it took us barely forty-five minutes to condition our professor with a new message, think of the effect on you of a lifetime of messages about money, or more precisely, about making money in the arts.

Begin familiarizing yourself with the voices in your head, those of your parents, teachers and culture, as well as your own. These are the commandments that orchestrate every move you make in regards to money. Look, too, at who is giving you advice, who is telling you what to do. What are *their* relationships to money? Is it what you want for *your* life?

Also, be aware of what you tell yourself. It is a form of hypnosis, whether what you tell yourself is true or false, positive or negative. "Our life always expresses the result of our dominant thoughts," said the philosopher Soren Kierkegaard. And if your head is filled with a tangled web of warnings and prohibitions that belong to someone else or to another time and place, you're operating on conditioning rather than conscience. More than any lack of money, these are the things that will hold back your writing career.

Consider these common exhortations and how they might affect your relationship to money, even your life as a writer:

- Creative types don't earn money. Get a "real" job.
- Money is dirty.
- There's never enough.
- What about the future? You're not getting any younger, you know.
- Don't talk to anybody about your money.
- You are what you earn.
- He who has the gold makes the rules.

- Put your "trust" in money, not in people.
- Save it for a rainy day. What if you get in an accident?
- Money is love. Or "Cheer up. Here's $50. Go buy yourself something."

Whatever messages you received, knowing what they are and how you feel about them can help you make better business decisions. For example, I have made a regrettable number of business and life decisions that started and ended with the statement "I can't afford . . ." (to visit my editors in New York City, to buy a new computer, to take writing classes, to pay my bills in full, to work on my essays . . .). In many if not most of these cases, I very well *could* afford it.

Telling myself repeatedly that "I can't afford . . ." grinds into my subconscious a message of self-imposed limitation. It is an abdication of my own desires, a surrendering of my power to money, the emotional equivalent of a rap on the knuckles at the cookie jar.

What is far more accurate is "I *won't* afford . . ." This adds to the situation an entirely new element: *Choice*. "I'd prefer to spend my money on car repairs than a new computer." Or "I'd rather write only part-time than quit my job and the luxury of eating out in restaurants for the next two years." This is not about semantics. It's about giving yourself back your power.

It's also about promoting evolution and improving the stock by reevaluating and upgrading the messages that get passed down blindly from generation to generation, passing along the favorable traits and leaving the dysfunctional ones for the fossil records. It's about breaking genetic codes, carving new furrows in our brains, reinventing ourselves.

Undoing the effects of these kinds of messages is a great challenge, though. Not only are you trying to change lifelong patterns, but historical, multigenerational patterns. These are attitudes that have been cultivated in your family and culture since well before you arrived.

The Protestant work ethic, for instance, has glorified for several hundred years the notion that poverty is punishment for idleness and incompetence, whereas self-denying work and material wealth put you in line to receive the key to the cosmic washroom. Needless to say, this bears reconsideration. Protestant, after all, means one who protests.

The Good American Novel: What Are Realistic Expectations?

One of the most suffocating dicta I know is contained in the injunction "Be realistic," an insidious bit of counsel that can easily wring the heart out of your dreams.

What is realistic to expect by way of success as a writer, or by way of income? Is making $10,000 realistic? $50,000? $100,000? And where do you draw the line? Is it realistic to expect to make a living as a magazine writer, a speechwriter, a novelist? If you have a vision of making $50,000 a year as a writer, is it more realistic to scale it back to $25,000, or is that a lack of faith in yourself? Is it realistic to consider you might write a Great American Novel? A Fair American Novel? And what is a realistic assessment of your talents?

As an old jazz song reminds us, "Real compared to what?"

I think being "realistic" starts with separating what is real (your current level of skill and know-how, your time constraints, how much money you have in the bank) from what you *believe* is real (writers don't make money, editors have all the power, money buys happiness).

I used to believe that you needed money to travel, for instance. It seemed like a realistic appraisal of the way things worked. But one of the great astonishments of my life has been the discovery that actually you *don't* need money to travel. You need enough credentials to convince others to pay for your travel.

In my first year of freelancing, I got an assignment from the Sunday magazine of the *San Francisco Chronicle* to write a story on local seaplane tours. With that "credential" I approached a seaplane outfit and got a free sunset-champagne tour (Dom Perignon, flute glasses) of the entire Bay area. Recently I went to the Amazon for a month, on somebody else's nickel. That was *very* real.

Being realistic is not the somber, calculating duty we make it out to be. The soundest business decisions are a combination of the assertions of the head *and* the heart. You must be smart and wise simultaneously. You cannot be realistic without a gracious and obeisant bow to your intuitions. Nor can you afford to be involved with your writing only romantically.

Though it's important to acknowledge your limitations and be "reasonable" in your expectations, it is equally vital to recognize that what any of us is capable of achieving is orders of magnitude beyond what conventional wisdom would indicate and probably what we ourselves think we can. With some 90 percent of our brain power yet untapped, it is impossible to get a definitive sounding on the depths of our potential. Besides, progress, personal or cultural, actually depends on "unreasonable" people, those willing to question authority, buck the trends, and blow their noses on the fabric of society.

The Insecure Way Is the Secure Way: Reevaluating Job Security

Many years ago, when I lived in Cincinnati, my car was broken into on the street outside my house. I lost nearly fifty cassettes that I had lovingly and laboriously taped myself from my favorite jazz radio stations over the course of a decade, as well as a few homemade recordings of my own music. That night, lurching back and forth between grief and vengeance, I played the piano for four hours straight, just to remind myself of what they *didn't* take.

This episode taught me a lot about the nature of security and the vulnerability of material possessions. Namely, that security is an inside job (and the more belongings you have, and the more expensive, the more you become a curator of your possessions rather than an owner).

This applies directly to anyone with a hankering to be self-employed as a writer, and who worries about the lack of security that accompanies it. True, it is an economic gamble, but the more you succeed at it, the more untouchable the security you possess.

As a freelance writer, I know I can always get work, I can live close to the edge if I have to, and I can never lose my job! I knew none of those things when I was employed. And of the bouts of insecurity I have weathered as a freelancer, none has rivaled the shock of losing a job. "The insecure way is the secure way," Joseph Campbell said. Or as a friend once told me, "It wasn't the poor people who were throwing themselves out of office windows during the Depression."

Furthermore, according to a *USA Today* survey of millionaires, the "insecure" way is also the way to make money. Seventy percent of millionaires work for themselves, 20 percent are retired, and only 10 percent work for someone else. You put a limit on your income in exchange for the dubious security and comfort of a regular paycheck.

And not even millionaires are secure. I know one personally who has been a millionaire four times—and gone broke three of them.

In the final tally, your best hedges against disappearing into an economic Bermuda Triangle are your own ingenuity and adaptability, traits that self-employed people learn by necessity.

The craving for security, anyway, has probably done more harm to progress than any other single factor. Everything about it is contrary to the central fact of life, that it changes. Security is about being safe and stable, free from worry, isolated and fortified. But life does not promise that kind of security; only death does. Life is about flux. By trying to protect yourself from change, you isolate yourself from living.

The more desperate you are to be secure, the less inclined you will be to want to get grass stains on your jeans, to spend money without guarantee of return, to take on risky (and exciting) writing projects, even to pursue your writing at all because it is not one of the world's notoriously high-paying professions. Although you certainly want to set aside money for a time in your life when you may not want to work so hard, if you have to do work you detest to make that money, then you are merely saving for a rotten future.

A hard worker with good ideas will always get work, and if you love your work—if you would do it even if you didn't get paid, or even if you won the lottery—you'll eventually make good money. But you've got to take risks. If you love writing plays and no one's paying you in New York, then you move to Kansas City where they *are* willing to pay you.

I was once a scab during a network strike. Producers called me for work, and

I got opportunities I never would have gotten otherwise. I was accused of whoring and was tarnished for a while. But you find jobs that keep your craft going. Just don't bad-mouth the strikers.

You have to be willing to go into debt to further your craft, to take one step back to make two steps forward. But you have to have faith that you'll make those two steps forward. There are a lot of writers in LA who are just dreamers, who just write without paying attention to the market, who go severely into debt, and who are in for big shocks. There are plenty of writers who will share a bitter attitude with you.

BILL CUNNINGHAM
WEST COAST PRODUCER, "GOOD MORNING AMERICA"

A total market orientation is the wrong way to approach writing. It doesn't produce interesting work. You survive best by doing what you want most, by developing your passions. The most unhappy writers I know are the ones going after the bucks.

HERBERT GOLD
AUTHOR, *A GIRL OF FORTY, LOVERS & COHORTS, DREAMING, TRAVELS IN SAN FRANCISCO*

I started freelancing way undercapitalized, with about two months' salary in the bank. I recommend at least a year's worth, and extra money to market yourself. You're not going to make a lot of money your first few years.

I make more money, and have more freedom as a freelancer, than when I worked in marketing for companies. I have a six-figure income (working ten to twelve hours a day, five days a week, and about eight hours on weekends), and I subcontract others to do projects I'm not crazy about, but want for the money. I just pay them a bit less than what I bid the projects for.

I'm also more secure now. When you work for a company, the marketing budget is the first to get slashed. Working for companies, I've been laid off four times in fifteen years.

SHELDON BAKER
PR WRITER, REAL ESTATE/FINANCE

Among artists, starvation is often a sign that you're clean, that you haven't sold out. Like people who inherit large sums of money, they often feel guilty for receiving money. But you *can* hold on to your integrity and get paid. If your business is an expression of your highest self and your deepest values, you can't lose. Prosperity comes.

But don't be foolish about financial savvy. Vagueness about money is a leading indicator of debt-proneness. Know what you spend, owe and have in the bank. For the first few years, work out a bare-bones lifestyle, until you have more predictable income. Have a track record of earnings before you raise your expenses, or you'll drive yourself back to work you don't want to do.

It's a big mistake, too, to spend money as soon as it flows in. Profits aren't all for spending. Set some aside for taxes, investments and savings. It's not important how much you save, just that you get in the habit. Those who say they'll start saving next year never do.

ANNE LIEBERMAN
FINANCIAL PLANNER
AUTHOR, *MASTERING MONEY*

I'm a successful writer, and I can't make a living solely from my writing. I earned $12,000 my best year, and about $8,000 most years, and I've been doing it about six hours a day for ten years. My husband is a businessman, and I keep him well dusted.

Success, to me, is selling 98 percent of what I write, and being able to call my editors and have them immediately know who I am. But it has taken me many years to get established. My biggest problem is sticking with one thing until it's completed. I wish I could publish a collection of stories that are just beginnings.

MARION WENTZIEN
SHORT STORY/CONFESSIONS WRITER
PEN FICTION AWARD-WINNER

On Money Management: A Message From the Patron Saint of Writers

The patron saint of writers, the aptly named St. Francis de Sales, exhorts his charges to practice "simplicity, simplicity, simplicity. Let your affairs be as two or three, not one hundred or one thousand, and keep your accounts on your thumbnail."

Whatever system you devise to track the flow of money into and out of your writing business, it had better be simple, or you won't use it!

My own bookkeeping consists almost entirely of a shoebox for receipts and a sheet of paper divided, each month, into two columns: Cash In and Cash Out. If it weren't for the fact that I have my accountant's blessing, I would be embarrassed by its simplemindedness. But it works, and that's all I care about. To say that I am weak in the numbers department is a bit like saying the Ice Age was a cold snap.

In fact, I do not even balance my checkbook. I long ago decided that spending two hours trying to reconcile 28¢ or $1.22, or whatever amount it was off that month, was not worth the grey hairs. So I stopped. It's not just that I value a sense of balance more than a balanced checkbook. It's also that it was hardly a cost-effective use of my time.

The point of bookkeeping is not to torment yourself. It is to keep your tax bite to a minimum and to provide your business with a progress report in the process. However, since preserving income is one way of making income, it is important to understand that whatever records and receipts you keep will determine how much of your money Uncle Sam gets at tax time — or how much he owes you. So don't be too busy making money to bother keeping an eye on it. "Praise Allah," says a Sufi proverb, "but first tie your camel to a post."

Knowing how your money comes and goes also helps you get a grip on yourself, showing you a clear picture of where you stand, and what business decisions you need to make at any given time. Are you ready to quit your job? Do you need to take on part-time work? Are you working for clients that pay you enough? Is it time to raise your rates? Where can you cut expenses? Should you cut out that rental office and work at home for a spell? Should you consider a speed-reading or typing class? Do you need a loan? Can you afford a secretary, a transcriber, an accountant?

If you're not watching your financial records for portents, or keeping them at all, business decisions will be made *for* you rather than by you.

The most important money-management activity I have found is simply to *link the act of spending money with the act of recording it*. Make this habit second nature. Write down income when you get it and expenses when you pay them (and if you get paychecks that include reimbursements for expenses, separate the expense portion out; it's not income).

Also, keep records of writing income separate from those of other incomes (such as job or investment incomes), so that you'll begin to get a realistic picture of what you're making from your writing.

Because of the unpredictable nature of writing income, if you're relying on it to make ends meet, you must also practice the art of restraint. This means not following the financial advice of the Dutch theologian/writer Desiderius Erasmus: "When I get a little money, I buy books. If any is left, I buy food and clothes." It means keeping your mitts off the money when the money's good, so you'll have something to live on when it's not so good, maintaining discipline during the rich months and faith during the poor ones.

Although my own expenses remain roughly the same from month to month, my income does not. When I have a flush month, if I can resist the temptation to buy drinks for the house, I will have reserves to draw upon when I have a lean month.

In most kinds of writing, any projects you take on — and any risks — will register in your bank account in the months immediately following them. There is a big sales cycle in the writing profession, from when you first initiate contact with a client, through the writing and rewriting, to when you sign the check. You've got to plan on this time delay. This sort of budgeting, though, is fairly simple: If you spend $2,000 a month on average, then during a month when you make $3,000, save $1,000 for the next month when you only make $1,000.

And you can certainly count on this sort of income schedule. The waiting game is part of the writing game. When proposals are accepted, you wait months before you're paid. When you put together one-day writing workshops for the local colleges, you wait semesters before getting paid. When you write books, you can wait years before you get paid anything more than the advance—if! And even "payment on acceptance" falls into the same category of famous last words as "We can still be friends" and "If elected, I promise. . . ."

In nearly twenty years of writing, only one magazine has actually paid me on acceptance. They sent a check with their acceptance letter. It took me weeks to recover.

Death and Taxes: One of Them Is Avoidable

The old maxim that you cannot avoid death and taxes is not entirely true. You still can't evade death, but you *can* avoid taxes. At least temporarily.

All you have to do is be a freelancer with a profit motive—not what the IRS calls a hobbyist—and take a business loss. In other words, pay more in expenses than you make in writing income, and in three out of any five years you can avoid taxes altogether.

Obviously you would probably rather pay those taxes, because it means you're making a profit, but the fact is the tax advantage comes in handy in the beginning of a writing career, and it's Uncle Sam's way of helping you get off the ground.

Although the IRS says that you have to make a profit in two out of any five years to declare a business loss and so not pay taxes, in practice there is far more latitude than this. People have taken ten years of straight losses because they were able to demonstrate—by showing very skeptical auditors piles of business correspondence, contracts, ledgers, receipts, phone bills and rejection slips—that their intention has always been to make money, that they are productive, and that they are professionals, not hobbyists.

But the burden of proof is on you, and if you cannot prove that you are more than a hobbyist, you can only deduct expenses to the extent you have writing income. That is, if you have $5,000 in writing-related expenses, but only $1,000 in writing income, you can only deduct $1,000 from your taxes that year.

As long as you can prove you're not a hobbyist, you can also take a stunning number of deductions in this profession (even while you work a regular job), thereby reducing your taxes considerably. So although you may earn less as a writer than you could in other professions, you can also keep more of what you earn.

But the burden of proof again rests with you regarding these deductions. You have to show cause and effect, an actual business relationship between deduction and profit. If you can establish that weekly Swedish massage is an "ordinary and necessary" part of your professional life, you can deduct it. If you're studying to be a scriptwriter, you can deduct movies—but only if you study movies, take notes and can show those notes to the IRS.

Because the writing profession features such a fine, porous line between work and life, nine-to-five and five-to-nine, virtually anything can be considered research, if you can make a substantial enough case for it, and if you believe strongly enough in the propriety of the deduction.

I have had students in my classes ask me if they could deduct the cost of their musical instruments, or lessons thereupon. Some claim that sitting down to the piano for an hour puts them in the proper frame of mind for writing. Others insist, quite rightly, that practicing piano *is* practicing writing, that they are both leavened with the same ingredients: composition, tone, structure, phrasing, drama, surprise.

The argument is impeccable; the problem is documentation. If you write music reviews or can show the IRS articles you have written on the subject of creativity or the parallels between music and literature, you will likely be granted the deduction. But simply declaring that you are inspired by music will not suffice, though to some unpredictable degree, even this depends on your auditor, and on which side of the bed he or she arose that morning. Like the criminal justice system, it depends on the judge you get.

It also depends on the accountant you have, because a good one will help you identify and pursue deductions militantly. A good one is also a monetary mentor who regularly deals with, if not specializes in, the self-employed and takes writers seriously!

Anyone who, like myself, can't even balance a checkbook has no business stepping into the ring with tax forms. Hire out such a weakness to someone who knows the ropes. An accountant can get you tax breaks you might never uncover on your own and can help you analyze your future needs (what a whopping advance, for example, or a couple of years of royalties might do to your tax bite). Think of an accountant as someone who makes you more money. And whose fees are deductible.

The way I work with my own accountant is brazenly simple. I add up my yearly income and deductions (takes me one afternoon), type it up and mail it to him. He does all the rest.

I pay quarterly estimated taxes, like most self-employed people. Here's why: If you're working for someone else, they're withholding your taxes every payday, so Uncle Sam gets his cut ongoingly. But without someone to take taxes out of your paycheck for the government, you would get to keep—and earn interest on—all of it until April 15. Uncle Sam doesn't approve of this. Thus the quarterly payments. You (or your accountant) must estimate your income for the coming year and make advance payments. If, at year's end, your guess was low, you owe. If it was high, they indemnify.

For Whom the Bills Toll: Getting What's Owed You

Just as we must render unto Uncle Sam that which is Uncle Sam's, so must our own clients render unto us that which they owe us. And on those occasions when they don't, we must protest.

Although I have had to pursue deadbeats only a handful of times in my years as a writer, it has happened, and I have no compunction whatsoever about giving chase, even as far as bankruptcy court. It's not so much the principle of the thing, it's the money.

A phone conversation I had early in my career with an editor at the *Washington Post* helped cement my convictions around this issue. A check was late, so I called. He traced the problem to accounting, said he would put a lean on them, and then apologized. "It's OK," I said, "it happens."

"It's *not* OK," he shot back. "If I were a freelancer, I'd be pissed! Writers should be paid on time."

Writers should also have more editors like that.

Fortunately, there are more people out there crusading for writers' rights than ever before, including writers who are tired of feeling powerless. Many years ago *New Age Journal* folded temporarily, owing its writers many thousands of dollars, myself included. The publisher pleaded poverty, said he couldn't even pay his creditors, no less his writers. Luckily no one at the National Writers Union believed him, because it was the union to which the writers turned to spearhead a class-action suit against the magazine—what the union rather unabashadly referred to as a "smear campaign." Within two months, I had my check.

In the 1980s alone, the union's grievance teams collected over a half million dollars owed to writers by magazine and book publishers. The Author's Guild, too, now randomly audits the royalty statements of two books a year, chosen by lottery so as not to single out any particular publishers. In other words, writers are coming into their power, making sure they get what is owed them.

In these matters, prevention is always the best defense. If you have good relationships with editors, you generally don't get stiffed, and if a check is late, a single phone call will usually suffice. As in any commercial transaction, if you are a "preferred customer," you receive preferential treatment.

When tracking down overdue money, do it in crescendo fashion, starting softly and building to a roar if necessary. Begin directly with the editor you worked with on the project and assume innocence. Or at least point the finger at accounting first. "It probably got hung up in accounting," you might say with a sporting tone. "Have they received the check requisition yet?" Editors rather instinctively blame accounting anyway, and if they do, ask to speak with the department yourself. Track down the glitch.

Also, document all your inquiries. Get names, dates, amounts, invoice numbers and quotes. If it ever reaches the courts, those with the best case usually win.

These things often take time, though. Sometimes years. When Vantage Press, the largest "vanity" publisher in the business, lost a suit brought against it by 2,193 authors who claimed they were hoodwinked, the $3.5 million settlement split among them ended the longest lawsuit in New York history—twelve years.

When all good-faith efforts fail, it's time to haul out the big guns. Companies are far more likely to respond favorably if a collection agency, union or lawyer steps in. Sometimes just sending your client a letter "cc'd" to an attorney will persuade them to reprioritize their to-do list. They respect power.

People like to throw around the threat of a lawsuit, but the fact is that going to court is time-consuming and occasionally expensive, especially if you hire the services of an attorney. And not everyone will fare as well as the photographer who sued American Express, owner of *Travel & Leisure* magazine, when they lost 248 of his slides (the customary price for that offense is $1,500 per slide). He settled for a reported $350,000.

As for last resorts, you might even consider the example of one London collection agency that takes the art of "making a stink" to new lengths. Called Smelly Tramps Ltd., it uses a phalanx of foul-smelling tramps (paid professionals, actually) who, dressed in shabby clothes and doused with some putrid chemical, simply pay a visit to the debtor's office and wait until a check is forthcoming. This usually takes about ten minutes.

Twenty Ways to Save Money

1. Don't be impulsive with the telephone. Make phone calls, faxes and phone interviews when the rates are cheapest. When my brother lived in Colorado, I once called him in the middle of the day just to tell him a joke. "Expensive joke," he said. I now have a Post-it note slapped on my telephone that says "Think!"

    It's also surprising how many clients and interview subjects are perfectly willing to talk to you in the evening from home rather than at the office.
2. Don't be impulsive with paper, either. Use it all the way up. Don't throw it out because it's half typed-on. Use wider margins, single space, and double-side your photocopies. Reuse manila and padded envelopes.
3. Reply to letters by writing right on them, trading formality for speed and savings. Editors do it all the time.
4. Use postcards instead of letters or even SASEs. Editors can simply check off a box for acceptance or rejection and not bother with sending proposals or manuscripts back if they're not interested. If you stick with SASEs, use smaller envelopes.
5. Join magazine subscription pools. Split the costs.
6. Don't call the operator for information you can get from the phone book.
7. If you're on assignment and find that you need certain books that you cannot get at the library, call the publisher. Mention your affiliation, say that you'd like a review copy, and that you'll be mentioning the book in your story. You should have it within two weeks, free.
8. If you own a computer and need several copies of one of your stories, print it out at home instead of photocopying it.

9. Buy in bulk. And if you can, from wholesalers, not retailers.
10. Recycle your computer ribbons. If you use dot matrix cartridge ribbons, ship them to the SW Ribbon Company in Austin, Texas. They'll replace the nylon with new ink material and send them back—for half the cost of new ribbons.
11. Pay bills at the last minute. If you pay $1,000 a month in bills at the time you get them, you lose $50 in interest that you would have in your 5.5 percent bank account if you wait a month to pay them.
12. Also, don't necessarily pay debts off all at once. When the interest your cash can earn by being invested is higher than the interest payments on your debt, it pays to pay the loan back slowly.
13. When setting up phone interviews, ask for 800 numbers, or explain that you're a freelancer on a limited budget and ask if the interviewee could call *you*. Same with editors with whom you work regularly. Or try this: If you've set up an expensive long-distance phone interview with a businessperson for, say, one o'clock, call at 12:45 when your interviewee may still be at lunch or in a meeting. Ask the secretary to have him or her call you back.
14. Similarly, if you need to call a company, especially out of state, call after five o'clock or, better yet, after eleven. Leave a message if you can, and let them call *you* back.
15. If it doesn't create problems, do not return phone calls to anyone who is bound to call you again because they need to get hold of you (creditors, for instance).
16. Get cheap furniture and office equipment by haunting business liquidation sales, police auctions, estate sales, secondhand stores and moving/garage/ yard sales.
17. Get cheap services of all kinds—clerical work, haircuts, auto and appliance repair, animal grooming, you name it—by patronizing vocational schools. The students need the hands-on training, come cheap, and are only limited by how far their curriculum has taken them at the time of your call.
18. If you're going to splurge on something, try doing so on a deductible item. Buy a book or go to a movie instead of going out to eat. Or if you plan a trip, throw in some business: an interview, a city to profile, a visit to an editor, a workshop. And then deduct whatever percent of the trip was business.
19. Barter. Money is whatever people agree to use to pay for things: goods, services, labor. I've used my writing and consulting services to pay for ad space, writing seminars, legal and financial advice, even travel.
20. And finally, save money by saving it. Take 1 percent or 5 percent or 10 percent out of every paycheck you get and sock it away in a high-yield, hands-off account (only 5 percent of a $20,000 salary will put $1,000 in the bank in a year). This is as much for psychological reasons as economic, since you demonstrate to yourself that you have enough money to be able to save. Savings shouldn't happen when there's money left over, because

there's no such thing as money left over.

It's also for the day when you don't want to work anymore. As one retirement-fund ad says: "When you're ready to go out to pasture, make sure you own the pasture."

Some final ruminations on the writer's relationship to money:

I work mornings on my novel and afternoons on my freelancing. That is, I work for love in the morning and for money in the afternoon. It's an exhausting schedule, but I wouldn't do it any other way. I make a pretty good living. I could make up to $80,000 if I did the educational writing full-time, but success to me is really whether my novel gets published.

Sometimes I'm proud of the books I've written—and they do help my novel writing—and sometimes I say to myself, yeah, but look at what kind of writing it is. I flip back and forth. It's hard to feel validated as a writer. I don't get evaluations, merit raises, promotions, notes from the boss. And even if my novel got published, even successful novelists don't necessarily make a living at it.

Money always seems to be there, though. I always panic and I always get good jobs. Sometimes I get nervous about money and take lump sums up front rather than negotiating for royalties, which might be worth more. I get chicken. But it's chancy. You get a lot less up front if you go for royalties.

LUCY BLEDSOE

TEXTBOOK WRITER, SIMON & SCHUSTER, HARCOURT BRACE JOVANOVICH

It's difficult to make a living as a writer, especially a black writer. You have to be very busy and versatile: novels, plays, poetry, songs, articles, lectures, teaching. You have to be constantly expanding your readership. I'm learning Japanese and a West African language so I can sell more abroad, and I publish a magazine for multicultural literature. I also buy other authors' remainders and sell them at my lectures, to get the word out, and for the money.

ISHMAEL REED

PLAYWRIGHT, NOVELIST, POET

AUTHOR, THE LAST DAYS OF LOUISIANA RED, MUMBO JUMBO, THE TERRIBLE TWOS

It's not that artistic people have an inherent inability to manage finances. It's that there's a market failure involved. The economics of the society are against them. They often can't make enough money to support a living, and they experience inferiority complexes about their ability to make ends meet. They end up with a frustrated relationship to money, and have to measure their value by other than economic standards.

As far as managing money, you can handle most of your finances just by keeping detailed records of transactions and appointments, and a drawer for receipts which you divvy up at year's end. Also, you've got to go after deductions in an aggressive way or pick an accountant who will. Also pick one who is sensitive to creative/self-employment activities. If you went to a doctor to have your appendix out, you'd want the one who does a hundred a year, not ten.

RON VINCENT
CPA, SPECIALIZES IN THE SELF-EMPLOYED

My relationship to money has changed since I became a full-time freelancer. I've become almost mystical in my assessment and appreciation of money. It's just an instrument, and reflection of, your consciousness. You attract what you believe. When I shut down, feel there's not enough money, get scared and tight, the money gets tight, too. I set myself up. Wallace Stegner once told me that in selling your writing, you're selling energy and receiving it in the form of money. And it's out there in nearly infinitude.

Though I have no best-seller, and have had to take intermittent part-time work to get a steady paycheck, it's getting better and better. I feel enormously successful. You can tell how successful you are by how you feel, and by the way you treat others. I feel more joyful than not. You just give it your best shot and cumulatively those shots add up to something bankable. Always be reaching, stretching. What you can make depends on your sense of daring.

Learn to bend your work, to find new markets. I write articles, movie scripts, fiction, poetry, as well as teaching, lecturing and doing readings. Reselling your work is good, though only up to a point. Sometimes you can feel like a musician who gets tired of singing the same hit. It can get old.

So can writers. And though you become more valued, if not valuable, the older and more bloodied you get, and you can work well past what others think of as retirement age, it's also awful how we throw out our elderly in this society. Having money prevents that from happening. So it's good to save money. My grandfather in Mississippi always said to save ten cents on every dollar. You'd be amazed how putting just the change from your pockets into a jar each night can add up.

AL YOUNG
NOVELIST, POET
AUTHOR, *SEDUCTION BY LIGHT*, *SITTING PRETTY*

CHAPTER SEVEN
The Art of Negotiation: How to Get Paid What You're Worth

M any years ago, one of my magazine editors left his coveted spot on the masthead to become a fellow freelance writer—an irony only a writer could fully appreciate.

Needless to say, he was now considerably easier to reach, and during one of our subsequent telephone conversations he told me something he never would have told me as an editor, for the same reason that politicians, prostitutes and celebrities don't list their numbers in the phone book: They'd never hear the end of it.

He said, "You writers never asked for more money. You always took whatever we offered. On the rare occasion that one of you did bargain for anything, I almost always gave it to you. If you're turning in good, consistent copy, you're worth more, but you've got to ask for it. Editors aren't going to offer it to you spontaneously."

I was guilty as charged. Up until that telephone conversation, my general approach to asking editors and other writing clients for more money, or more anything, could best be described as approach-avoidance: If I didn't approach the subject of negotiation, I could avoid having to take no for an answer, which I generally assumed I would get, probably in one of the following forms:

1. "Hey, I'd love to pay you more, but my hands are tied. Company policy, you know."
2. "If you don't like our rates, you don't have to write for us."
3. "I've got plenty of writers who'd be happy to write for this amount."
4. "We only pay more to our best writers."
5. "What makes you think you're worth more money?"

In order to break into assignments, writers usually take whatever terms are offered, which is fine—at the start. But continuing this practice after establishing relationships with editors and clients costs you money. *What you're negotiating for is your paycheck, and not negotiating is like turning down raises.* Furthermore, if you're living on a financial cushion that's beginning to lose some of its stuffing, not negotiating will eventually spell real trouble: p-o-v-e-r-t-y.

For most people, the fear of asking for money is in direct proportion to their fear of rejection, whether they're asking the bank for a loan, the waiter to take back an undercooked hamburger, or an editor for an extra $500. It is undoubtedly a fear sunk into the deep end of the gene pool, something about asking your parents for more allowance or the keys to the car on Saturday night, about self-worth and selfishness, about our relationship to power and the pecking order.

In fact, I would submit that, to be able to negotiate on your own behalf as a businessperson, you will need to examine the voices in your head, the admonitions of old role models. Sometimes you have to move backward in order to move forward. You don't pull a hook out of a fish without backing it up a little first.

Writers also struggle with an additional dilemma about negotiating: They think only Mack-the-Knife types can pull it off, and they don't think of themselves that way. However, the very qualities that make them writers and make them feel they would be eaten alive in a negotiation—sensitivity, thoughtfulness, creativity—are actually vital negotiation skills, and those writers who combine them with assertiveness become the best negotiators of all.

The sobering conversation I had with my former editor, augmented by a bit of soul-searching, filled me with new insight and indignity, and I began experimenting. When a trade magazine editor asked to reprint one of my stories for $75, I screwed up my courage and said, "How about $125?" He said, "How about $100?" I said OK.

I hung up the phone shaking my head, amazed and disgusted all at once: amazed at how simple it was, and disgusted at the thought of how much money I would have had in my bank account by then had I been negotiating all along. Still, on my first try, I made $25 for less than ten seconds of talking. That would make a dandy hourly wage.

Not all my negotiations have been this easy, of course, but each time I managed some success I was emboldened, and within a year I was negotiating with some of the buck-a-word magazines for money and rights that would double my income. In short order, I learned three important lessons:

1. It is astonishing what you can get if you ask. One editor I know told me that nine out of ten writers never ask for anything, and to the one out of ten who does, she almost always says yes.
2. The worst they will say is no. Not one editor in over fifteen years has refused to do business with me because I asked for more money.
3. Everything and anything is negotiable. Mickey Hart, drummer for the Grateful Dead, recently created a sensation in the publishing world by getting Harper & Row to agree to a "tree clause" in the contract for his latest book: They will plant two trees in the rain forest for every tree consumed in producing his book.

Not only is anything negotiable, but anyone. As a writer, you will be negotiating with more than just clients and editors. I have negotiated with suppliers and printers for extended-payment plans that were supposedly contrary to company policy; with photographers and illustrators on collaborative works; with attorneys and accountants about bartering; even with an old landlord to knock the rent down fifty dollars a month in exchange for light maintenance work around the apartment building.

You will also be negotiating for more than money. In any bargaining session, in fact, it is crucial to involve other negotiables such as expenses, rights, payment schedules, kill fees, deadline, length, tone, the use of company car/credit cards/secretaries/computers/office or parking space, benefits (for longer projects), work hours, editing and editorial space, and even whether you will work on retainer. If, for instance, an editor offers you little money, try negotiating for shorter length, longer deadline, or payment on acceptance instead of publication.

One fact, though, remains constant: You've got to ask for what you want — otherwise, you won't get it. And if the idea of negotiating rubs you the wrong way, remember that friction is a fundamental property of nature, and nothing changes without it. That includes what you get paid for your writing.

Collaborative Bargaining: Playing to Win-Win

There are more than a few writers who feel they couldn't warm to editors if they were burned at the stake together, and are equally cool to the idea of negotiating with people they consider to be in the same category as cardsharps and carpetbaggers.

If they do it at all, it is in an atmosphere of trust not unlike that surrounding two nations exchanging spies at the border.

Successful businesspeople, however, know that customers (and editors are your customers) are not the enemy. They are hard-working people usually stuffed into small office cubicles, trying to do good work and be recognized for it, who eventually move into their own offices, ones with a window and a door. They are just people. There is no conspiracy.

The word *negotiate*, in fact, comes from the Latin for "to trade" and refers to a give-and-take situation. But the most successful negotiations are not give-and-take in the sense of minimizing give and maximizing take — the typical approach to negotiation — but in the sense (the original sense) of compromise, which is to "promise together."

Negotiations must be collaborative. If you win at somebody else's expense, they will resent it, and this will come back to haunt you. Editors are not people you're buying used cars from. You must negotiate with long-term relationships in mind, because the more steady customers you have, the more steady income you have.

Also, the more you enter into negotiations in the spirit of cooperation and mutual benefit, the more you will enjoy those relationships. And you might as well, because they are going to become important ones in your life.

Even if you are negotiating a onetime project for a onetime client, a reputation for uncivilized tactics may not stop there. Gossip travels, competitors talk among themselves, and editors turn over faster than burgers at a fast-food stand. An editor of mine at the *San Francisco Chronicle*'s Sunday magazine, for instance, suddenly turned up one day as an editor of mine at *Vogue*, and I was damn glad there was no bad blood between us.

Therefore, *negotiation must preserve the relationship over any given assignment.* What you want is a win-win outcome in which you find equitable agreements that honor both parties' needs and don't damage the relationship.

The Perception of Power: Turning the Bargaining Tables

So how do you manage a win-win outcome when editors have all the power? How do you win even just for *yourself* when, as writers so often protest, it's a buyer's market, with hordes of hungry scribes clamoring after a handful of vainglorious publishers?

First, you must understand a crucial distinction: It is a buyer's market for some writers and a seller's market for others—and what determines this is the good old law of supply and demand.

If there are half a million writers, all offering roughly the same thing— passably good writing, fairly good ideas, occasional reliability, a modest stamina for rewrites, and a deep-seated fear of asking for anything more than whatever editors offer them—it's a buyer's market, and they buy the cheapest. I would.

But when you begin giving editors what they want most—bang-up writing, imaginative ideas, a firm grasp of the audience, punctuality and a product that will sell—and when you ask for payment commensurate with that quality of performance and get it, suddenly it starts becoming a seller's market, with editors favorably disposed to negotiating in order to keep you. In fact, the only reason editors will ever negotiate with you is because they want what you're selling.

If the writing profession is as much of a buyer's market as writers perceive, editors would have no reason ever to negotiate. The fact is, they do it all the time, with writers who give them what they want.

No matter what the power dynamics, though, any market with both buyers and sellers will (despite the best collaborative efforts) have a few inherently adversarial components that negotiation must take into account. Here are some that are typical of the writer/editor relationship:

1. *The fear of vulnerability:* Neither side wants to show the other any weakness, afraid that it will be taken advantage of. The unfortunate outcome of this is that in negotiations, and even throughout the working relationship, both writers and editors act cool and disinterested, so as not to tip their hand that they're eager to buy or sell.

Editors understate their enthusiasm for writers' work even when they like it, so as not to let writers think they're worth more, lest they ask for more. And writers play poker-faced so as not to let on that they're amazed they landed the assignment at all, lest an editor think less of them and offer less.

The net effect of all this playing-hard-to-get is that the relationship itself loses a measure of the excitement it should have when people work on an exciting and mutually beneficial project together, and neither side feels fully appreciated.

But don't be so afraid of asking for, and administering, feedback and strokes—though this is most effective and least suspect when you're not in negotiation mode, when no one's dukes are up.

2. *The profit motive:* The publishing industry, like writing, is a business and is out to make a profit. It is your duty not to sell yourself so cheaply that you go out of business in helping your clients to stay in business.

For example, contracts are drawn up by *their* attorneys to benefit *their* bank accounts, not yours. You must negotiate to win back some of the money they will keep if you go along with the standard contract.

3. *Human nature:* Editors don't like rejection any more than you do, and if they want to offer you more than their budget allows, they will then have to negotiate with *their* bosses for the extra money, and they may not succeed. Saying no is safe. Saying yes means somebody has to *do* something.

On the other hand, editors regularly engage in creative budgeting, moving monies around between editorial, art and travel budgets. Ask them about it.

4. *Nothing is sacred:* Editors often admit to being frustrated writers, and one of the few places they get to write is on your copy. Granted, a staggering amount of the writing editors see is god-awful, and the changes they make are intended to improve it. But more than occasionally I have found my writing changed but not improved, and occasionally downright diminished. In this latter case, you should defend the honor of your writing. You will not always win—in fact, you will seldom win—but it is important to protest slash-and-burn editing that compromises your writing in substantial areas like clarity or accuracy.

Toot Your Horn: Using Your Bargaining Power

Negotiation is not an event but a process. It is more than just a sales pitch; it is the whole sales campaign.

It begins not when you pick up the telephone to talk with a client about an assignment, but when you pick up the relationship, and bargaining power is the cumulative effect of everything you do in that relationship.

Because writers often don't recognize this fact, most of them greatly underestimate their bargaining power. (On the other hand, those who overestimate their power have failed to recognize that the best time to negotiate is when you *have* some power.)

Nevertheless, everything is potential bargaining power. Here are five "power tools" writers should gather and put to good use in building their cases. Call them the five Ps.

Performance

Not long ago, one of my regular buyers of short pieces, the editor of Allied Publications, called to say, "The cupboard is bare. Send more ideas." I said I would be glad to and would also like to renegotiate my fee, which for two years had held steady at $25 per piece. He said, "Put it in writing and let me think about it." I sent him the following letter:

"Dear Richard — It was nice chatting with you on the phone today. I look forward to putting together more pieces for Allied. As for the business: After having written eight or ten pieces for Allied over the course of two years, at $25 each, I am hoping we can consider a higher fee: $50 each. I hope that, given the consistent quality, fast turnaround, and minimum of editorial work involved in my articles, this will seem like a fair price. Give me a ring and we can discuss it."

His reply: He raised my rate from $25 to $35 and suggested we could talk about another readjustment in six months. Meanwhile, a 45 percent raise.

When you deliver the goods and give clients more than they bargained for, do not let it go unnoticed at bargaining time. You might even send them samples of work you've delivered for other clients. They like to know they're dealing with working writers.

Also, try quantifying your performance for a client. I am in the habit, for example, of calling on people or companies I write about to gauge the response they receive as a result of my articles. If it is anywhere from favorable to overwhelming, I tell my editors, so they know that my articles are giving their readers something they want and need.

Presentation

From the first impression on, your presence should communicate enthusiasm, self-motivation, attention to detail, resourcefulness, humor, patience and, above all, confidence (fake it if you must; it has a way of becoming a self-fulfilling prophecy anyway).

You reveal a great deal about yourself (whether you know it or not) through your tone of voice, phone manner, assignment proposals, stationery, writing and even grooming and attire (for those in corporate enclaves).

Professionalism

During the negotiation of my first piece for *Pursuits Magazine*, one of the glossies owned by the Whittle Communications empire, the editor wanted me to pay the expenses up front for a trip to Seattle to do the piece, for which she would later (much later) reimburse me.

I understand the logic: The longer they can keep their money in the bank, the more interest it earns. I explained, though, that I was currently on assignment for two other national magazines, both of which wanted me to pay out-of-pocket expenses for trips—one of which was to South America—and that it was fast depleting my savings account.

I therefore asked if she would reconsider her request and instead send me a check before the trip to cover my expenses; I assured her that I would be happy to provide her with a thorough list of what I anticipated spending.

She sent a check for $600 that week.

What I did was demonstrate—in this case by implication—that I was a credible and competent professional, that I was *worth* sending not just to Seattle but to South America, and that I nonetheless had a limited bank account.

Bringing excellence, integrity and self-esteem to your business and writing affairs has a commanding effect. "Professional" writers, for instance, are those most likely to succeed at changing a payment-on-publication clause to payment-on-acceptance simply because they know that in no other business do people, professional or not, tolerate not being paid their wages on time, and that the main reason it happens is that writers let it happen. (Ask an editor if he would approve of being paid six months late and see what he says.)

If they couldn't get the policy changed, these writers would still appeal to an editor's sense of logic, fairness and business principles by pointing out that it is a time-honored tradition with all deferred-payment plans (such as credit-card payments) that a buyer pays a higher price for delayed payment, and a seller gets a higher price for waiting. So why not with the payment-on-publication policy?

Polish

This is the willingness to go the extra mile for clients, to burn the midnight oil in order to give an assignment that extra shine.

You might help them track down art to accompany your copy; do your own editing so editors won't have to do it; keep costs down; double-check your facts; oblige all reasonable requests for rewrites; and get work in *before* deadline.

And remind editors of the extra mileage at negotiation time.

Personal Contact

Personal (not just professional) contact, both on the phone and in person, is highly regarded. As a rule, people enjoy doing business with those they identify with, so the more opportunities you can give clients to identify with you as a person, the better. Go meet them. Break bread, laugh at their jokes, listen to them, pick up the tab.

Because editors are also team players as well as cogs in giant corporations, they, too, have professional relationships that need personal tending. So anything you can do to help them look good to their teammates and superiors will go a long way.

Here are a few more tips from the trenches on bargaining power:

Editors are like Pavlov's dogs: They go back to what feels good. If you place as few obstacles in editors' paths as possible, do what you're asked, when, and don't make them rewrite, it allows them to take longer lunches, and they'll overpay you just to keep you in the stable.

Writers are very insecure, though. They fear that making so much as a peep will cause an editor to can the whole deal. It's not true. In fact, it raises an editor's respect for you, though it also raises their expectations of what you'll then deliver. Still, for most beginning writers, it's a mistake to press the limits.

ADAIR LARA
FORMER EDITOR, *SAN FRANCISCO MAGAZINE*
COLUMNIST, *SAN FRANCISCO CHRONICLE*

Give an editor exactly what he wants. Meet deadlines. Save him money. Help him shine. Call and say, "Here's what I've dug up so far on this story. Here's the direction I'm planning on taking it. Are we on the same wavelength?" And listen for his behind-the-scenes agenda. If an editor reveals he's backed up on deadlines, get *your* story in before the deadline. All this translates to bargaining power.

Also, remember that for what most writers do and for the work they put in, they're worth more than they'll probably ever get paid. Believe you're worth it.

DAVID BRILL
FORMER EDITOR, *WHITTLE*
AUTHOR, *AS FAR AS THE EYE CAN SEE: REFLECTIONS OF AN APPALACHIAN TRAIL HIKER*

The biggest problem I have with writers—and it's really both our faults—is communication. Be very clear up front what is expected of you. Keep asking questions until you understand. Also, take some initiative to come up with creative ideas, new angles, your own twists on things. I welcome that. Don't just do everything by rote.

SUSAN BAKER
WRITING DIRECTOR, BLANC & OTUS, PR FIRM

I am willing to pay for peace of mind. If I can count on a writer, he or she becomes extremely valuable. But I don't want anyone who is doing this kind of writing just to earn extra money.

They must be interested in the work. It's an art form. Ninety-nine percent of those who send me resumes are not really interested in learning the craft. It's not something to throw off while you're waiting for your novel to sell.

JULIE LEVAK
SENIOR CONSULTANT, MEL WARWICK & ASSOCIATES
DIRECT-MAIL FIRM

Thinking Big: Even Left Field Is Still in the Ballpark

Several years ago, an editor at *Vogue* called me about a story proposal I'd sent on nutrition. She wanted to buy the *idea*, though, not the story. They had a staff writer who handled the nutrition beat.

"How much do you want for the idea?" she asked.

"Uhhhh," was all I could muster by way of stalling for time.

What is a story idea worth? They're a dime a dozen—$100? I did save them a lot of time, though, by already outlining the story—$200? And now they wouldn't have to pay me to write it—$300?

"How about $400?" I finally said, thinking myself the shrewd and quick-witted negotiator.

"Sold!"

There was a moment's silence, then I thought to myself, "Damn!"

Any time a buyer accepts your first offer, you blew it. You undersold yourself. And writers are chronic undersellers. Most magazine writers, for instance, get paid coolie wages for their labors because they consider it a fair trade for the "privilege" of being published.

The fact is, editors need writers the same way service stations need parts suppliers. They cannot do their job without our part, and we must recognize the value of our contribution. A recent strike by Hollywood television script-writers demonstrated this with sobering effect. There was nothing on TV but reruns for a month.

So, what is your writing worth? *Whatever someone will pay for it.* And that is determined by several factors: how much they need it; how valuable they perceive it to be; the going rate for the kind of writing you do; the amount of money in the budget; and the kind of bargaining power you have.

What someone will pay for a writing project, however, is not determined by how much they initially offer. In almost every case, there is room beyond that to negotiate. You must test the limits. Once you know a client's pay range (if you haven't worked with them before, talk with people in the business, ask for your client's "writer's guidelines," and check *Writer's Market*), take the initiative and come in with a price first. But set high aspirations and suggest a price that is greater than you expect to get, or expect them to pay. Often your expectations of both are way too low.

Do not feel arrogant coming in high and negotiating down. It is the way the game is played; the rule, not the exception.

By coming in high, you increase your shot at making more money, and when you eventually "settle" for less, your client or editor will have the satisfaction of having brought your price down. That's win-win.

But remember: *Aspirations can always be lowered in negotiations, but once stated they cannot be raised.* When my *Vogue* editor said, "Sold!" I could not then say, "Wait a minute. Did I say $400? I meant to say $700."

(What I should have charged, by the way, was something much closer to what I would have been paid to *write* the piece, since by selling her the idea, I sold my right to write it. And that figure, it still pains me to recall, would have been closer to $1,500.)

Do not start out with an extreme position, though, an absurdly high price that is guaranteed only to irritate your client. He'll think you're trying to dupe him, or that you don't know the true value of your writing, and it only builds resentment, not credibility. Set a *reasonably* high price—I generally set my sights between a third and a half higher than I expect to get—*and be able to explain why you feel the project and you are worth that much.*

Also, if an editor says, "Our range for this kind of piece is $300 to $500," take the higher amount and without missing a beat say, "I can do it for $500 if you'll cover my phone expenses."

In setting your aspirations you must, at the very least, know what your *time* is worth, in an hourly wage. This will be a valuable reference point for negotiation.

Take the last project you wrote. Divide the price you got for it by the number of hours you put in. Include time spent:

- Putting the proposal together.
- Following up on it.
- Negotiating.
- Researching.
- Interviewing.
- Traveling.
- Writing.
- Rewriting.
- Tracking down photos/illustrations/charts/graphics/maps/cartoons/etc.

If your figures come out anything like mine did in the beginning, this hourly wage will point to the lowest price you can afford to take without having to cheat your kids out of birthday presents.

A Novel Approach: Plotting Your Negotiation

You're negotiating with an editor to get payment-on-publication switched to payment-on-acceptance. Quick, what would you say if he told you, "Nope, can't do it. Company policy"?

If you didn't plan for that possibility, you would probably be reduced to immediate impotence, stammering out weak-kneed responses like "Well, it doesn't hurt to ask, huh?"

But having anticipated a few worst-case scenarios *before the negotiation*, you might have offered a more studied response, such as inquiring into why that particular company policy exists, and then seeing what your editor says. On the following pages (pages 163-164) there is a transcript of a negotiation I

This Business of Writing

Sample Negotiation

The following dialogue demonstrates the kind of tone I find most workable in negotiating with editors. It is excerpted from a phone call I had with an editor for whom I had written a half-a-dozen articles and was about to write another. After receiving the contract, I decided I wanted to tackle their payment-on-publication policy.

I sat down and made a list of questions to ask and possible responses to make. What I wanted from this particular negotiation was to get an agreement from him to be paid on acceptance, and I was willing to settle for simply making him aware of my displeasure about the current policy, which I consider to be of questionable ethics. (In this exchange, I am designated by the letter *G*, the editor by the letter *E*).

G: "Hi, Mike. This is Gregg Levoy. Have I caught you at an opportune moment?" (Start out on the right foot; be considerate.)

E: "Sure. How are you?"

G: "Great. Just got back from a weekend of skiing" (keep it personal), "and I'm rarin' to go on the 'Offbeat Museums' story. I'd love to chat with you about it for a minute, though."

E: "Shoot."

G: "I got the contract and it looks great, and I wonder if you'd consider a change in it?"

E: "What's that?"

G: "The payment-on-publication clause. I'd like to see if we" (stress the collaborative) "can arrange payment-on-acceptance" (state your case clearly and succinctly). "I find it a bit difficult waiting six months for payment. I'm sure you can understand" (create a sense of being on the same side, looking at a common problem).

E: "Well, um, it's kind of our policy, Gregg. I don't think there's much I can do about it."

G: "Can you tell me the rationale for the policy?" (Ask open-ended questions; get him talking.)

E: "Well, if I'm not mistaken, the fellow who started the magazine several years ago was having trouble being paid on time by his advertisers, and I guess he just passed it along to the writers."

G: "I can certainly understand why he'd do that. Is he still having the problem?"

E: "Actually, no."

G: "But the policy's still in effect?"

E: "Yeah."

G: "Mike, how would you feel about approaching him on my behalf, and mentioning that, since the problem isn't so pressing anymore, perhaps he could let a check slip out early for me." (Not for everybody; start small.) "It would be greatly appreciated. I'm hoping that, given the consistent quality of my work, you'll agree that I've earned the raise" (stress bargaining power).

E: "Yeah, your stuff's been great. I've appreciated the work you've done for us. And I hate being in between the writers and publisher on this issue."

G: "That must be uncomfortable" (acknowledge his position).

E: "It is. I just don't think I should approach him at the moment."

G: "What do you think would happen if you pointed out that the policy no longer reflects his financial situation, and that since the magazine is doing well, he might want to move toward a payment-on-acceptance policy" (appeal to logic). "The magazine relies on writers, and he'd be making them a lot happier."

E: "Look, rather than doing that, why don't I just agree to move you up a month? I'll pay you a month earlier."

G: "That would be great. And if you can do that, why not move it up to paying me on acceptance?" (Stick to your guns; recognize room to maneuver.)

E: "Why is payment-on-publication such a problem, anyway?" (He actually didn't know.)

G: "Well, it's being paid for my services six months after I render them. If I did that with the guy who fixes my plumbing, he'd wrap a monkey-wrench around my backside" (humor goes a long way in negotiations). "It would be like you getting your paycheck six months late. It wouldn't be fair, would it?" (Appeal to his sense of ethics.) "Mike, I like working for you, and I want to keep working for you, and being paid on time really encourages me to do my best work. Let's find a way to work this out so we both feel good about it." (Stress importance of relationship and mutually beneficial outcome.)

E: "Well, it's not like the publisher looks over my shoulder or anything. How about if I paid you two months early?"

G: "Again, Mike," (use his name liberally, to personalize the negotiation) "if you can pay me two months early, why not on acceptance?" (Keep bringing negotiation back to the issue.)

E: "Look, I don't want to rock the boat too much. I'll pay you at halftime, between acceptance and publication. But I can't do any more for now."

G: "OK, I respect that. It's a deal." (Know when to stop.) "I really appreciate your willingness to negotiate with me, Mike, and to be flexible" (acknowledge his concession). "And if you can slip a little letter of confirmation to me in the mail" (get it in writing), "I'll put my skis away and get to work on that museum piece. I think you're going to like it."

conducted recently with an editor on just this subject.

The general rule here is not to go into negotiations with the attitude that you'll just see what happens, figuring it out as you go, relying on your genius for quick comebacks and thinking on your feet.

Rely instead on a well-thought-out strategy, based on doing some homework, on practicing what you're going to preach, and on knowing what you'll say if an editor invokes "company policy." Get your facts and figures together. Role-play with a friend. Write out a script if need be.

Knowledge is power, and you must know:
- What you want out of a negotiation.
- What you're willing to settle for.
- What you'll do if you can't reach agreement.
- What kinds of negotiables there are.
- What your client's pay range is.
- What your bargaining power is.
- And what an editor is likely to say given his or her relationship to *you*.

No matter what the negotiation, the more prepared you are, the better you will fare. If you're about to negotiate a book contract with a publishing house, for example, ask the editors and marketing people about their projections for the book.

If you're negotiating a public-relations assignment, brainstorm all your media contacts beforehand. Well-connected writers are worth more.

If you negotiate with magazines, call ahead for their writer's guidelines, which will give you a sense of the pay range for rank-and-file writers (celebrity writers command more, of course).

If you'll be negotiating a big contract with a corporate client, you might even drive by the day before and check out what the employees are wearing. Those in start-up companies, for instance, often sport jeans, not pinstripes.

Planning a negotiation involves everything from the grand designs to the subtlest details you glean from clients in unguarded moments. I take notes during all my conversations with editors, for example, and keep in my Rolodex tidbits that might come in handy during negotiations. And they do come in handy.

Several years ago, an editor of mine at *Health* magazine mentioned during a phone conversation that rates were probably going down for shorter pieces like columns, but up to a dollar a word for the longer features. I jotted it down in my "Pearl Harbor file."

Four months later, she called with a go-ahead on a story I had pitched, and offered me $1,500 for 2,000 words.

I pulled out my file and there was the note about a probable rate change. I asked her about it. "Oh yeah, right, um, right, the rate change. Yeah, that, uh, that did go through . . ." she squirmed. "So, uh, OK, how about $1,800 for 1,800 words?"

Sold!
Less work, more money.

It is easy to be caught by surprise on the telephone and find yourself suddenly — and ill-preparedly — bargaining. But if you're up to your armpits in something else, don't wing it. Postpone the conversation: "I wonder if we could discuss the project later today. I'd like to devote my full attention to it, and presently I'm finishing up another assignment." Then marshall your forces and prepare a proper defense.

Don't let an editor or client bully you by saying, "Look, I'm in a hurry. We need to talk about this now." That's a pressure tactic. There is always time. If you simply must negotiate then and there, at least make sure you have a list posted near your phone of the common negotiables (fee, expenses, rights, payment schedule, deadline, story particulars) so you remember to cover the bases and don't forget anything that might cost you money down the road.

As it is, negotiations are typically faster and more competitive on the phone than in person. There is usually less time available, less information exchanged (including nonverbal cues), and it is easier to be refused when they don't have to look you in the eye. So the more important and pricey the negotiation, the better off you are doing it in person, if you can.

Also, hold off negotiating until you have developed a good working relationship with a client. If you do it right, this can happen by the end of the first assignment. Then, by the time you begin negotiating for more, they have devoted time, energy and faith in you and have a vested interest in keeping you satisfied.

Editors don't want to spend their days breaking in new writers. There is thus a link between time invested and willingness to compromise.

The spirit of compromise is also crucial to planning your negotiations. Because there will often be two competing needs, *it is essential to brainstorm solutions that meet both parties' needs.* For example, both sides usually want more money, and conventional wisdom suggests that more money for you means less for them, and vice versa. But not necessarily. The pie is not limited. You can expand it. Here are three solutions I often bring to negotiations when I plan to ask for more money:

1. When I must travel on assignment to a city where I have friends, I offer to stay with them instead of a hotel, if the editor will kick back half the savings into my fee.

2. With phone expenses, I agree to make as many calls as I can at night, early in the morning or on weekends, again, if the editor will split the proceeds with me.

3. If I know a hot young photographer who is still paying dues and is willing to work for less, I offer to connect him or her with the editor, if he'll split the difference (between the young photographer's rates and those of the more seasoned pro he might otherwise hire) with me.

Another potential deadlock that has required collaborative forethought on my part accrues from the fact that many magazines insist upon exclusive ownership of stories, and to ensure this they buy all rights from writers. This means you are denied the opportunity to resell your work and make extra income.

One solution I have found workable with several major magazines is to suggest that I retain syndication rights, meaning that I can sell my pieces again, but only to newspaper syndicates (middlemen who offer freelance material to newspapers) that agree to put at the top of the article "Originally appeared in *XYZ Magazine*." The magazine gets its exclusivity, and I get my extra income.

But the point is to think of these solutions *before* the negotiation. During it, you may not have the composure.

Ultimately, negotiating is like taking a test. The more prepared you are, the better you do, and the less likely you are to have to go back and repeat the same material.

A few more tips from veteran strategists on planning negotiations:

Listen carefully to how editors phrase their offers. If an editor says, "How does $1,400 sound?" you should respond, "How does $2,000 sound?" Their question is a wide-open invitation to counter-offer. You can feel when there's a cushion. "We can pay you $1,400" is only semi-open.
BEN FONG-TORRES
MAGAZINE WRITER
AUTHOR, *THE MOTION PICTURE ALBUM*

I seldom negotiate. I put a price on a project and I don't care how long it takes you. The only way to get more money is to either work on a bigger project for me or convince me that I've underestimated what's involved in a project.

Three other points will help make a writer valuable to me. 1) Listen! Be concerned with my objectives and strategies, not just how you're going to come across. New writers especially need to learn this. Creativity seems to breed arrogance. 2) Be willing to take criticism and not get pissed off at having to rewrite. 3) Do research. You damn well better understand our industry if you're going to come in here and write for us.
SCOTT HOLMES
EVENTS PRODUCTION MANAGER, APPLE COMPUTERS

Think of negotiation as sales, and sell a piece to me. Tell me why it matters. Be convincing—that is, be writerly. And if you're going to take a risk negotiating, start with a small piece.
DAVID WEIR
SENIOR EDITOR, *MOTHER JONES*

When asking for a "raise," don't say, "Can I . . . ?" Say, "My rates have gone up to . . ." If that's too high for them, cut back your hours, not your price. Also, don't take a cookie-cutter approach to negotiating. Each one is different."

MIKE BALLARD
PR WRITER

Strategic Command: Tactics for Win-Win Negotiating

The most artful negotiator I have ever known is my own mother; somehow she managed to raise twin boys without letting them kill each other in the process.

The one peace-keeping tactic I consider her most elegant was what I call the Dessert Strategy. Whenever my brother and I squared off over splitting dessert, my mother would step in, hand one of us a knife, and issue the following command: "One of you cut it . . . and one of you choose it!"

To this day, the Dessert Strategy continues to work miracles for my brother and me, but mainly because the negotiation has remained essentially the same; the players are merely bigger versions of the way they were.

Since you will most likely be negotiating with many different clients over a multitude of negotiables, you must have a multiplicity of strategems. Few will work across the board. Some editors, for instance, have gone for my syndication-rights solution, and some have not. Some clients have company cars, credit cards and secretaries that can become negotiables, others do not.

But it is not just the content of a given strategy that's important; it is also the principle of the thing; the spirit in which you administer it. Like the Dessert Strategy, it must convey that your interests are in maintaining diplomatic relations and helping each side feel good about what it's getting.

The following, then, are ten negotiation strategies that are, if not based on collaborative principles, at least not contrary to them, and can be applied both before and during most bargaining situations.

Listen

When people are tested for listening skills, they routinely hear between 25 and 50 percent of what was said, and that's under test conditions, immediately after listening to someone.

Retaining only a fraction of what is communicated, though, is not good enough for successful negotiations, or for relationships. Nor is listening only for cracks in the other guy's defense.

I know more than a few editors whose primary beef against writers is that they're more concerned with how they present themselves than with listening to clients' needs and objectives.

Remember, listening is not necessarily agreeing, but if the other side feels they've truly been heard, it goes a long way toward softening them. In fact, about the cheapest concession you can make in a negotiation is simply letting someone know they've been heard, and even repeating to them what they've said ("So, if I understand you correctly, you're saying . . .").

Listening attentively is especially tactical during telephone negotiations, because there is no opportunity to pick up telling body language such as folded arms, drumming fingers and legs vibrating like tuning forks. You must listen for these signals in the voice. The *way* someone says "company policy" may hold the key to how close they are to their limit or to the end of their patience.

Be Quiet

Nature abhors a vacuum. People will naturally rush in to fill silences, and if that person is not you, this phenomenon can be to your advantage.

During a negotiation about payment on acceptance with an editor at one of the in-flight magazines, I mentioned that as a business practice it didn't seem fair or professional. And then I shut up for a moment. In the awkward silence that ensued, the urge to blurt out something, anything, to ease the tension, was excruciating. He broke first, and when he did, he did so with a compromise, effectively talking himself right out of his own position.

This is a difficult tactic to pull off, especially in person. Silence is uncomfortable enough even among friends. But if silence is going to be broken by a compromise, it should at least be theirs, not yours.

Attack Problems, Not People

In the in-flight magazine negotiation, I made sure to focus my attention and displeasure on the issue, not the editor. It was the payment-on-publication policy that was unfair, not the person trying to uphold it, even against his own principles.

The point is to place you and your co-negotiator on the same side looking at a common problem — "How can we solve this to our mutual benefit?" — and not put the problem between you.

Personalize the Negotiation

It is easier to reject someone when you can depersonalize him. That way you don't feel as guilty. But you can counteract this phenomenon by personalizing your business relationships and negotiations as much as possible.

Before the negotiation: Keep the tone of all your correspondence personal and conversational; call clients to let them know how projects are going; send them clips and ideas you think may be of interest to them; send them thank-you notes and compliments at the end of projects and when articles appear; visit them — shake hands and kiss babies.

During the negotiation: Refer to your good working relationship and your interest in continuing it; remind them of your file bulging with more story ideas; use their names (it is the most singularly harmonious sound in the universe to a person); whenever you agree on a negotiable say, "I'm glad we agree," "This arrangement feels good to me," "Excellent idea," or anything else that strikes you as collaborative and complimentary.

People like to work with others they perceive as personable and appreciative. They don't want to undermine the good vibes.

Ask Open-Ended Questions

The more information you have about a client's needs, interests and dilemmas, the better your bargaining position. So get them talking by asking open-ended questions, those that elicit more than just a yes/no answer: "What would happen if we . . . ?" or "How would you feel if . . . ?" or "What would you like to see more of coming across your desk?" or "Are there improvements I could make in my writing that would make it work better for you?"

Have a Concession Strategy

There is a fine line between conceding too much and not conceding enough. On one hand, you don't want to give in just to avoid conflict. You'll get run over that way, and besides, the only people who make any sort of living bending over backwards are acrobats.

For that matter, if you come in with a price of $900 and your editor counters with $500, don't immediately start whittling away at your initial offer by offering $800. Instead, say, "Well, let me tell you why I think I'm worth $900 for this assignment."

On the other hand, don't dig your heels in and refuse to move, biting when a simple growl would do. The hand you bite might be the one that feeds you.

Instead, enter a negotiation knowing what your asking price is, and your walk-away price (the one you won't go below). Remember what psychologists call the "barrier theory": The harder it is to achieve something (within reason), the more we want it. Make clients work a little for their concessions.

And when conceding, make small concessions. Don't go, for instance, from asking for $1,500 to backing off to $1,000 in one giant step. It will appear that you can be bought even cheaper than *that*. Go instead to $1,300, and the closer you get to your real bottom line, the smaller your increments should be. If your bottom line is $950, start with $1,500 and go to $1,300, then $1,150, $1,050, $1,000, $975, $960, and so on. They will see by those increments that you're nearing your walk-away price.

If you're going to put up any numbers, put up odd numbers, not round, even ones. One thousand dollars sounds like one you just threw out there; it's itching to be challenged. Nine hundred fifty sounds more solid, more considered, less negotiable.

You might even decide to concede entirely on fee, as a strategy aimed at encouraging your editor to concede during the next negotiation. If you're concerned with appearing a pushover, try taking some lesser negotiable home with you; expenses, rights or deadline.

Conceding a first negotiation, though, doesn't automatically brand you a patsy. It may, more importantly, give you a reputation for being flexible and agreeable (especially if you put up an intelligent fight).

Discuss Fee Last

If you can steer the negotiation that way, try saving discussion of fee for last. It is the area about which you are most likely to disagree, so build up goodwill first by focusing on the more easily agreed on areas.

If your client suggests a three-month deadline, say you can get it done in two and a half. If she says $50 is all she can give you for phone expenses, tell her you'll only need $30 because you plan to make the calls in the evenings and early mornings. Tell her about that hot young photographer you know who is still working for peanuts because he hasn't been discovered yet.

Then, once you have built up some common ground and warmed the editor's heart with your conciliatory nature, talk price. You may have earned a concession or two by then.

Recognize Advantage

There will be those rare and delirious occasions when a client owes you one. Don't let the opportunity to garner a return favor slip by.

Perhaps you helped him fill an editorial hole when another writer left him high and dry by not coming through on deadline. Maybe you worked a graveyard shift one night to get out a rush-order brochure for a client with a late-breaking conference. Or let's say an editor lost your slides (you did have dupes, didn't you?).

When an editor at *American Way* magazine (the in-flight of American Airlines) lost a manuscript he had commissioned me to write and then took two months to tell me about it, he was considerably apologetic by the time he called.

I generously shrugged it off and agreed to send him another copy, but first I asked for a small benefaction: "While I've got you on the phone," I said, "I wonder if we could discuss a minor readjustment of one of the clauses in our contract."

"Sure," he said, "which one?"

"The all-rights clause. I'd love to change it to first rights."

He agreed without skipping a beat.

When You Stop Negotiating—Stop!

Make sure you discuss all negotiables in one session, not piecemeal. And when you make your final agreements (even if they're not completely agreeable to you), don't bring it up again unless, for instance, there are cost overruns that must be discussed.

Get It in Writing

When you finish negotiating, make sure you commit your agreements to paper, whether in a written contract or a simple letter of agreement.

If an editor suggests that you forgo a written contract and just leave it at a friendly handshake, politely tell him or her that you'd like to *keep* the relationship friendly, so you would much prefer to work with a contract—company policy!

Stand By Me: The Role of Agents and Attorneys

There is a saying in the legal profession that the man who represents himself has a fool for a client.

Although you are generally best off negotiating on your own behalf, and it is important not to deny yourself the experience of negotiating with clients head-on, there may be times when you are *not* the best person to represent yourself.

At these times you will want a pinch hitter, a professional negotiator, and that means either an agent or a literary lawyer.

The most promising occasions around which to employ these paladins of the publishing world are when you are facing complex or pricey contract negotiations like those involved in selling a book, play, film, television, or even computer software property.

There must generally be substantial money at stake, because agents, who are essentially freelancers, charge 10 to 20 percent for their services; it isn't worth their time to handle articles, essays, short stories, poetry, ad copy, greeting cards or anything else that doesn't render upwards of at least $5,000. Attorneys charge as much as $250 an hour, and since negotiations take several hours at least, it isn't worth it to *you* if the deal offers much less than five grand.

Some publishers—most notably Hollywood producers and major publishing houses—even refuse to negotiate directly with writers. They consider most to be just too poorly informed on the vicissitudes of contract negotiations and would rather talk to someone who knows the business. In fact, nearly 80 percent of all book manuscripts sold to major publishers come through agents.

Agents and attorneys are also for those writers who feel—and not all do—that they do not have the wherewithal to handle the complexities inherent in, say, book and movie deals, and therefore wouldn't mind the middleman; who would rather write than fight; who have the money to spend; or who consider it an expensive but worthwhile investment in their future (which I for one consider it to be).

"Literary" writers, however, are not the only ones who seek or receive representation. There are agents who specialize solely in technical writers and even comic-book writers, and Hollywood agents regularly pitch their scriptwriters to the corporate world for part-time work, because there's more money in corporations than in Hollywood.

There are distinct advantages to third-party representation at the bargaining table:

- Agents and attorneys know how to negotiate!
- They save you time you could spend writing.
- They do the "dirty work" for you, helping you keep your relationships with publishers and editors "clean." When writers drive hard bargains, editors often feel they're being obnoxious, but when agents and lawyers do it, they're just doing their job.
- They know the publishing market (and in the case of agents especially, the shifting personnel) much better than most writers.
- They provide a certain measure of credibility. Your representation by an agent or attorney says to a publisher that at least *someone* thinks your work is worth fighting for. Whether an agent's or attorney's representation is considered clout, though, depends on his or her reputation. You should investigate: Ask what kinds of properties they handle, what authors they've agented, what books they've placed, with which publishers, and whether you can talk with a few of their clients.
- They do your boasting for you, which writers often find distasteful.
- And they are your employees. They do your bidding. But to give them proper instructions, you must know what you want. It also helps to know something about publishing contracts, even if it's only book-learned.

There are, however, differences between the two species. Many agents will take you on even if you don't have a track record or an interested publisher, just a manuscript; attorneys only go to bat for you when you already have a contract to negotiate, though you may hire one just to review a contract before you sign it.

Whereas attorneys tend to limit themselves to the contract negotiation, agents take on the whole enchilada, becoming both sales rep and business consultant to writers, helping them develop works, evaluating manuscripts and markets, pitching scripts and book proposals around town, resolving author/publisher conflicts, negotiating contracts, keeping the books, following up on movie/book-club/video/foreign-rights sales, and generally doing a fair amount of hand holding.

Some types of agents, such as those for technical writers, exist only to connect writers and corporate clients. They keep a database of writers — usually with very specific skills — match them to jobs as they become available, negotiate for writers on longer projects (those that are considered "temporary"), and take up to a 25 percent commission.

Agents, because their income depends on your income, can run the risk of losing perspective on what is best for the writer. The best deal is not always the one offering the most money.

Agents often know the publishing field better, while attorneys tend to have a firmer grip on the law. But the best agents and literary attorneys are steeped in both, and a good agent will know when a property has legal problems (libel, copyright infringement, breach of contract) that are best handled by a lawyer. Whatever you do, though, do *not* go with a nonliterary lawyer. Publishing contracts are unique.

The easiest way to find representation is to have something worth representing. Beyond that, finding agents and literary attorneys is best done by word of mouth: Get referrals from other writers, editors, publishers, writers' club directors, even bookstore owners; find those who agented your favorite books; attend writers' conferences where there are agents' or lawyers' panels.

Or call trade organizations like your local bar association for attorneys. For agents, try the Independent Literary Agents Association, or the Society of Authors' Representatives (both in New York City), or the Writer's Guild of America in Los Angeles. Agents are also listed in the annual *Literary Agents of North America*, and some in *Writer's Market*.

Some final observations about the services of agents and attorneys:

Fiction writers are especially vulnerable in business dealings like negotiations. We spend so much time in imaginary worlds that our hard-reality skills are somewhat lacking, though after your first book you learn quickly.

Still, agents are a real boon. For me, I wanted to *build* a career, so I wanted the guidance a good agent provides. Most importantly, though, they know the business. They know what money is appropriate for a particular kind of work, what book editors are looking for, and what publishers will make what concessions. Besides, I'd rather let someone else be in the adversarial role, and help me keep my relationships with editors smooth.

MARILYN WALLACE
NOVELIST, *A CASE OF LOYALTIES, PRIMARY TARGET*
EDITOR, *SISTERS IN CRIME* ANTHOLOGY SERIES

There's no secret to getting an agent: Just show us a salable product. But agents won't necessarily handle all properties. Most won't touch textbooks, scholarly books, small press or poetry books. There's no money in them. Consider a lawyer.

The time to engage an agent, though, is before you have an interested publisher, when you're ready to submit.

FELICIA ETH
LITERARY AGENT

You make a bigger impression with an agent. But I'm most effective after you've gotten your foot in the door, once there's a career to begin with. I can't make money with beginners because I work on commission.

MIKE FRIEDRICH
AGENT, COMIC-BOOK WRITERS/ARTISTS

If a writer is not up to the task of negotiating a book, it can be a contractual disaster. And that kind of negotiating is hard for creative people. They live in their heads; their imaginations drive their lives. When they ask for more money, they imagine nightmare scenarios. I don't.

Through a third-party representative, writers can preserve their good relations with publishers. Their ego is kept hidden, rejections are said directly to the attorney or agent, and greed is communicated through *them*, not you.

Writers' biggest fear about negotiating, though, is making waves. They're afraid editors will withdraw their offers. But it never happens! I've made over a thousand publishing deals and it's a phantom fear. By the time an editor picks up the phone with an offer, he's already invested a lot of time and energy. He's convinced an editorial committee and the marketing department that your book would make enough money to make it worthwhile. The whole agency has decided that it's a good book. It's very unlikely he will blow all that investment because you, or your attorney, asks for a change in the initial offer.

BRAD BUNNIN
LITERARY LAWYER
CO-AUTHOR, *THE WRITER'S LEGAL COMPANION*

Writers should definitely not negotiate for books. They're just not good at it, and they're often taken advantage of. But if you're going to hire anyone, hire an agent who is also an attorney.

ALAN RINZLER
BOOK EDITOR, SIMON & SCHUSTER, MACMILLAN, BANTAM

Writers often have a greater need to be published than to be treated well. This is a situation we deplore, of course, but if writers need help *after* negotiations—if they have grievances about getting paid or being mistreated—we do handle that. We've also done class-action negotiations with entire magazines, such as *Mother Jones* and *The Nation*, to set minimum standards in the industry.

Most publishers assume that the writer is alone and that no one else cares what happens to him or her. The union disabuses them of that notion.

KIM FELNER
EXECUTIVE DIRECTOR, NATIONAL WRITERS UNION

CHAPTER EIGHT

Research: The Happiness of Pursuit

G iven three wishes, one of mine would certainly be to have the power to lay my hand on any book and instantly absorb everything in it.

Writing, like science and detective work, is a research career, and such a skill would be worth a king's ransom.

But other aptitudes are even more valuable to the writer-researcher: a desperate regard for the truth, imagination and tremendous forbearance for your own company. You must also love questions more than answers and be willing always *not* to know; to be continually the child, the student, the fool. Albert Einstein once said, in fact, that mystery is an emotion, and that to be creative one must be able to feel wonder.

Above all, *you need the temperament to enjoy—not just tolerate—doing research.* For almost any kind of writing—whether ad copy, magazine articles, or what Henry Miller called "huge, labyrinthian soul-struggles" such as the novels of Dostoevsky—if you do not like research, you are in the wrong profession.

Unfortunately, research can feel an awful lot like homework, and for me, homework was always what I had to do before I could go out and have fun. "Do your homework" was right up there with "Clean up your room" as among the most exasperating parental commandments of my formative years. They were good for me, but I hated them anyway. And being a writer sometimes feels like doing homework for a living.

But research becomes exciting in direct proportion to whether a writing project includes:

1. A subject I am passionate about.
2. A hands-on experience.
3. The chance to use my own voice.

When all three are present, research is no longer something to get through, but half the fun of writing. In fact, writing itself can be a surprisingly small part of what a writer does (with my nonfiction, I spend barely a third of my time writing), so you must enjoy the gathering and assembly of raw materials, not just the finished product; the building process, not just the building.

You must relish reading, thinking deeply, getting out and doing your own field testing, and persuading people to confide in you things they wouldn't tell their father confessor. You must be willing to follow a straying trail of clues for weeks until you find a dusty old book in the backwater of some public library and, sitting right there in the aisle, submerge yourself in it for an afternoon even though your deadline looms.

The three ingredients for excitement may be different for different writers, but when you are engaged in the right writing for you, research will be anything but boring. Here is a brief list of some of the "homework" I have been called upon to do in my line of writing:

- Paddle a dugout canoe in the Amazon rain forest.
- Raft the fiercest white-water river in America.
- Fly in a seaplane right up to the thundering face of the world's highest waterfall in Venezuela, close enough to get spray on the windshield.
- Scuba dive into an undersea scientific-research habitat in the West Indies that would turn Jules Verne green with envy.
- Sit in on a sex-change operation.
- Ride an elephant bareback at the head of a Barnum & Bailey circus parade.
- Hurtle through the aquamarine waters of the Caribbean on the back of a giant sea turtle.
- Watch an autopsy.
- Witness twins being born.
- Help birth a horse.
- Spend a month of Friday nights in strip joints in Newport, Kentucky.
- Pump bullets from a .357 Magnum into a target-silhouette of a man.
- Go helicopter skiing.
- Spend a full-moon night in a hospital emergency room.
- And scariest of all, venture into the jungle of my own soul in pursuit of essays I could not research in any other way.

Although the primary and most common use of research is to put together your writing, it is really a survival skill. Like the consumers you write for, you need information in order to make informed decisions about your business and your life. What you don't know can hurt you.

Therefore, research—the search for knowledge—is also what you will use to set goals, study the marketplace, find subjects to write about, keep your costs down, buy the best tools of the trade, negotiate with editors, design your writing proposals, and prepare for the future, since that is where you will be spending a lot of your time.

And because writing, like any business, is a confidence game—and confidence comes both from knowing your stuff and from the faith readers and editors place in you—without solid research, you cannot play to win.

Presearch: Planning Your Research

Researching a subject without knowing what you're looking for is like shopping for food on an empty stomach. You end up buying things on impulse like marinated artichoke hearts, crabmeat cocktail and Norwegian sardines in mustard sauce.

Without planning your research—that is, defining your subject and your method of attack before you begin — you can end up with far too much or far too little material, not cutting the task to fit your deadline, reading when you should be skimming, or letting yourself get carried away on too many intriguing but irrelevant tangents.

Without setting some limits on what you're looking for, you can easily be overwhelmed with the task or confused as to where to start. You need a big picture of the project up front, so that when you're immersed in the details, you won't lose sight of your goal.

Answering a few simple questions will help clear the runway:

- What *exactly* are you writing about?
- Who are you writing it for?
- How much do they already know?
- Where can the material you need be located?
- Whom do you need to interview?
- What hands-on experience does the piece demand?
- How much time and space do you have?
- What are you being paid?

Whether you're researching how to paper train puppies or the poetic imperialism of fifteenth-century Europe, your approach should be the same: Make a list of what you're looking for and where you're most likely to find it.

Recently, I put together a story for *Omni* on something called "debt-for-nature" swaps, in which conservation groups buy up Third-World debt in exchange for commitments from those countries to set aside land for conservation.

I listed the topics I needed to investigate: debt-for-nature swaps themselves, Third-World debt, conservation groups involved in debt relief, debt-for-equity swaps (similar to debt-for-nature swaps, except that debt is exchanged for ownership in local companies, not for conservation), and the World Bank (a key player in Third-World debt).

Then I listed where I might find information on these subjects: conservation-group literature, public and business libraries, computer database searches, Congressional records (for any pending bills on debt relief), Third-World consulates in this country, World Bank offices, and interviews with conservationists, bankers, foreign-affairs officers, and professors of foreign policy.

Another approach that will give you a bird's-eye view of both your topic and your task is what Gabriele Rico, author of *Writing the Natural Way*, calls "clustering," a technique that uses free association to generate a batch of ideas related to your subject.

It is a technique for those whose eyes glaze over at the mere mention of a formal outline, who want a painless way to organize their thoughts.

You begin clustering by circling a word or short phrase that best describes your subject, then brainstorming and circling all individual associations that spring to mind from that word. The result can serve as a rudimentary or preliminary outline for your research endeavors. (The illustration on page 180 shows a clustering I used to consolidate my thoughts for this chapter.)

At the far end of your research, when all the data are in hand, you can again use this "outline" to assist you in writing. If ever writers wished for a literary version of Rumpelstiltskin, someone who could magically turn a heap of notes into a coherent story by deadline, it is when they are sitting before reams of research material.

The formidable task of weaving flax into gold, though, doesn't require magic or sorcery, only stamina and another simple organizing trick: assign each sub-topic of your cluster a letter. Then go through your notes and next to each section or sentence write the letter that applies. This will greatly simplify and speed up your writing.

As for your plan of attack, take a lesson from resourceful celebrity biographers who are refused direct interviews. They learn quickly that the front door is not the only way into a house.

Make use of all angles in coming at a subject. Given the confines of space, deadlines, and dollars, make use of public and specialized libraries, city and government agencies, PR and professional associations, clipping services, investigative reporters and private eyes, university research departments, computer database searches, phone and in-person interviews, firsthand experience, personal journals and a generous helping of your own familiarity with a subject. But do library research before interviews, so you know what questions to ask and can go beyond rote answers.

The research you do will determine the questions you ask, and the more interesting your questions, the more interesting the responses, and ultimately the stories.

But as with goal setting, do not bite off more than you can chew. Before you propose a writing project, and certainly before you sign on the dotted line, have some idea how much research a project will demand. Do not trade massive treatises for meager fees.

Finally, do not let planning take the spontaneity out of research. Any exploration of the unknown involves the unexpected, and you must be open and alert to it. Be willing to follow your curiosity to out-of-the-way places; to ask the odd question; to dig up an out-of-print book because something tells you it may contain the answer you're looking for; to talk to someone seemingly on the fringes of a subject; even to pursue the occasional intriguing and irrelevant tangent.

An old Ceylonese folktale called "The Three Princes of Serendip" gave us the word to describe the often startling, delightful and "accidental" discoveries that can accrue from following this intuitive path: serendipity.

Here are some tales a few other folks can tell you about planning research:

Before you start researching, ask yourself, "Why is it important to me to investigate this subject?" Think through what it will stir up in you. The clearer

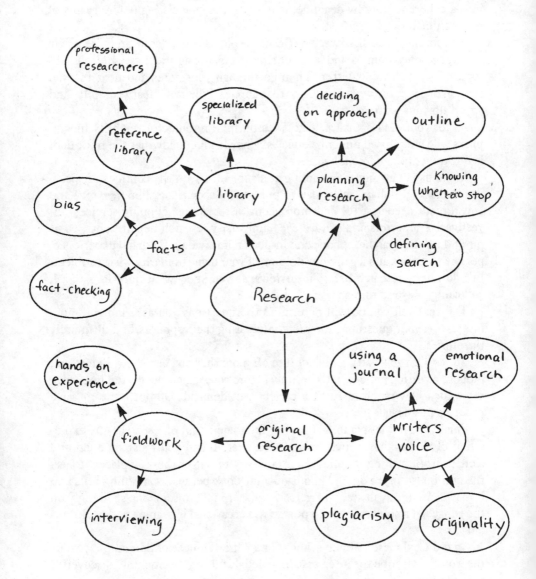

professional researchers

specialized library

deciding on approach

outline

reference library

library

planning research

Knowing when to stop

bias

facts

defining search

fact-checking

Research

hands on experience

using a journal

emotional research

fieldwork

original research

writers voice

interviewing

plagiarism

originality

This Business of Writing

you are about your emotional involvement in a subject, the less emotion will be flying around in your story like loose luggage in the baggage compartment of an airplane. But bring your full presence to a piece and draw on your own experience and emotions. If you feel vague dissatisfaction, or an editor tells you a piece is flat, it may be the emotional dimension is missing.
CAROLYN FOSTER
WRITING INSTRUCTOR
AUTHOR, *WRITING FROM YOUR ROOTS*

Your level of distaste for research is relative to your system. If you're badly organized, you'll dread it. You have to decide what angle you're going to take, what your purpose is, and how much research you can do by deadline. Also, take control of your subject with an outline of some kind. Good writing is determined by good reporting.
LINDA JUE
INVESTIGATIVE REPORTER, "MACNEIL/LEHRER NEWSHOUR," *GEO,*
LOS ANGELES TIMES

An absolutely essential part of research is studying other writers, for technique, economy of style, sense of focus, use of language and how they get their effects.
MAUREEN EPPSTEIN
POET

I spend at least 50 percent of my time researching: doing interviews, collecting newspaper clippings, keeping files on different health issues, subscribing to health newsletters, going to the library, doing computer searches. I also get out into the field as often as I can. I sit in on surgeries, wander hospitals, and take medical tests myself.

And when I'm done I take the example of my favorite painter, Georgia O'Keeffe, by pulling out of the research material only the essence, nothing extraneous. When I send a pitch-letter to a medical reporter at, say, the *Wall Street Journal*, to get him excited about a subject, it hurts to communicate too much. I have five seconds or I lose him. He gets four hundred pieces of mail a day.
BOBBI FISCHER
PRESIDENT, PR AGENCY, HEALTH-CARE INDUSTRY

The Branch Office: Making the Most of Libraries

Many years ago, I called my local library with a question I was certain would stump the reference librarian: "What is the specific gravity of olive oil?"

Several hours later she called back, and in a voice tinged with just a trace of swagger, she asked, "Would that be Italian or California olive oil?"

The library is the single greatest repository of all our recorded history, and in it there is virtually nothing you, or a reference librarian, cannot find information about, if you know what to ask and how to look. And since libraries are like branch offices to most writers, and you will likely spend a sizable chunk of your waking hours in them, it pays to know your way around. Entire books are written on how to do just that (see the Appendix). Permit me to simplify it greatly: *Ask the reference librarian.*

Reference librarians are willing to answer an astonishing number and variety of questions right over the phone, assuming the information you want does not require a Senate subcommittee investigation to unearth, and they are rigorously trained not to laugh at you if you ask (and people do) such innocent questions as:

- "What kind of trees do croutons grow on?"
- "How many acres were there in the Garden of Eden?"
- "Do you carry a book called *Roget the Sorcerer*?"

Big-city libraries receive several million reference questions a year, and any that require voluminous research you will have to handle on your own, along with medical or legal advice, lists of books, math homework or business referrals. The only thing they ask of you when you call is to be specific. Tell them not just what you want, but why. Reference librarians can best help those who help themselves.

If the library doesn't have a particular book, or if you live in a town with little more than a bookmobile, ask about interlibrary loans. Most libraries nowadays are linked via computer to most other libraries, and certainly to others within the same branch. Depending on the popularity of a book (magazine, microfilm or even audio tape) and the distance it has to travel, it may take anywhere from a day to two months to arrive.

While you're at it, ask about checking out reference books. You're allowed to do it, if it isn't one the reference librarians or patrons use with any regularity.

Given their inherent affinity for all things literary, including writers, reference librarians are natural allies. Introduce yourself, tell them your areas of interest, ask for a private tour of the grounds. If they got up on the right side of the bed that morning, they're generally happy to oblige.

Your relationships with reference librarians should be cultivated in the same manner as your relationships with the "gatekeepers" at a magazine or company (secretaries and receptionists). They wield power disproportionate to their status, and they can make your task far easier for you or far more difficult and time-consuming, depending on your attitude toward them. Remember, they are public servants, not servants. I have gone so far as to send reference librarians clips of articles they have helped me research.

Reference librarians are like tourist guides in foreign countries, and libraries can be every bit as confounding, given the sheer magnitude of the information contained in them and the multitude of media in which it is contained—books, magazines, newspapers, microfilm, annual reports, government publications, phone books, audio and videotapes, catalogs, recordings, newsletters, trade publications, photographs, maps, rare books, films, computers, patent collections and more.

Some libraries, of course, are more intimidating than others. The Library of Congress, the world's largest, has 327 miles of aisles, and even walking at a good clip it would take you three solid days to cover them.

In addition to public libraries, there are also specialized libraries: medicine, business, science, education, music and law. There are libraries in museums, corporations, historical societies, bar associations, law firms, medical centers, social service agencies, and newspapers (they're called morgues, because that's where all the old, dead newsclips wind up). For academic, scholarly and historical research, nothing beats university libraries, especially since they're usually open nights and weekends.

Libraries nowadays also have a great deal more going on in them than just things to look up or track down. There are language and literacy classes, puppet shows and storytellers, fax machines, tutors, computerized card catalogs in a dozen different languages, museum passes, lecture series, classes, rental typewriters and computers, even tool-lending services.

The following handful of recommendations may help you further streamline your library research:

• Get used to using computers. They make research push-button simple. The old *Readers' Guide to Periodical Literature*, for instance, is going the way of the wooly mammoth and is now computerized at most libraries. It's called Infotrak, and with five minutes of practice you can save yourself hours of page flipping.

You punch in the subject you're looking for, and the computer searches its file of over four hundred magazines going back roughly ten years. You can then print out citations for any article contained therein.

Many libraries can also provide computer database searches, either free or for a modest fee (depending on their budget), giving you access to several thousand databases on every conceivable subject. Computer searches can be used for any kind of question but are best for complex, cross-referenced topics or for material that is very old or very new (not in the library yet). Only a few databases currently provide anything more than citations for research material, so you must still hunt down the material (e.g., the entire text) yourself.

You can, of course, do your own computer search if you have a computer and modem, and want to subscribe to a network such as CompuServe, one of the cheapest and largest.

• Devise some form of shorthand to expedite note-taking. Use *g* for "ing," *w* for "with," = for "equals," etc. (for et cetera). Shrtn wds. Spd thngs up. It cms in hndy fr intrvws, too.

• Do not sit near the children's section. Certain areas of the library are noisier, busier and more distracting than others and should be avoided if you have, like me, a Sesame-Street attention span. These forbidden zones include anything near the reference desk, the checkout counter, the children's section, the microfilm machines and the magazine rack where every time you glance up from your studies you're seduced by a swarm of cover photographs specifically *designed* to grab your attention.

Unfortunately, many writers (including me) have spent too much time writing in cafes and are used to people-watching when they work anywhere outside of home. Perhaps it's the lonesomeness of the business. But every time you allow yourself to be distracted, it takes another moment to refocus your attention, and you often find yourself rereading the same paragraph half a dozen times.

• Avoid photocopying research material whenever possible. Unless the library is about to close or you really need an entire passage, photocopying only moves the research from the library to your house. It also costs you money.

On the other hand, if you want a copy of a magazine article but don't want to pay for it, do not tear it out. Sit down and take notes. I've seen people do this: They cough violently while simultaneously ripping out an entire article and slipping it in their briefcase, leaving nothing but a jagged hole for the next reader. If it weren't for the fact that I've done it myself, I'd tell on them.

• Broaden your peripheral vision. Browse the shelves on either side of the book you're after. One of the most insightful and relevant books I found on the subject of research—although it was about scientific research—was sitting a few books down from the one listed under "Research—Writing" in the card catalog.

• Get in the habit of perusing the bibliographies at the end of books for other sources of research material.

• If you need to find out-of-print books, go to secondhand booksellers. For a modest fee they can often track it down for you.

• To find photographs to accompany a writing project, try libraries, historical societies, museums, stock-photo agencies, tourist boards, professional associations, government agencies and PR departments. Some charge, some don't. Some need permissions, some don't.

• The U.S. government is the largest publisher in the country, each year rolling out thousands of free consumer how-to booklets, cookbooks, guidebooks, government speeches, posters, magazines, dictionaries, indexes and statistics. You might as well use them. You're paying for them.

• Reference librarians are not the only people who can assist you with research. There are professional researchers and information brokers (*Literary Market Place* and the Yellow Pages both list them), and the majority of them have computer search skills. There are university press offices, professional associations and public relations people who may be willing to help you with some legwork if it's in their interest. And there are even magazine and company interns who can often take some of the burden off a weighty research project.

Seeing for Yourself: Hands-On Research

A writer whose research emanates solely from libraries is like a botanist who never leaves the laboratory to smell the flowers. He ends up compiling, not creating, and his writing rings with the hollow clank of the classroom.

In fact, library research is to writing what classroom learning is to education: half the story. The rest takes place out in the world (or deep within yourself), and quite often what is learned in school has to be unlearned in life anyway.

Part of the appeal of the writing profession is that it offers the opportunity to step out from behind a desk and meet the world head-on. It is therefore incumbent on writers to take advantage of this advantage, or else what is the "free" in freelancing for? Do not become, as Henry Miller once cautioned, "a writer who never leaves the birdcage; who writes about life without ever living it." Besides, the more you get out, the more you will be able to tolerate the solitude.

Therefore, *if there is an experience to be had in a writing project, have it.*

If you have a novel set in Little Italy, sublet a studio there for a month, get to know the old shopkeepers, try out the pizza and cannoli, dance the tarantella at the street fairs.

If you're writing about a product, use it, observe people buying it, break it and take it back to the store to see how customer relations handles it, study drawings and specs, talk to customers, assembly-line workers, even the competition.

If you aspire to playwriting, get some acting experience, even if it's only in the classroom.

If you're putting together an essay on team sports in school, drive yourself to the core and remember how it felt to be last on the phys-ed lineup when they were choosing sides for basketball. Get mad all over again. Tape it.

Nothing brings authenticity to my writing more than reporting from the trenches, turning on the senses, being there.

No amount of bookworming will bring to a story on self-defense classes the sight of a woman screaming at the top of her lungs and kicking a heavily padded "assailant" in the groin hard enough to buckle him like a ruptured metal pipe.

No secondhand description of the durability of a new line of toys will substitute for the feeling of personally hurling one against a wall in the toy-company test lab.

No amount of hearsay will prove to you that dowsers are for real until you witness someone use a fishing pole for a dowsing rod and find underground water where a team of geologists could not.

There are two kinds of truths that must be brought to bear upon your writing. One is academic truth, the kind that can be fact-checked. The other is visceral truth, the kind you know in your gut. Recognizing visceral truth comes from bringing the emotional and sensory elements into your research, the wisdom of the road, the insight that comes only from having been there yourself.

It is hard to describe, but readers know it when they see it, the same way that people do not need to "understand" classical music or abstract painting in order to be moved by it. What gives it authenticity is simply recognition, a reader saying, "I know that feeling."

My story about the use of atom smashers to cure cancer—which has sold and resold more times than almost anything I've ever written—is a good case in point. Here was a supremely informative piece, an impeccably *factual* story—and one in dire need of the human element to bring it to life.

This was provided by watching a young woman with a brain tumor being strapped beneath one of these huge and inconceivably complex machines by a phalanx of shirt-sleeved physicists. I was struck by two things: the sight of her breath rising and falling gently in the long moment before they turned the machine on; and the image of her sister, sitting in an adjacent lead-lined room, anxiously fingering the binding of a book she thought she might read during the hour-long session.

Being there in person was the only way I could hope to communicate what the story was really about: how utterly fragile we are, and how monumental are our efforts to attenuate that fact; what a fingers-crossed affair technological progress really is; how oddly poetic this particular science is, using the invisible to battle the invisible.

Interviews are no different. They demand, as often as you can manage it, the personal touch.

Advertisers spend billions trying to figure out what makes people tick. Your task is to do the same, tempered with a keen and compassionate regard for the dramas that orchestrate all our lives, the unspoken desires and dreads that move just below the surface.

Most people, I believe, despite their protestations, want to be revealed or, more to the point, recognized. And interviewing, I think, is largely the ability to make people feel safe enough to be themselves in your presence. If they trust you, and if you are utterly attentive, your problem will not be getting them to open up but quite the opposite.

For this reason, here are two good excuses to bring a tape deck to interviews: 1) People talk at roughly 130 words per minute, faster when they're excited, and it's impossible to even type that fast. And 2) you can let the machine catch their words while you catch what is in between them: the nervous tics, the fidgeting, the way they breathe or shift their eyes, where the lines are on their faces, that little muscle at the back of the jaw, beneath the ear, that flexes and twitches . . . when their teeth are clenching.

You must be ready to capture the subtlest gestures that issue from people's normally guarded faces, the blips of emotion that otherwise escape unnoticed—like the particles that flash into view for a billionth of a second when atoms are smashed together at the speed of light and then disappear again into the cosmic soup. You must be a photographic plate on which the slightest trace of drama leaves an imprint.

Take note, also, of the surroundings, what my old journalism professor called the "environmental details." Trophies, paintings, quotes tacked up on the refrigerator, the position of furniture, the books on the nightstand, the food in the icebox, the doodles on the desk blotter. These things often say more about people than what people say about themselves.

Caveat: There will be times when you'll tell yourself that it would be quicker and cheaper to do interviews over the phone than to shower, dress, get in the car and slog through traffic there and back. And when you feel backed up with deadlines or pinched for cash, you will probably be right.

Doing it in person is not as convenient. But you can easily slip into the habit of never leaving the house, the office, or the library and thereby rob yourself of much of the delight and diversity of the job, and rob your research of the full weight of authority.

Your move.

In or out of the office, however, a writer is constantly researching. The Argentinian novelist Jorge Luis Borges used to read encyclopedias, for example, the way some people read books. Hemingway used to say that he learned as much about how to write from painters—in his case Heironymus Bosch, Goya, Cézanne, van Gogh and Gauguin—as from writers. Composition, he said, is composition, and harmony is harmony. The novelist Bernard Malamud claimed to have learned about rhythm, timing and comic presence from studying Charlie Chaplin.

Just like the greening of bargaining power, research is ongoing and ideally all-encompassing, and it begins when you take up the reins of the writing profession. You are always gathering knowledge, always tearing up magazines and newspapers and stuffing your idea file to the bursting point, always eavesdropping, always the voyeur.

The depth of your writing is a function of how absorbent you are. Writers must first inhale the world, and then exhale it as writing. Art, it has been said, is the discharge of experience, and the more deeply informed you are by your receptivity, by your life's experiences, the richer your writing. The more of the world you "in-spire" (literally "breathe in"), the more you are capable of inspiring the world.

Therefore, living well is not only the best revenge, but the best research material.

Undo Influence: Removing Bias

In research, as in goal setting, you are far more likely to find what you're looking for. So it pays to be clear about what you're looking for.

But not so clear that you become blind to anything except the facts, figures and testimony that will support your foregone conclusions, with little regard for the whole truth, or what radio commentator Paul Harvey calls "the rest of the story."

This is not research. It is manipulation.

The truth is not simple. It is also not convenient. And although most people chafe at the thought of diluting the power and sanctimony of their opinions by admitting contradictory evidence, a fair trial demands it. Only when people are given all the facts are they capable of making truly informed decisions.

Therefore, be aware of your biases. Research shouldn't prop up your preconceptions; it should reveal the truth.

(Also be aware of the distinction between fact and opinion, and of the editorializing that turns one into the other. "The writer Hemingway" is fact. "The great writer Hemingway" is opinion.)

Ultimately, a writer cannot serve if he or she resents the truth for its inconvenience and overlooks a full accounting of things because one ugly little fact threatens to undo some boast you made to an editor in trying to sell a piece.

Early in my career, I pitched a story around on the search for a male birth-control pill, an incarnation of which was then widely used in China. In the 1950s, the Chinese had discovered that men who had a diet high in cottonseed oil had very low fertility rates, and with a population fast approaching a billion people, they had plenty of incentive to try and develop a birth-control pill based on this observation. What they came up with is called gossypol and is made out of the ordinary cotton plant.

They claim it does everything scientists have always wanted a male birth-control pill to do: It stops the production of sperm without stopping sex drive, it's reversible and it's nontoxic.

Unfortunately, I saw what I wanted to see: a hot story about how the male birth-control pill is right around the corner. The trouble was, after I got the go-ahead from a major national magazine, my research kept unearthing profound reservations within the American medical community about both the true toxicity of gossypol and the clinical integrity of the studies conducted by the Chinese. It would be a decade, if ever, they insisted, before gossypol became available in the States.

But this information didn't jibe with the story I had promised, so I underplayed it.

Miraculously, nobody saw fit to fire off an indignant letter to the editor when the piece appeared, and I was spared the humiliation of admitting to the shabby integrity of my own studies.

I would like to think of this as merely a sin of enthusiasm, but given the small matter of professional ethics, I'm afraid it was more than that.

Impartiality is tough to come by, and objectivity, as any honest journalist will tell you, more the ideal than the real. But it is the only way to make an *honest* living as a writer.

Authenticity and the Voice of the Author

Having said all this, I still insist that a writer must be in the writing. Research at its most authentic—and the word refers to "one who does things himself"—does not distract you from using your own voice.

Research is not about dictation, taking down word for word what others have said. It is about discovery—discovering what you have to say. "I hate quotations," Emerson once griped. "Tell me what you know."

Confucius say "Learning without thinking is useless." And indeed, nothing substitutes for original research, for thinking deeply about a subject. The greatest store of information at your disposal is your own library of knowledge: the things life has taught you, the things you have been willing to learn from it.

Writers are not merely fact collectors, but extrapolators and synthesists. By not throwing yourself into the fray, you are no more involved in the process of learning than when you had to memorize schoolbooks and spit the information back out at test time.

Unfortunately, that is precisely what we were trained to do. I recall a sociology class in college in which the professor asked how many students would prefer multiple-choice tests and how many would rather have essay-type exams. I was the only student who raised my hand in favor of essays—in favor of thinking instead of memorizing—and everyone glared at me in disbelief.

To hell with 'em. Step out from behind the stacks and think out loud. Get in on the action. When you've finished your library research, your interviews, and your fieldwork, sit down and ask yourself how *you* feel about the subject. Draw conclusions, make conjectures. Theorize, interpret, translate, decipher, opine. Draw out meaning, identify patterns, kindle relationships, become connective tissue in the body of knowledge.

Ask the questions that haven't been asked, find the angles that haven't been slanted, assume the positions that haven't been assumed. Take the past and breathe the present into it. Answer the question, "So what?"

Communicate not just the facts, but the emotions. "We know so much," said D.H. Lawrence, "and we feel so little." Writing lives only with the life you put into it, he said. If you put no life into it—no thrill, delight or discovery—then it is a dead thing, and no amount of "thorough and scientific work" will revive it.

This, too, is what imparts originality to your writing, what separates you from everyone else, what makes it impossible for anyone to steal your work. Facts may belong to everyone, but the voice, the spirit, of a piece is solely yours; nobody else has lived your life. Research, therefore, should also be the search for your own voice. The more personal your writing, the more universal its appeal.

Over the years, in fact, I have found that the writing into which I pour my most authentic voice is always my best. It is the most satisfying, the most work, and the least edited. It is also the writing that has won me whatever honors and awards I have achieved in this profession.

It is for this reason that, to me, the single most infuriating and discouraging aspect of writing has been editors who take out that voice and leave only the facts, even if they do so for the perfectly legitimate purposes of fitting to space or leaving room for the advertisers. The writing then becomes like freeze-dried food; it fills the stomach and starves the senses.

Do not just take from the body of knowledge on a subject, but add to it, so that somday another writer calling up a citation of yours during his or her own research will find there not just a recitation of other people's research and ideas, but a few of your own; not just the facts, but the soul of the person who wrote it. When writers talk about leaving something behind, about "making a difference," that, I believe, is largely what they're talking about.

Journal-ism: The Diary as a Research Tool

About the best way I know to practice speaking in the first person as well as generating some of that "original research," is to keep a journal. In order to "write what you know," you have to remember what you know (re-search?).

Furthermore, writing for yourself is an indispensable part of writing for others, something more than a few famous writers have discovered: Anaïs Nin, F. Scott Fitzgerald, John Dos Passos, Oscar Wilde and Virginia Woolf. John Steinbeck kept a journal during the writing of *East of Eden*, and it, too, became a book: *Journal of a Novel*.

Here, then, are half a dozen good reasons why I think writers should also be journal-ists:

1. There is a built-in guinea-pig factor to a journal. It is a safe place to rehearse thoughts before articulating them or unleashing them onto the world.

2. A journal is a fabulous back file, providing you with a greatly expanded repertoire of anecdotes, revelations, observations, conversations and impressions; all the rich but forgettable details that make life, and writing, come alive.

It also makes a good scrapbook for pictures, poems, fortune cookie and horoscope messages, letters, cogent quotes, newspaper headlines, doodlings, drawings and graffiti. It's all grist for the mill.

3. Keeping a journal is good practice for researching. A certain portion of any journal will entail confrontations with yourself, and in hashing out a problem, you are in essence doing research: you are digging, thinking an idea through, playing the devil's advocate, and asking questions that may lead to answers.

4. Journaling is good for your shorthand. When you're in the midst of a fast and furious stream of consciousness, you want your hand to keep up with your synapses. You learn to write tight.

5. Writing in a journal just before bed provides great fodder for dreams,

since whatever is on your mind then is most likely what you will dream about. And dreams, if you record them in the journal as well, represent one of the most profound ways of knowing. Dreams tie in to events, patterns emerge, guidance is offered, memories are dredged up. And all of this is research material. Why sleep through it?

6. Finally, journaling is a wonderful antidote to writer's block. Writing in a journal is writing unabashedly. You say whatever you want, without the constraints of audience or editor, or even moral, linguistic, or space considerations. Just make sure to hide the journal from your kids, your creditors, and your ex.

Gullibles' Travels: Don't Believe Everything You Read

I recently read that a sizable number of people questioned in a large survey thought Chernobyl was a ski resort, DNA a food additive, and protons something you put on salad.

It is astonishing the amount of erroneous information floating around out there.

It is equally appalling how often writers contribute to it by not bothering to verify their facts, by believing everything they read, and by slothfully accepting another writer's research as gospel. They thereby pass errata not just from writer to writer, but from generation to generation, and even from century to century. I, for one, have plenty on my hands just repeating my own mistakes, without having to repeat someone else's.

Just as scientists and lawyers cannot go public with insufficient evidence, neither can writers. Responsible research must demystify, not confound. Writers must cultivate a healthy skepticism for even the most time-honored truths. After all, what were facts five hundred years ago—the Earth is flat, for instance—have since been disproven; which of our current crop of certainties will meet the same fate?

Facts are not always facts. I have even heard the public library described as "an ammunition dump of unexploded arguments." Therefore, writers must authenticate their facts, even if it means bringing legends crashing down to earth, like the apple that supposedly inspired Sir Isaac Newton to discover the law of gravity and that most biographers consider an apocryphal story.

In the course of auditioning facts, I have run across a startling array of misconceptions, misquotes and misinformations, and have come to the conclusion that "fiction" is not much farther from the truth than fact. Some examples:

- George Washington never chopped down a cherry tree, and Galileo never dropped weights off the Leaning Tower of Pisa.
- Water does not always flow downhill. It flows uphill in trees.
- Samuel Johnson never said, "The road to hell is paved with good intentions." He said only that "Hell is paved with good intentions." And Lord

Acton never said, "Power corrupts, and absolute power corrupts absolutely." He said, "Power *tends* to corrupt, and absolute power corrupts absolutely."

- Etymologically, a radical and a fundamentalist are exactly the same thing: one who goes to the root, foundation or underlying principle of a thing.

Verification means second-guessing the "experts," even asking them for the names of colleagues who disagree with their views and interviewing them. It means finding out the proper spelling of people's names, even when they seem obvious. It means double-checking statistics or anecdotes that seem incredible to you.

Often you will find three completely different statistics on the same subject in three different articles, and it doesn't mean any of them are wrong. It could mean that each researcher used different criteria. The circulation of a magazine, for example, might be a million if you're counting only the number of issues printed each month, or three million if you're counting the number of people who read it, which includes what are called "pass-along" readers (family members or people in doctors' offices).

It also means updating facts. I lost a valuable client once because I neglected to update my information in reselling a piece; I was informed by an irate editor after the piece ran that the organization I wrote about went belly-up—over a year earlier.

Verification also means that writers follow the example of Theseus, who laid down a trail of string in the labyrinth of the Minotaur so that he could retrace his steps once he had slain the beast. We must write down all our sources, so that we can backtrack and retrieve material when an editor, shaken to the roots by the revelation that Galileo didn't really drop weights off the Leaning Tower of Pisa, wants to see proof.

Purloined Letters: The Spell of Plagiarism

Originality, it has been said, is the fine art of remembering what you heard, but forgetting where you heard it.

One of the dangers of research is discovering that others may have written about your subject more eloquently, humorously, insightfully—better—than you can, and the temptation to shoplift from the store of knowledge is tremendous. By doing so, your writing suddenly comes into possession of new power, and like being drunk, you feel more articulate than you really are.

In classical times, a "plagiary" was one who kidnapped children. Writers' words are their children, and you cannot adopt them without permission.

Although trafficking in stolen goods is illegal, what is more at issue than the exigencies of the law is your integrity as a writer, and your belief in yourself. In making a shambles of the Eighth Commandment, in taking another person's writing as your own, you demonstrate a tremendous lack of faith in yourself, an admission that you will never be good enough to be noticed.

Think ahead. Ask yourself how you would feel if you were caught, if the person you pirated were to write a scathing review of your book, if your colleagues (whose esteem is the main one that counts to writers) were to scorn you, if publishers were to blacklist you. When people become famous, the public and the press delight in digging up their every dirty little secret, and with writers the first thing they scrutinize is your writings.

Also, ask yourself how *you* would feel if someone filched your favorite lines and put their by-line above it.

Ultimately, plagiarists are like kleptomaniacs, who for the most part do not really need what they steal. There is an element of the self-destructive in it. But just as one business may not appropriate another's logo, motto or jingle with impunity, a writer cannot loot the literary past without paying a price. If the law or the profession doesn't catch you, your conscience will.

And yet, it is abundantly clear that literature abounds—nay, swarms—with lootings and grave robbings, often with the barest attempts at cover-up. Samuel Coleridge was not only accused, but proven to have plagiarized. Gail Sheehy (*Passages*) and Alex Haley (*Roots*) both paid hefty compensatory damages for plagiarism. Even the immortal phrase, "Ask not what your country can do for you . . ." was swiped by John Kennedy from a line by Oliver Wendell Holmes.

A few thousand years of such indiscretions, however, have confirmed that there is a fine line between influence and plagiarism, and that the naturally imitative phase writers often go through in their careers can turn into a plagiaristic temperament without proper restraint.

So if you are going to steal, at least fuse it into your own experience and make it new. Don't just switch by-lines.

Hold That Thought: Knowing When to Stop Research

In a short story by Leo Tolstoy called "How Much Land Does a Man Need?" a man is given the opportunity to own as much land as he can run around in a day. At the end of that day, having run himself to a frenzy, the man collapses and dies of exhaustion. It turns out that six feet is about all he really needs.

What there is to know about most subjects is inexhaustible. You are not. It is therefore imperative to know when to stop researching and start writing.

In research, as in nature, one thing flows into another, one inquiry leads into the next and the next and the next, and you must draw the line somewhere. You must know the boundaries of your time, your tolerance and especially your search. *If you don't know the questions you want answered, you won't know when you've answered them*, and research can go on 'til the cows come home. At some point, you must stop and write—even though a hundred books still lay unread, a score of witnesses could still testify, and a small infinity of things remain to be learned about your subject.

One reason it is often easier to continue researching is that, for most writers, researching is easier than writing. It is also difficult to know when you are procrastinating and when a story has simply not revealed itself to you yet. Still, there is a temptation to hide in the research phase of a project, the same way that some people stay in school as a way to avoid stepping out into the real world, putting themselves on the line.

At some point, though, you get only diminishing returns. Studies even show that students who study more than thirty-five hours a week earn poorer grades than those studying under thirty-five hours.

Judging when to stop should be based on how much time you have, how much money you're being paid, how important the project is to your career, how complex the project is, and your own judgment as to what the story demands.

With the nuclear-free zone story, I had to strictly limit the scope of my research or I would have been quickly overwhelmed with the sheer proportions of the undertaking. As it was I had to wade through great heaving mounds of "literature" on political and antinuclear campaigns, corporate financial records, lengthy treatises on the American city's role in foreign policy and the economics of military spending, and government statistics that could put an actuary into a coma.

I stopped researching this piece when I had answered all my interview questions, when I noticed that I had more information in my notes than in the articles I was digging up, when my allotted research time was running out, and when I simply reached my saturation point.

In this case, as in most, the research displayed the iceberg effect: Only a small portion showed and the bulk stayed under the surface. That is, you will generally gather a great deal more information than you will ever use. Gold is usually embedded in ore.

Research is also demanding enough that by the time you finish, you're tempted to show it all off. Resist. Studies with laboratory rats show that overcrowding leads to confusion and aggression. Learn to be discriminating, to know what goes in and what stays out.

"How many books do we read from which the writer lacked the courage to tie off the umbilical cord?" asks the writer Annie Dillard about the tendency of writers to cram their writing with research just because they suffered to get it. "How many gifts do we open from which the writer neglected to remove the price tag? Is it pertinent, is it courteous, for us to learn what it cost the writer personally?"

If you do it right, you will inevitably end up using only a fraction of the research material you generate. And once you begin to write, you must use the eye of a sculptor, to help you carve away what you don't want and reveal the true story beneath it.

Some final field-notes on calling it quits:

If I'm interested in a topic, I do more research than I really need, just out of curiosity. This has advantages and disadvantages. On one hand, knowing more gives me a deeper perspective, and I discover more dimensions than I thought were there at the start. A piece on environmentalists versus loggers will turn out to have many more than just the two sides: scientists, politicians, even carpenters. On the other hand, there is more technical material to have to step away from, and more material to organize.

SETH ZUCKERMAN
ENVIRONMENTAL WRITER, *NEWSWEEK, SIERRA, NATION*
AUTHOR, *SAVING OUR ANCIENT FORESTS*

I usually err on the side of too much research, being too conscientious, and only stop when I begin to know more than the people I'm interviewing. Sometimes it's just a form of procrastination. That's why deadlines are important.

Before I start writing, I make a list of the main facts I want to make sure to get into the piece. Then, for a big feature, I may spend several days poring over my material to start getting it up in my head, up in the air, like a juggler, working myself up into a state where I've got all this material wound up, and then I write.

PAUL RAUBER
POLITICAL REPORTER, *MOTHER JONES, SIERRA, THE NATION*

Ideally I like to stop researching before I write, because once I get into a book I shift into writing mode, I'm in my characters' heads, and I don't want to step out to do more research. It never works, though.

I do roughly three months of research for nine months of writing, and I always research more than I need. The problem then becomes the urge to spell it all out, to lard up the book with details. A few months later, I go back and cut it out because by then I can see what I've done. There is an inordinate likelihood, for instance, that some character with an arcane profession will be telling my detective every little detail about his profession—details I slaved to find.

SUSAN DUNLAP
MYSTERY WRITER, *DETECTIVE JILL SMITH* SERIES

POSTSCRIPT

To succeed in this business of writing, to reach the goals you set for yourself, you must be convinced that what you want to write is the single most important thing in the world, though of course it isn't. But you will need just such a foolish, arrogant and vital faith to go the distance, along with an ample sense of humor.

In the early years, you will undoubtedly feel like a house of cards while fate holds its breath. But in sticking with it, this uneasy feeling passes. You feel stronger and stabler each year, more indomitable in your resolve, more certain of your staying power.

Still, as an acquaintance of mine—a writer well into his eighth decade—once told me: If you are determined to be a writer, just remember that the first sixty years are the hardest.

Annuit Coeptis

A P P E N D I X
Books, Organizations and Resources

This appendix of books, organizations and resources for writers is by no means exhaustive. It is I who is exhaustive.

I am still, however, holding out for that extra hundred years, just to read.

Books

Chapter One

Growing a Business, Paul Hawken, Simon & Schuster, 1987.

An inspiring and unusual business book, full of unconventional wisdom about the hidden qualities that make small businesses succeed, primarily that business is an expression of who you are.

The New Venture Handbook, Ronald E. Merrill and Henry D. Sedgwick, American Management Assn., 1987.

The subtitle sums it up: "Everything you need to know to start and run your own business." A comprehensive, readable guide, low on jargon, high on practicality. I give it an *A*.

Running a One-Person Business, Claude Whitmeyer, et al, Whitmeyer/Raspberry/Phillips, Ten Speed Press, 1988.

One of the most personable books I've seen on being self-employed. As attuned to the emotional/human side of business as the managerial/financial.

Ambition: The Secret Passion, Joseph Epstein, Dutton, 1980.

A thorough examination of what the author considers the engine of achievement, its pros and cons, and the price we pay for it. Many in-depth profiles, including several famous writers. An intriguing chapter about the power of money.

Swim With the Sharks Without Being Eaten Alive, and *Beware the Naked Man Who Offers You His Shirt*, Harvey Mackay, William Morrow & Co., 1988 and 1990 respectively.

These books, especially *Sharks*, are standouts among business books. Filled with brilliant insights and anecdotes, sharply written and singularly entertaining, they are gospels of great advice on being in business, even if they are a bit

Machiavellian. They won't bore you to death with business-school platitudes and complicated charts.

Pathfinders, Gail Sheehy, Bantam, 1981.
An epic-sized exploration of the characteristics that enable some people to overcome life's predictable and unpredictable crises and passages. In-depth profiles and interpretation of what Sheehy (author of *Passages*) calls people of "high well-being."

Transitions, William Bridges, Addison-Wesley, 1980.
A timeless book that has come back to inspire me repeatedly over the years. It perfectly describes where growing people always seem to find themselves — in transition — and suggests that chaos and uncertainty are essential stages of growth. A beautifully and simply written book explaining the art of making changes.

The Path of Least Resistance, Robert Fritz, Stillpoint Publishing, 1984.
A wonderfully convincing argument for "going with the flow," for changing your orientation from reacting to life's circumstances and your own urgings, to creating what you want in a very straightforward manner. Pain is inevitable, he believes; suffering is optional.

Solitude, Anthony Storr, Ballantine, 1988.
The best book I've seen on the role, and importance, of solitude in the creative life. Particularly appropriate for writers.

Rotten Rejections, Edited by Andre Bernard, Pushcart Press, 1990.
A true friend to the writer, this little gem is a compilation of famous kiss-offs throughout literary history. A comfort on dark days, it will remind you that editors don't necessarily know it all.

Chapter Two
Wishcraft, Barbara Sher, Random House, 1979.
A classic among the hordes of "make-your-dreams-come-true" self-help books. Powerfully and humorously written, it is an indispensable guide for people who have lost their way and want hopeful, but not at all pie-in-the-sky, advice on realigning with their missions in life. Two thumbs up!

What Color Is Your Parachute? A Practical Manual for Jobhunters and Career Changers, Richard Bolles, Ten Speed Press, 1990.
Four years on the *New York Times* bestseller list, and deservedly so, this is a standard-bearer among job-hunting guides. Written with tremendous wit and warmth, it is filled with illustrations, charts, cartoons, drawings, and some of the most cogent and concise life-planning strategies on the market.

Procrastination, Jane Burka and Lenora Yuen, Addison-Wesley, 1983.

Written by two psychologists, it is a tour de force on the phenomenon of why we procrastinate, along with plenty of how-to for overcoming it.

Career Opportunities for Writers, Rosemary Guiley, Facts on File, 1985.

One of the most comprehensive guides to jobs in the writing/editing/publication fields. Nearly one hundred distinct jobs are described in terms of responsibilities, salaries, employment prospects and experience needed. Includes a fabulous appendix of trade associations and publications, as well as colleges and universities that offer studies in communications.

Opportunities in Writing Careers, Elizabeth Foote-Smith, National Textbook Co., 1982.

A how-to book that is also that rarest of things: a page-turner. Delightfully personal and thoughtful and loaded with anecdotes about famous writers, it is entertaining, if a bit superficial.

Jobs for Writers, Kirk Polking, Writer's Digest Books, 1980. (Out of print.)

A solid, informative volume broken into short sections on over forty different writing jobs, from advertising and book reviewing to public relations and speechwriting, each written by a pro in the field.

Chapter Three

In Search of Excellence: Lessons from America's Best-Run Companies, Thomas J. Peters and Robert H. Waterman, Harper & Row, 1982.

An exemplar among books on what makes successful companies tick. Though focused on Fortune 500 companies, its management, marketing and business strategies are eminently applicable to the small-business person.

CareerTracking: 26 Success Shortcuts to the Top, James Calano and Jeffrey Salzman, Simon & Schuster, 1988.

A highly distilled, readable book filled with digestible, cut-out-and-tack-on-the-bulletin-board tips on succeeding as an entrepreneur. Snappy and entertaining.

What They Didn't Teach You at Harvard Business School, Mark McCormack, Bantam, 1984.

A friendly, unconventional, people-oriented book that picks up where business schools leave off, with street-smart teachings from the school of hard knocks.

The Writer's Handbook, Sylvia Burack, The Writer Inc., 1988.

Dozens of short articles by famous writers on selling everything from poetry to fiction. Very readable.

Ogilvy on Advertising, David Ogilvy, Crown Books, 1983.

The crown prince of advertising, Ogilvy (of Ogilvy & Mather) gives the lowdown on the ad business, with his trademark outspokenness and wit. A great read not just for those interested in ad writing, but for anyone who has to sell a product. Good copy.

The Complete Book of Scriptwriting, J. Michael Straczynski, Writer's Digest Books, 1987.

Broken into four sections on writing for TV, radio, film and theatre, this thorough, insightful, and conversational guide to breaking into these markets is also an enjoyable read.

Sell Copy, Webster Kizwa, Writer's Digest Books, 1978. (Out of print.)

A thorough if slightly dated look at the world of "sell copy": ad, brochure, direct-mail, speech and publicity writing designed to sell ideas and products.

The Craft of Copywriting, Alastair Crompton, Prentice-Hall, 1979.

A behind-the-scenes look at the craft of ad writing, full of professional advice, how-to and wit.

Corporate Scriptwriting Book, Donna Matrazzo, Communicom Publishing Co., 1985.

A plainly written, step-by-step book on writing scripts for corporate films, video sales presentations, slide training programs, and so on.

Travel Writer's Handbook, Louise Purwin Zobel, Writer's Digest Books, 1984. (Out of print.)

A wonderfully anecdotal and thorough book, one of the best, on what you need to know to fulfill the almost universal dream of making money by traveling.

How to Get Your Book Published, Herbert W. Bell, Writer's Digest Books, 1985. (Out of print.)

Simple, insider advice on every stage of the publishing game and on creating a mutually beneficial partnership with publishers, whose viewpoint is amply portrayed.

Chapter Four

Working From Home, Paul and Sarah Edwards, J.P. Tarcher, 1987.

Encyclopedic in scope, easy to read, loaded with everything you could ever want to know about working out of your house, making the transition to doing so, coping with the drawbacks, and enjoying the rewards. This doorstop of a book has it all, from the practical to the psychological.

Stay Home and Mind Your Own Business, Jo Frohbieter-Mueller, Betterway Publications Inc., 1987.

A simple guide to running a cottage industry, with generous coverage of setting up and maintaining an office.

The Home Office, Peg Contrucci, Prentice-Hall, 1985.

A detailed how-to book on financing, designing and capitalizing on a home-based office.

How to Qualify for the Home Office Deduction, Katherine M. Klotzburger, Betterway Publications Inc., 1985.

A fast and easy-to-read guide to qualifying for a home office deduction. Written in extremely lay terminology, with plenty of elucidating court cases of people who did and did not qualify, and why.

Home Offices & Workspaces, Sunset-Lane Publishing Co., 1986.

One of the series of home improvement books by the publishers of *Sunset Magazine*. This is a picture book with loads of ingenious and inspiring ideas for converting unused space into office space.

Chapter Five

The Writer's Guide to Self-Promotion and Publicity, Elane Feldman, Writer's Digest Books, 1990.

A treasure trove of ideas on getting attention for your writing, mostly geared toward book and magazine writers. Especially good for novelists who tend to believe you can't publicize fiction. Ain't true.

Guerrilla Marketing and *Guerrilla Marketing Attack*, Jay Conrad Levinson, Houghton Mifflin, 1985 and 1989 respectively.

Among the cream of the crop in the area of promoting small businesses, whatever they are. A real underliner, full of simple, do-able strategies, as well as a discussion of the attitudes that make for good promoters. A book that will make you want to jump up and get things going.

Expose Yourself, Melba Beals, Chronicle Books, 1990.

A clear, concise guide to using public relations skills to promote your business and get your message across, whether to your next door neighbor or to national TV.

How to Write Irresistible Query Letters, Lisa Collier Cool, Writer's Digest Books, 1990.

Probably the definitive book on the subject. A breeze to get through, pared to the bone, and filled with sample proposals. An excellent reference book on an essential sales tool.

The Writer's Digest Guide to Manuscript Formats, Dian Buchman and Seli Groves, Writer's Digest Books, 1987.

Looks count. And here's a thorough, down-to-the-pica description of how to submit professional-looking manuscripts, proposals, cover letters, and anything else you want an editor to have a good first impression of.

Chapter Six

Prosperity Handbook, Michael Fries and C. Holland Taylor, Communications Research, 1984.

A beautifully distilled and entertaining book about basic economics and how it affects the average person. Focuses on the role of money in our lives and the power of a little knowledge about it.

Hunger for More: Searching for Values in an Age of Greed, Lawrence Shames, Random House, 1989.

Written by the ethics columnist for *Esquire* magazine (what an appropriate last name, Shames), this is a wry, fascinating investigation of America's obsession with money, success and acquisition, at the expense of deeper values. A brilliantly drawn portrait of a national addiction on the brink of major change: a reevaluation of the definition of success.

Moneylove, Jerry Gillies, Warner Books, 1978.

One of the better among the crop of books on "prosperity consciousness," this book is a short, exciting read. Makes a convincing case for reconsidering the typical person's poverty orientation, the feeling that there is never enough.

Prospering Woman, Ruth Ross, Bantam, 1985.

Another of the "prosperity consciousness" books, this one is based squarely on the axiom that "what you believe is what you achieve." It prescribes a multitude of ways to go about reprogramming the way you think about money and abundance. Not for women only.

Less Is More: The Art of Voluntary Simplicity, Goldian VandenBroeck, Harper, 1978.

A far-ranging anthology of quotes on living the life of voluntary simplicity, this book presents as eloquent an argument as there is for reexamining the rat race.

Wisdom of Insecurity, Alan Watts, Random House, 1968.

Subtitled "A Message for an Age of Anxiety," this is essentially a book of philosophy that argues that the mad scramble for security in life can only make you feel more insecure. Not a breezy read, but a valuable one full of insight, especially for anyone heading away from the "security" of a job.

The Seven Laws of Money, Michael Phillips, Random House, 1974.

Though somewhat dated, this is an unusual money book, based on the ancient concept of "Right Livelihood"—the idea that, among other things, money is a by-product of doing your "right work." Heavy on intuition and optimism.

Wealth Addiction, Philip Slater, E.P. Dutton, 1980.

A provocative expose of the pervasive addiction to money and the ill-fated belief that money buys happiness. A keen diagnosis of a widespread problem and the ways in which we can kick the habit.

Do What You Love, the Money Will Follow, Marsha Sinetar, Dell, 1989.

A book that has developed nearly cult status. It is for those who want confirmation of something they have either suspected for a long time or have already discovered to be true. Or who want guidance on how to make it happen. It is a book about integrating love and work and making it pay off.

Writer's Legal Companion, Brad Bunnin and Peter Beren, Addison-Wesley, 1988.

If you're going to get only one book on the relationship between writers and the law—contracts, copyright, collaborating, libel, and so forth—make it this one. A practical, nonjargony how-to guide to keeping your wits about you in legal matters and keeping your money in your own pocket.

Chapter Seven

Getting to Yes: Negotiating Agreement Without Giving In, Roger Fisher and William Ury, Penguin Books, 1981.

One of the best books about the subject of win-win negotiating, despite the implications of the subtitle. Applicable to all kinds of conflict resolution, from domestic to business to political.

Art of Negotiating, Gerard L. Nierenberg, Simon & Schuster, 1984.

A more in-depth handbook on negotiation, with a strong psychological approach and scores of case studies. Dry, but thorough.

You Can Negotiate Anything, Herb Cohen, Bantam, 1983.

For those who like their negotiations a bit more cutthroat. This book is loaded with usable, if occasionally brash and irreverent tactics. An entertaining read, and one that is dedicated to proving that negotiation isn't the prerogative only of diplomats and corporate buccaneers, but a practical skill available to most anyone.

Winning the Salary Game: Salary Negotiation for Women, Sherry Chastain, John Wiley & Sons, 1980.

Although focused primarily on salary negotiations in full-time employment — from job interviews to raise requests — this nuts-and-bolts book is fully applicable to anyone negotiating for more money, in almost any situation.

Literary Agents, Michael Larsen, Writer's Digest Books, 1986. (Out of print.)
Written by one of the top agents on the West Coast, this is a basic how-to book on getting and working with an agent.

The One Minute Manager, Kenneth Blanchard and Spencer Johnson, William Morrow, 1982.
One of the paragons of business management, this little book is really a guide to the effective "management" of all kinds of relationships, professional and personal.

How to Sell Your Ideas, Jesse S. Nirenberg, McGraw-Hill, 1989.
A thorough exploration of the fine art of persuasion. Big on the psychological, between-the-lines subtleties that go on when trying to win someone over to your side.

Chapter Eight
Knowing Where to Look: The Ultimate Guide to Research, Lois Horowitz, Writer's Digest Books, 1988.
As thorough a reference book on the art of research as exists. How to find just about anything, and how to find your way around a library.

The Modern Researcher, Jacques Barzun and Henry F. Graff, Harcourt Brace Jovanovich, 1985.
One of the most eloquent books written on the subject of research, by two historians. Thought-provoking, engaging and witty, filled with vivid examples that bring research to life. Also an excellent examination of the biases and assumptions that researchers typically bring to their research.

Research Shortcuts, Judi Kesselman-Turkel and Franklyn Peterson, Contemporary Books, 1982.
Not a tedious roadmap of the public library, but a simple, easy-to-read list of research tips to help streamline your explorations. Though geared toward students, it is not beneath anyone else's dignity.

Study Smarts, Judi Kesselman-Turkel and Franklyn Peterson, Contemporary Books, 1981.
Again, geared to students and test-taking, but highly applicable to the writer's profession. Short and lightfooted.

From Dream to Discovery: On Being a Scientist, Hans Selye, Ayer Co., 1975.

Written by the father of research on stress, this is a beautifully written treatise on the nobility and value of research, and on the very human elements of the craft. Although it is directed at scientists and has sizable chunks of technical exposition that you will want to skim, it prominently addresses anyone deeply involved in a research career and a creative career.

Stolen Words: Forays into the Origins and Ravages of Plagiarism, Thomas Mallon, Ticknor & Fields, 1989.
A lurid and fascinating portrayal of the "crime" of plagiarism. A touch on the scholarly side, but a gripping and eye-opening read nonetheless.

Keeping Your Personal Journal, George Simons, Paulist Press, 1978.
Inspired by the pioneer journaling work of Ira Progoff ("At a Journal Workshop"), this is a simple manual on starting, maintaining and using a personal journal as a toll for growth and creativity.

The Craft of Interviewing, John Brady, Writer's Digest Books, 1976. (Out of print.)
Probably the most comprehensive book around on the subject, a fast and funny look at getting interviews, doing your homework, going face-to-face, and even getting tough. A tough book to beat.

Miscellaneous

Writers at Work, Edited by George Plimpton, Penguin Books.
An ongoing series of books composed of interviews culled from the *Paris Review* of celebrated writers (mostly novelists and poets) talking about their lives and work, their methods and their madnesses. Great reading.

The Writer on Her Work, Edited by Janet Sternburg, W.W. Norton, 1991.
I recommend this because the above-mentioned "Writers at Work" features so few women writers. This book, though, is a compilation of essays by women about being writers, again, primarily of fiction.

The Writer's Chapbook, Edited by George Plimpton, Viking, 1989.
Drawn once more from interviews in the *Paris Review*, this is a substantial collection of witty outtakes and wisdom from famous writers, on subjects such as inspiration, motivation, publication, writer's block, security, even vicious gossip.

On Being a Writer, Edited by Bill Strickland, Writer's Digest Books, 1989.
A book of profiles filled with compelling advice from many of the literary heavyweights of the twentieth century. These are dispatches from the front lines of the writing profession, as only those who have waged the good fight

can testify. One of the most accessible collections of contemporary literary interviews around.

Creative Process, Edited by Brewster Ghiselin, New American Library, 1955.
A collection of remarkable essays by renowned writers, artists, musicians, and others on what makes the creative mind tick. Not always easy reading, but instructive and inspiring.

Zen in the Art of Writing: Essays on Creativity, Ray Bradbury.
Exuberant essays from one of history's most prolific writers, all of which share a common theme: that writing is, or should be, a joy, not a chore. A wonderful read, especially the title story.

If You Want to Write, Brenda Ueland, Graywolf, 1987.
Subtitled "A Book About Art, Independence and Spirit," this little gem speaks to the heart of writing, the imagination, as well as to the danger of criticism, the "great destroyer" of the imagination. It is a book about the creative process, about the intrinsic rewards of writing, not the extrinsic ones. Heartful and hopeful, it is a love letter from a gentle teacher who believes that everyone is talented and has something to say.

A Whack on the Side of the Head, Roger von Oech, Warner, 1983.
With its sequel, *A Kick in the Seat of the Pants*, this book is a rambunctious and whimsical manifesto on unblocking your creativity, filled with exercises and based on von Oech's job as a creativity consultant to Fortune 500 companies.

The Writing Life, Annie Dillard, Harper & Row, 1989.
An insightful and literate look at "the dedication, absurdity and daring" that are part of the working life of a writer, described in one metaphor after another. As usual, beautifully written, and both delightfully and painfully recognizable.

An Open Life, Joseph Campbell, in conversation with Michael Toms, Larson Publications, 1988.
Anything by or about Joseph Campbell is worth reading, in my estimation. His work in the area of mythology, his belief in "Following your bliss" and especially his seminal book *The Hero's Journey* are by now legendary. This collection of interviews provides a splendid introduction to his ideas.

Writers' References

Writer's Market
From Writer's Digest. Annual directory of thousands of writing markets,

from magazines and syndicates to book publishers and greeting cards, complete with descriptions of editorial needs, submission details, contacts, pay rates, and tips from editors.

Offshoots include *Novel & Short-Story Writer's Market*, *Poet's Market*, *Songwriter's Market*, and *Photographer's Market*.

Literary Market Place, and *International Literary Market Place*, and *Literary Agents Directory*
Annual directories of book publishers, syndicates, agents, contests, writer's organizations and editorial services for writers.

Ulrich's International Periodicals Directory
Annual listing of publications worldwide.

Working Press of the Nation
Annual, probably the most comprehensive directory of publications within the U.S. But unlike *Writer's Market*, it only lists vital statistics: addresses, circulations, editorial staff.

Publisher's Directory
Lists nearly 10,000 book publishers, including trade, textbook, scientific and alternative.

Editor & Publisher International Yearbook
Annual directory of newspaper and newspaper editors worldwide.

Editor & Publisher Annual Directory of Syndicated Services
Annual directory of syndicates and syndicated properties, listed by subject.

Dramatists Bible
Sourcebook for playwrights, includes lists of theatres, script requirements, artistic directors, play producers, market information, agents, grants and writer's organizations.

Markets Abroad
Market and submission information for writers interested in markets outside the United States and Canada.

Trade magazines: *Writer's Digest*, *The Writer*, and *Poets & Writers*
Magazines with want-ads for writing jobs: *Publishers Weekly*, *Editor & Publisher*, *Folio*, and *The Chronicle of Higher Education*. Also check out the National Arts Job Bank (207 Shelby St., Suite 200, Santa Fe, NM 87501).

Writer's Organizations

American Advertising Federation. 1225 Connecticut Ave., Washington, D.C. 20036. 202-659-1800.

American Society of Journalists and Authors. For nonfiction writers. 1501 Broadway, Suite 1907, New York, NY 10036. 212-997-0947.

Associated Writing Programs. For writers associated with academia or looking for creative writing programs. Old Dominion University, Norfolk, VA 23508. 804-440-3839.

Author's Guild. For writers of fiction, nonfiction and poetry. 234 W. 44th St., New York, NY 10036. 212-391-9198.

Copywriter Council of America. Building 102, LMP-15, Middle Island, NY 11953. 516-924-8555.

Direct-Mail/Marketing Assn. 6 E. 3rd St., New York, NY 10017. 212-689-4977.

The Dramatists Guild. For playwrights, composers and lyricists. 234 W. 44th St., New York, NY 10036. 212-398-9366.

International Association of Business Communicators. Mostly public relations writers. 870 Market St., Suite 940, San Francisco, CA 94102. 415-433-3400.

Mystery Writers of America. 236 W. 27th St., Rm. 600, New York, NY 10001. 212-255-7005.

National Association of Home Based Businesses. P.O. Box 30220, Baltimore, MD 21270. 301-363-3698.

National Writers Club. For all writers. 1450 S. Havana, Suite 620, Aurora, CO 80012. 303-751-7844.

National Writer's Union. Provides grievance procedures, collective bargaining, peer counseling. 13 Astor Place, New York, NY 10003. 212-254-0279.

PEN American Center. Part of international writer's organization in over sixty countries that champions freedom of expression worldwide. 568 Broadway, New York, NY 10012. 212-334-1660.

Poets & Writers. 72 Spring St., Rm 301, New York, NY 10012. 212-226-3586.

Public Relations Society of America. 845 3rd Ave., New York, NY 10022. 212-826-1250.

Romance Writers of America. 13700 Veteran's Memorial Dr., Suite 315, Houston, TX 77014. 713-440-6885.

Science Fiction Writers of America. P.O. Box 4236, West Columbia, SC 29171. 803-791-5942.

Small Business Administration. Government agency that counsels small businesses. Services include SCORE (Service Corp of Retired Executives), a volunteer group of people experienced in running small businesses. Offices in most major cities. 1441 L St. NW, Washington, D.C. 20416. 800-368-5855.

Society of American Travel Writers. 1100 17th St. NW, Suite 1000, Washington, D.C. 20036. 202-785-5567.

Society of Children's Book Writers. Box 296, Mar Vista Sta., Los Angeles, CA 90066. 818-347-2849.

Society for Professional Journalists. 840 N. Lake Shore Dr., Chicago, IL 60611. 312-649-0060.

Society of Technical Communication. 815 15th St. NW, Suite 506, Washington, D.C. 20005. 202-737-0035.

Writers Guild of America. Labor union representing writers for film, TV and radio. 555 W. 57th St., New York, NY, 10019. 212-245-6180. Also West Coast branch: 8955 Beverly Blvd., Los Angeles, CA 90048. 213-550-1000.

Volunteer Lawyers for the Arts. 1560 Broadway, Suite 711, New York, NY, 10036. 212-575-1150.

INDEX

independence with, 48
part-time, 10-11
See also Self-employment
Friedrich, Mike, on agents, 174

G

Garfinkle, Perry, on goals, 42
Generalist, vs. specialist, 71-73
Genre, researching specific, 60-61
Goals
  attainable, 41-42
  chart for breaking down, 40
  focusing, 35-36
  importance of reevaluating, 17-19
  long-range vs. short-range, 38-39
  new, making room for, 43
Goals, setting, 32-33
  exercises for, 50-51
Gold, Herbert, on developing passions, 143
Goldberg, Ceil, on writing, 35

H

Hendin, David, on syndication, 136
Hilsinger, Judy, on self-promotion, 110
Holmes, Scott, on working with writers, 167
Home-based office, 75-79
  deductions for, 87-88
Houston, Jim, on writing, 17
Howe, Tom, on finding unique niche, 71

I

Income
  average of writers', 129
  output and, 8
  from resale, 130-131
Influence, ability to, through writing, 48
Information gathering. *See* Research, Market research, Interviews
Infotrak, 183
Interlibrary loans, for research, 182
Internship. *See* Apprentice, promotional nature of
Interviews, using personal touch during, 186-187

J

Jobs
  part-time, 10-11
  selling out by taking, 133-135
  to supplement writing business, 9-12
  in writing field, 11
Johnson, Fenton, on self-promotion, 108
Johnson, Tyler, on networking, 124-125
Journal, keeping, 190-191
Jue, Linda, on research, 181

K

Kane, Carole, on organization, 95
Kane, Joe, on earning living, 137
Keaton, Diane, on writing, 16-17
Keen, Sam, on self-promotion, 108
Knox, John, on renting office space, 77-78
Kristoff, Ray, on setting rates, 136

L

Lara, Adair, on negotiation, 160
Lead, dramatic, for proposal, 112-113
Letter of agreement, 172
Levak, Julie, on working with writers, 160
Librarian, reference, working with, 181-183
Library
  importance of, 181-184
  market research at, 56-57
  personal, 92
Lieberman, Anne, on managing finances, 143-144
Location
  of office, 75-79
  of writer, 70

M

Machines
  answering, 84-86
  fax, 86
  photocopying, 86

Press kit, 103
Priorities
  adjusting, for new projects, 43
  charting, 44
Procrastination, 33-35, 90
Professionalism, 158-159
Promotion
  necessity of, 98-100
  various methods of, 102-111
Proposal
  as first impression, 111-118
  multiple submission of, 118
  See also Query
Publications, success of new, 5
Publishing
  desktop, 82
  facts about, 59-60

Q

Query
  directing, to proper person, 116
  finding right time for, 117
  reporting time on, 117
  sample chart of, 96
  sample letter of, 114-115
Questions
  to ask self, 49-50
  asking open-ended, of clients, 170
  for market research, 56

R

Radio, as method of promotion, 107-108
Ramey, Joanna, on corporate writing, 71
Ranalli, Carol A., on writing, 16
Rate
  advice from Ray Kristoff on setting,
    136
  determining, 131-133
Rauber, Paul, on research, 195
Recognition, for writing, 48
Reed, Ishmael, on earning living, 151
Reference librarian, getting help from,
    181-183
Rejection
  form, 28
  handling, 27-31
  trying again after, 116-117

Reporting time, on query, 117
Research, 176-177
  hands-on, 185-187
  library, 181-184
  overdoing, 193-195
  planning ahead for, 177-181
Research, market. *See* Market research
Reselling writing, 130-131
Resources
  for doing market research, 56-57
  drawing on, 43-46
Resume, and press kit, 103
Rights
  ownership of, 130-131
  syndication, 167
  writer's, 148
Rinzler, Alan, on agents and attorneys,
    175
RoAne, Susan, on networking, 124
Roseman, Janet, on competition, 68

S

Salary. *See* Income, Rate
Sale, of rights, 130-131
SASE. *See* Self-addressed stamped enve-
    lope
Sautter, Carl, on promoting script, 109
Scriptwriting, advice from Kerry Cox on,
    66
Self-addressed stamped envelope, rule
    for, 117-118
Self-employment
  features of, 7-9
  security of, 141-142
  and taxes, 88
Self-promotion. *See* Promotion
Selk, Merry, on competition, 68
Setterberg, Fred, on competition, 68
Shavelson, Lonnie, on goals, 42
Shepard, Sally, on home-based office, 78
Singer, Bruce, on writing, 16
Skills
  finding hidden, 51-54
  writer's, checklist of, 51-52
Slack, Michael, on writing, 30
Software. *See* Computers
Solitude, of writing profession, 23-25
Specialist, vs. generalist, 71-73

Other Books of Interest

Annual Market Books
  Artist's Market, edited by Lauri Miller $21.95
  Children's Writer's & Illustrator's Market, edited by Lisa Carpenter (paper) $17.95
  Guide to Literary Agents & Art/Photo Reps, edited by Robin Gee $15.95
  Humor & Cartoon Markets, edited by Bob Staake (paper) $16.95
  Novel & Short Story Writer's Market, edited by Robin Gee (paper) $19.95
  Photographer's Market, edited by Sam Marshall $21.95
  Poet's Market, by Judson Jerome $19.95
  Songwriter's Market, edited by Brian Rushing $19.95
  Writer's Market, edited by Mark Kissling $25.95

General Writing Books
  Annable's Treasury of Literary Teasers, by H.D. Annable (paper) $1.00
  Beginning Writer's Answer Book, edited by Kirk Polking (paper) $13.95
  Discovering the Writer Within, by Bruce Ballenger & Barry Lane $17.95
  Freeing Your Creativity, by Marshall Cook $17.95
  Getting the Words Right: How to Rewrite, Edit and Revise, by Theodore A. Rees Cheney (paper) $12.95
  How to Write a Book Proposal, by Michael Larsen (paper) $10.95
  Just Open a Vein, edited by William Brohaugh $15.95
  Knowing Where to Look: The Ultimate Guide to Research, by Lois Horowitz (paper) $16.95
  Make Your Words Work, by Gary Provost $17.95
  Pinckert's Practical Grammar, by Robert C. Pinckert (paper) $11.95
  12 Keys to Writing Books That Sell, by Kathleen Krull (paper) $12.95
  The 28 Biggest Writing Blunders, by William Noble $12.95
  The 29 Most Common Writing Mistakes & How to Avoid Them, by Judy Delton (paper) $9.95
  The Wordwatcher's Guide to Good Writing & Grammar, by Morton S. Freeman (paper) $15.95
  Word Processing Secrets for Writers, by Michael A. Banks & Ansen Dibell (paper) $14.95
  The Writer's Book of Checklists, by Scott Edelstein $16.95
  The Writer's Digest Guide to Manuscript Formats, by Buchman & Groves $18.95
  The Writer's Essential Desk Reference, edited by Glenda Neff $19.95

Nonfiction Writing
  The Complete Guide to Writing Biographies, by Ted Schwarz $6.99
  Creative Conversations: The Writer's Guide to Conducting Interviews, by Michael Schumacher $16.95
  How to Do Leaflets, Newsletters, & Newspapers, by Nancy Brigham (paper) $14.95
  How to Sell Every Magazine Article You Write, by Lisa Collier Cool (paper) $11.95
  How to Write Irresistible Query Letters, by Lisa Collier Cool (paper) $10.95
  The Writer's Digest Handbook of Magazine Article Writing, edited by Jean M. Fredette (paper) $11.95

Fiction Writing

The Art & Craft of Novel Writing, by Oakley Hall $17.95

Best Stories from New Writers, edited by Linda Sanders $5.99

Characters & Viewpoint, by Orson Scott Card $13.95

The Complete Guide to Writing Fiction, by Barnaby Conrad $17.95

Cosmic Critiques: How & Why 10 Science Fiction Stories Work, edited by Asimov & Greenberg (paper) $12.95

Creating Characters: How to Build Story People, by Dwight V. Swain $16.95

Creating Short Fiction, by Damon Knight (paper) $10.95

Dialogue, by Lewis Turco $13.95

The Fiction Writer's Silent Partner, by Martin Roth $19.95

Handbook of Short Story Writing: Vol. I, by Dickson and Smythe (paper) $10.95

Handbook of Short Story Writing: Vol. II, edited by Jean Fredette (paper) $12.95

How to Write & Sell Your First Novel, by Collier & Leighton (paper) $12.95

Manuscript Submission, by Scott Edelstein $13.95

Mastering Fiction Writing, by Kit Reed $18.95

Plot, by Ansen Dibell $13.95

Spider Spin Me a Web: Lawrence Block on Writing Fiction, by Lawrence Block $16.95

Theme & Strategy, by Ronald B. Tobias $13.95

The 38 Most Common Writing Mistakes, by Jack M. Bickham $12.95

Writer's Digest Handbook of Novel Writing, $18.95

Writing the Novel: From Plot to Print, by Lawrence Block (paper) $11.95

Special Interest Writing Books

Armed & Dangerous: A Writer's Guide to Weapons, by Michael Newton (paper) $14.95

The Children's Picture Book: How to Write It, How to Sell It, by Ellen E.M. Roberts (paper) $19.95

Comedy Writing Secrets, by Mel Helitzer (paper) $15.95

The Complete Book of Feature Writing, by Leonard Witt $18.95

Creating Poetry, by John Drury $18.95

Deadly Doses: A Writer's Guide to Poisons, by Serita Deborah Stevens with Anne Klarner (paper) $16.95

Editing Your Newsletter, by Mark Beach (paper) $18.50

Families Writing, by Peter Stillman (paper) $12.95

A Guide to Travel Writing & Photography, by Ann & Carl Purcell (paper) $22.95

Hillary Waugh's Guide to Mysteries & Mystery Writing, by Hillary Waugh $19.95

How to Pitch & Sell Your TV Script, by David Silver $17.95

How to Write Action/Adventure Novels, by Michael Newton $4.99

How to Write & Sell Greeting Cards, Bumper Stickers, T-Shirts and Other Fun Stuff, by Molly Wigand (paper) 15.95

How to Write & Sell True Crime, by Gary Provost $17.95

How to Write Horror Fiction, by William F. Nolan $15.95

How to Write Mysteries, by Shannon OCork $13.95

How to Write Romances, by Phyllis Taylor Pianka $15.95

How to Write Science Fiction & Fantasy, by Orson Scott Card $13.95

How to Write Tales of Horror, Fantasy & Science Fiction, edited by J.N. Williamson (paper) $12.95

How to Write the Story of Your Life, by Frank P. Thomas (paper) $11.95

How to Write Western Novels, by Matt Braun $1.00

The Magazine Article: How To Think It, Plan It, Write It, by Peter Jacobi $17.95

Mystery Writer's Handbook, by The Mystery Writers of America (paper) $11.95

The Poet's Handbook, by Judson Jerome (paper) $11.95
Powerful Business Writing, by Tom McKeown $12.95
Successful Scriptwriting, by Jurgen Wolff & Kerry Cox (paper) $14.95
The Writer's Complete Crime Reference Book, by Martin Roth $19.95
The Writer's Guide to Conquering the Magazine Market, by Connie Emerson $17.95
Writing for Children & Teenagers, 3rd Edition, by Lee Wyndham & Arnold Madison (paper) $12.95
Writing Mysteries: A Handbook by the Mystery Writers of America, Edited by Sue Grafton, $18.95
Writing the Modern Mystery, by Barbara Norville (paper) $12.95

The Writing Business
A Beginner's Guide to Getting Published, edited by Kirk Polking (paper) $11.95
Business & Legal Forms for Authors & Self-Publishers, by Tad Crawford (paper) $4.99
The Complete Guide to Self-Publishing, by Tom & Marilyn Ross (paper) $16.95
How to Write with a Collaborator, by Hal Bennett with Michael Larsen $1.00
How You Can Make $25,000 a Year Writing, by Nancy Edmonds Hanson (paper) $14.95
This Business of Writing, by Gregg Levoy $19.95
Writer's Guide to Self-Promotion & Publicity, by Elane Feldman $16.95
A Writer's Guide to Contract Negotiations, by Richard Balkin (paper) $4.25
Writing A to Z, edited by Kirk Polking $22.95

To order directly from the publisher, include $3.00 postage and handling for 1 book and $1.00 for each additional book. Allow 30 days for delivery.

Writer's Digest Books
1507 Dana Avenue, Cincinnati, Ohio 45207
Credit card orders call TOLL-FREE
1-800-289-0963

Prices subject to change without notice.

Write to this same address for information on *Writer's Digest* magazine, *Story* magazine, Writer's Digest Book Club, Writer's Digest School, and Writer's Digest Criticism Service.